SHAPING AMERICA

The Politics of Supreme Court Appointments

GEORGE WATSON

JOHN A. STOOKEY

Arizona State University

 HarperCollins*CollegePublishers*

For our mothers
Lela Parker Watson and
Sallie Weisenburg Stookey

Acquisitions Editor: Marcus Boggs
Cover Design: Anne O'Donnell for Ruttle, Shaw & Wetherill, Inc.
Photo Researcher: Judy Ladendorf
Electronic Production Manager: Angel Gonzalez Jr.
Publishing Services: Ruttle, Shaw & Wetherill, Inc.
Electronic Page Makeup: Heather Parke
Printer and Binder: R.R. Donnelley & Sons Company
Cover Printer: R.R. Donnelley & Sons Company

Shaping America
The Politics of Supreme Court Appointments

Library of Congress Calatoging in Publication Data
    Watson, George
        Shaping America: the politics of Supreme Court appointments/George Watson and John A. Stookey.
            p. cm.
        Includes bibliographical references.
        ISBN 0-06-500863-4
        1. United States. Supreme Court—Officials and employees—Selection and appointment. 2. Judges—Selection and appointment—United States. 3. Political questions and judicial power—United Sates. I. Stookey, John A. II. Title.
    KF8742.W385—1995
    347.73'0634—dc20
    [347.3073534]   94-18637
                                                                    CIP

95 96 97 98   9 8 7 6 5 4 3 2 1

Contents

Preface

> I, Clarence Thomas, do solemnly swear that I will administer justice without respect to persons, and do equal right to the poor and to the rich, and that I will faithfully and impartially discharge and perform all the duties incumbent on me as associate justice of the Supreme Court of the United States, according to the best of my abilities and understanding, agreeably to the Constitution and laws of the United States; So help me God.

With this oath came to an end one of the strangest confirmation battles in the history of Supreme Court appointments. The solemnity of the Thomas oath-taking ceremony was in stark contrast to the confirmation process that just a week earlier was described by many as a political and media circus.

An Oklahoma law school professor, Anita Hill, had alleged that Thomas had sexually harassed her when she worked for him at the Equal Employment Opportunity Commission. Hill's explicit description of the sexual discussions that Thomas allegedly had with her captured the public's attention in a way unprecedented in the annals of Supreme Court nominations. Thomas vehemently denied the charges and characterized them as a politically motivated "high-tech lynching of an uppity black."

While the charges of sexual harassment were a unique aspect of the Thomas nomination, the fact that controversy emerged about a nominee's suitability for the Court was not unique. Over the history of the country approximately one in every five Supreme Court nominees has been the subject of considerable controversy.

Although such sensational nominations will play an important part in this book, we want to emphasize that this is not another "Thomas" book or even another "Bork" book. That is not to disparage such books but merely to say that ours is a different enterprise. In fact, we began the research that led to this book in response to one of the more noncontroversial of modern nominations: Sandra Day O'Connor. We started from a desire to witness history—the appointment of the first woman to the Court—and we were immediately intrigued with the role of politics in a presumably nonpolitical pro forma confirmation process. That beginning evolved into a broader interest in nomination politics as we observed and studied the ebb and flow of nomination controversy through such nominees as Scalia, Bork, Kennedy, Souter, and Thomas. Thus, rather than focusing on merely the controversial, we seek to ask the more fundamental questions of when, how, and why controversy emerges and what implications that emergence or lack thereof has for the political dynamics of the nomination process.

We began this book with the intention of writing a scholarly treatment of nomination politics. We hope to have met that goal. However, as work progressed we found more and more of the material appropriate for our classroom teaching. How justices reach the Supreme Court is not just of interest in courses dealing with the Court; the process by which appointment and confirmation occur is fundamental to understanding the legislative process, interest-group activities, executive decision making, and legislative-executive interactions.

Similarly, general public interest in the appointment process reached unprecedented levels with the nominations of Robert Bork in 1987 and Clarence Thomas in 1991. While we were pleased with the interest shown, we were concerned with the apparent lack of knowledge and understanding about the process. Therefore, in our writing we have tried to address the interests and needs of these additional audiences. Specifically, we have included context and detail that may not be needed for a scholarly audience. In addition, we have tried to minimize the use of academic jargon. Finally, while we do use some quantitative methods, we have combined them with explanations and visual presentations that will make them accessible to all audiences.

We address more fully in Chapter One why understanding the selection of Supreme Court justices is such a significant topic. However, the selection and confirmation of the 43-year-old Clarence Thomas in 1991 makes the point well. Justice Thomas likely will serve on the highest court in the land well into the twenty-first century. During that time he and the Court will make decisions that will affect you for the rest of your life: Do you, a friend, and/or family member have the right to an abortion or to interfere with those who seek to exercise such a right? Is it permissible for your employer or potential employer to use an affirmative-action program in making hiring decisions? Under what circumstances can you be stopped and searched as part of the war on drugs? Do you or members of your family have the right to choose the time and manner of your death? Will you or your children have the right to make genetic decisions involving the characteristics of future generations? In short, because the Supreme Court shapes the America in which we live, the process by which the justices of that court are selected is of vital interest to us all.

The remainder of the book is structured to follow the nomination process as it unfolds, beginning with when a vacancy occurs on the Court. As straightforward as that seems, Chapter Two reveals there is much more to a vacancy than simply an empty seat on the Court. The timing and nature of a vacancy are critical to all that follows. In particular, they establish the setting in which the resulting nomination will take place. By so doing, the initial seeds of consensus or controversy are sown.

Chapter Three describes the factors that motivate a president to select a nominee and the processes by which those factors are considered. Confronted with a particular political situation, the president's selection and initiation of the nomination discourse will do much to determine whether the nomination will generate controversy or produce consensus.

The selection of the nominee moves the nomination into the public forum, at which point a variety of constitutional and non-constitutional actors investigate, analyze, and evaluate what positions and which actions are appropriate for them to take with regard to the nomination. In Chapter Four we discuss that period of time between the president's selection of a nominee and the beginning of the Senate's consideration. Specific attention is paid to the important roles of advocacy groups, the media, the public, and others during this period.

Chapter Five follows the nomination to the Senate Judiciary Committee. In the modern era, Judiciary Committee hearings have come to serve as the focal point of a nomination. It is here that opponents and supporters focus their attempts to define the nominee as unacceptable or acceptable, respectively. Even in the absence of controversy, however, we shall discover that a number of politically significant activities occur within the hearings.

From the Judiciary Committee, a nomination eventually reaches the full Senate. Chapter Six describes the process and analyzes those factors that influence the outcome of the confirmation vote. It is here that the various elements of the political model we develop throughout the book come together in the "moment of truth" for the nomination.

In Chapter Seven we recap the process by suggesting how the information in this book can be used to observe and understand future nomination processes as they unfold. We conclude with a systematic evaluation of recent criticisms and calls for reform of the nomination process that have resulted from the Bork and Thomas nominations.

George Watson
John A. Stookey

CHAPTER ONE

Politics, Language, and Court Appointments

> Robert Bork's America is a land in which women would be forced into back alley abortions, blacks would sit at segregated lunch counters, rogue police could break down citizens' doors in midnight raids, school children could not be taught about evolution, writers and artists could be censored at the whim of government, and the doors of the federal courts would be shut on the fingers of millions of citizens for whom the judiciary is—and is often the only—protector of the individual rights that are the heart of our democracy.
>
> *Senator Edward Kennedy*

Whether this characterization of Robert Bork was fact, hyperbole, or gross distortion is subject to considerable debate. However, what is not subject to debate is the assumption upon which the statement is based—in our society, the U. S. Supreme Court and, therefore, the justices serving on that Court affect our daily lives. To a considerable extent, they determine whether we have the rights to speak freely, to publish material critical of the government, to be provided with an attorney if suspected of a crime, to attend a college with an affirmative action program, to have an abortion. The justices truly have the power to shape America.

As a result, Senator Kennedy is right to remind us that who is placed on the Supreme Court is an extremely significant political question. It follows, then, that how justices are selected and evaluated is similarly important. The constitutional description of the process is deceptively simple. Supreme Court justices are appointed for life tenure by the president with the advice and consent of the Senate. However, over the past 200 years a rich tradition of informal norms, procedures, and extra-constitutional actors has emerged. Only by understanding that tradition—the nomination and confirmation process in action—can we understand the process of selecting Supreme Court justices. Describing, analyzing, and evaluating that tradition is the purpose of this book.

This chapter begins the task by articulating why Supreme Court appointments have become so important. We then distinguish between the constitutional and extra-constitutional settings that do so much to structure the appointment process. Finally, we foreshadow much of the rest of this work by introducing the central theme that the appointment process is, above all, a political process, one which develops a political discourse that determines whether a nomination will or will not generate controversy and, ultimately, whether the nominee will be confirmed or rejected.

★ ★ ★ ★ ★ ★ ★ ★ ★

BOX 1.1

How a Single Justice Shapes America: David Souter Replaces William Brennan

Although it is often contended that the replacement of a single justice does not significantly affect the decisions of the Supreme Court, the 1990–1991 term showed otherwise. Below are five instances (arguably there are more) where the replacement of William Brennan with David Souter significantly affected the meaning the Court gave to sections of the Bill of Rights of the Constitution. In each of these cases, Souter joined a five to four majority that rejected constitutional claims by individuals, claims that Brennan, had he remained on the Court, in all likelihood would have supported, along with the four dissenters, producing five to four majorities in the opposite direction.

The Constitution	Souter's America	Brennan's America
First Amendment	*Barnes* v. *Glen Theatre*	
Congress shall make no law . . . abridging the freedom of speech. . . .	An Indiana law prohibiting totally nude dancing is not a limitation on expressive conduct that is protected by the First Amendment.	By banning an entire category of expressive conduct, the Indiana prohibition is so broadly drawn as to violate the First Amendment.
Fourth Amendment	*Riverside* v. *McLaughlin*	
The right of the people . . . against unreasonable . . . seizures, shall not be violated. . . .	A person who is arrested without an arrest warrant may be held for up to 48 hours without an initial court appearance.	A 48-hour detention with no judicial scrutiny of the basis for arrest gives too much discretion to the police and is an unreasonable seizure.

The Significance of Supreme Court Appointments

That passion should engulf the nominations of Supreme Court justices seems incongruous with Alexander Hamilton's depiction of the Court as "least dangerous to . . . the Constitution" (Hamilton 1987, 78:7) and with a view by almost all of the justices themselves that judging requires a dispassionate and nonpartisan interpretation of the laws of the land. The subordination of passion to legal reasoning is reflected in the solemnity of the Court's pro-

---

Fifth Amendment

No person . . . shall be compelled in any criminal case to be a witness against himself. . . .

Arizona v. *Fulminante*

Using confessions coerced from defendants as evidence against them, although always unlawful, . . . may be deemed harmless error and will not require convictions to be invalidated.

A coerced confession is never a harmless error and whenever such a confession has been used in court against a defendant, he is entitled to a new trial where the confession is not admitted as evidence.

Sixth Amendment

In all criminal prosecutions, the accused shall enjoy the right to a speedy and public trial by an impartial jury. . . .

Mu'Min v. *Virginia*

To insure an impartial jury it is sufficient to ask potential jurors who have heard about the case if their knowledge will bias them.

If potential jurors have been exposed to pretrial publicity the judge must determine what information the potential jurors have and make an independent judgment as to whether they can be fair.

Eighth Amendment

Cruel and unusual punishments [shall not be] inflicted.

Harmelin v. *Michigan*

States may impose life in prison without possibility of parole on first-time drug offenders who are convicted of possessing a large amount of drugs.

The Eighth Amendment requires a court review of the proportionality between the crime and the punishment. A life term for a first-time possession of drugs is a penalty disproportionate to the crime.

ceedings. The absence of partisanship is asserted by judges and Supreme Court justices, who are quite fond of telling how often they must decide cases in accordance with what the law dictates and against their own personal preferences and values. Justice Holmes reminded his colleagues "to learn to transcend our own convictions and to leave room for much that we hold dear to be done away with" (Marke 1964, 66). In the presence of such solemnity and objectivity, why then can it matter, and matter so ardently, who makes those judgments?

The answer to why it makes a difference and why people argue over such nominations is four-fold. First, of course, it simply does make a difference who makes decisions. No student of the Court doubts that the replacements of William Brennan and Thurgood Marshall by David Souter and Clarence Thomas, respectively, diminished the "liberal" bloc of the Court—that we have lost the "automatic" votes against the death penalty or weakened the opposition to scaling back what constitutes a coerced confession or an illegal search and seizure. As Box 1.1 reveals, the replacement of Brennan by Souter meant that several decisions of the Court during Souter's first year had different, and more conservative, outcomes than if Brennan had remained.[1] As Sam Ervin, the droll North Carolina senator who gained fame in the Senate's Watergate investigation, once noted:

> It is a very fortunate thing for us lawyers that we can read the same books and draw different conclusions from them, [otherwise] . . . we would not have near enough lawsuits to keep us all going. (Senate 1969b, 384)

A second reason appointments to the Court constitute high political stakes is that the Constitution, to paraphrase Chief Justice Hughes, is indeed what the Court says it is (Hughes 1916, 184, 307). Certainly there are many constraints on the judgments of the justices. The Court is not free to create its own version of the Constitution from whole cloth. Nevertheless, the fabric of the Constitu-

---

[1] While Souter made a significant difference in the conservative direction during his first term on the Court, during the 1991–1992 term (his second) he made an apparently moderate shift along with Justices O'Connor and Kennedy. Thus, in some key cases during this second term and in subsequent terms his voting was actually very similar to what we would have expected from Justice Brennan. For example, Souter joined a plurality opinion that while upholding several Pennsylvania restrictions on abortion, nonetheless reaffirmed, over vehement objections by Chief Justice Rehnquist and Justices Scalia, White, and Thomas, the basic holding of *Roe* v. *Wade* that a woman has a constitutional right to an abortion, at least before the viability of the fetus. (*Planned Parenthood of Southeastern Pennsylvania* v. *Casey* 1992).

tion is woven with intricate ideas and concepts that express the framers' commitments to freedom, equality, due process, and those rights endemic to citizens in a free society.[2] Much of the legislation of the Congress contains similarly broad and potentially ambiguous words and phrases. Whether by design or not, the Supreme Court is now vested with capturing the richness of these abstractions in concrete policies and rules of law.

 AMENDMENT I
Congress shall make no law... abridging the freedom of speech .
THE CONSTITUTION

The history of constitutional law is one of giving meaning to the language of the Constitution. That meaning changes over time and, particularly, with changes in the personnel of the Court. The First Amendment's protection of free speech has raised endless interpretations of what constitutes speech. In the 1990 *Glen Theatre* case, the justices argued about whether nude dancing is a type of expressive conduct that is covered by the free speech guarantee of the First Amendment. Justice Byron White said yes; Justice Antonin Scalia said no; Justice William Rehnquist said it was speech, but only marginally so, and therefore could be prohibited by states. Areas of symbolic speech, expressive conduct, and pornography have long precipitated definitional squabbles among the justices. Robert Bork was rejected as a nominee in 1987 in part because of concern about how he defined speech. At an early point in his academic career, he had written that the First Amendment protected only political speech (Bork 1971, 27–28). Knowing how a nominee will define speech is important because speech, in the final analysis, is what the Court says it is.

A third reason Supreme Court appointments elicit attention is that these interpretations of the Constitution by the Court provide

---

[2] The nexus between justices' views and constitutional interpretation was noted by one of the more prominent champions of "judicial restraint," Felix Frankfurter. "Constitutional interpretation is most frequently invoked by the broad and undefined clauses of the Constitution. Their scope of application is relatively unrestricted, and the room for play of individual judgment as to policy correspondingly broad" (Frankfurter and Landis 1928, 308). In addition, "The words of the Constitution . . . are so unrestrained by their intrinsic meaning, or by their history, or by prior decisions, that they leave the individual justice free, if indeed they do not compel him, to gather meaning not from reading the Constitution but from reading life" (310).

the most common path by which the meaning of the Constitution evolves. Formally, the Constitution changes only through the amendment process. That procedure, however, is cumbersome, requiring approval of three-fourths of the states, a feat successfully accomplished only 11 times in the past 120 years. Debates will rage over the interpretative concept of "original intent," a view that Constitutional phrases and concepts should be interpreted consistently with the meanings intended by the framers or some other subset of Constitutional contemporaries. However, the fact remains that the Court does alter the effect of the Constitution by redefining the words and by broadening or narrowing the scope of their application.

One of the key issues in recent Supreme Court nomination hearings has been the scope of the "equal protection" clause of the Fourteenth Amendment. Does it prohibit sex discrimination or economic discrimination as well as racial discrimination? The so-called Equal Rights Amendment that would have explicitly prohibited sex discrimination failed to secure ratification in part because of arguments that it was not needed—that women were protected already by the Fourteenth Amendment. Acceptance of some broader view of the Fourteenth Amendment beyond race is today virtually a prerequisite for confirmation to the Court.

> *AMENDMENT XIV*
>
> *No state . . . shall deprive any person of life, liberty, or property, without due process of law; nor deny to any person . . . equal protection of the laws.*
>
> THE CONSTITUTION

Fourth, the significance of Supreme Court appointments is heightened by the fact that appointments are, in effect, for life tenure. The median term of service for justices appointed in the twentieth century has been 13 years, but many have served much longer. Just prior to William Brennan's retirement in 1990 after 35 years of service, the Court still contained justices appointed by seven different presidents, dating back to Eisenhower in the 1950s. Presidents Reagan and Bush's new appointees to the Court have ranged in age from 43 to 51, justices we might expect to remain on the Court for 30 years or more. The position of Supreme Court justice is a considerable grant of power, one that is given only with increasing scrutiny—by the president, the Senate, and the public.

The Constitutional Setting

Any attempt to understand the process of selecting Supreme Court justices must necessarily begin with the president and Senate as the two constitutional actors in the process. As the process has emerged, when a Supreme Court vacancy occurs, the president selects a nominee whose name is forwarded to the Senate for consideration. That consideration ultimately involves a vote by the Senate to confirm or deny the appointment. If more senators vote for than against confirmation, the nominee is confirmed as a lifetime appointee to the high Court. If the vote for confirmation fails to gain a plurality of the votes, then the nominee is rejected and the president must submit another nomination.

 ARTICLE 2 SECTION 2

He [the President] . . . by and with the advice and consent of the Senate, shall appoint . . . judges of the Supreme Court. . . .

THE CONSTITUTION

This is the process in its simplest form, and while we shall cover it in considerable detail throughout the book, it is worth noting here that there is no formal procedure by which the Senate provides "advice," except in the sense that the failure to give consent is advising the president to do better the next time around. In response to a question from the Senate about how he wished to handle nominations, George Washington established the precedent that the president would submit nominations to the Senate in writing and that they should respond in kind. There would be no meetings between the Senate and the president. In other words, there would be no formal advice in "advice and consent" (Harris 1953, 38–39). As we shall see, however, many presidents have sought advice informally from key senators, and senators have seldom been reluctant to offer advice, even when it is not solicited.

The simple form of presidential nomination and Senate confirmation is not always followed. In fact, not all nominations even reach a vote before the Senate. As shown in Box 1.2, the Senate has simply taken no action on six nominations and effectively rejected four others by postponing consideration. All but one of the postponements or inactions came in the first 100 years of the nation, typically during the last year of a presidency and in lieu of an out-

★ ★ ★ ★ ★   ★   ★   ★   ★

BOX 1.2
The Numbers

Saying how many justices there have been on the Court is not a straightforward task. Stephen Breyer is the one hundred and eighth person to sit on the Court, though not necessarily the one hundred and eighth justice to be appointed. Here's why:

1. John Rutledge, one of the initial appointees to the Court, subsequently resigned from the Court only to be reappointed in 1793. Since the Senate was not in session at the time, he was issued an interim commission until the end of the next session of the Senate, and he presided as chief justice for the August 1795 term. When his name was submitted in nomination to the Senate in December 1795, he was rejected. Given that he actually did preside, we list him twice among those who have served, but he is also listed among the 12 who were rejected. He is the indicated by the 1 on the direct line from the president to the Court.

2. Edwin Stanton was appointed and confirmed to the Court in 1869, but he died four days after his confirmation and never actually sat with the Court. His commission was signed after his death by President Grant and given to his widow. Because Stanton did not take his oaths of office, he is not counted among the 108 who have served.

3. Charles Evans Hughes initially served on the Court from 1910 to 1916, but he resigned to run for the presidency. He was then reappointed to the chief justice position by President Hoover in 1930. Thus, one man filled two different vacancies.

4. Three sitting associate justices have been elevated to the chief justice position—Edward White in 1910, Harlan Fiske Stone in 1941, and William Rehnquist in 1986, simultaneously filling and creating a vacancy.

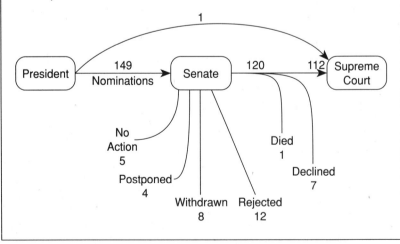

right rejection. Presidents have withdrawn seven nominations. Withdrawals usually anticipate a rejection,[3] most recently that of Douglas Ginsburg in 1987, and the nomination is withdrawn before the vote occurs. Such a move presumably saves the nominee embarrassment, allows the president to avoid losing a vote, and permits senators to avoid a public stance with the potential of alienating some of their constituents. Appendix B details these failed nominations, along with the 12 who were rejected in outright confirmation votes.

A failed nomination does not always result in another nomination right away. Five presidents (J. Q. Adams, Tyler, Fillmore, Hayes, and L. Johnson[4]) have left office with vacancies unfilled due to Senate recalcitrance. The rejection of a nominee near the end of a president's term may signal the Senate's resolve to save the nomination for the next president. That was an explicit consideration articulated by some Republicans in their refusal to consider Lyndon Johnson's nomination of Abe Fortas to be chief justice in 1968 (CQ 1968, 532).

The Extra-Constitutional Setting

The austere instructions of the Constitution about the appointment procedure have inevitably given rise to a more robust process. It has become considerably more complex than when George Washington, on September 24, 1789, submitted six names on a piece of paper as his nominees to the first Court (Box 1.3). The nominees were confirmed only two days later after discussion in the whole Senate, albeit a Senate not much larger than the 18-person Judiciary Committees of 1994. Today, while the submission of the nominee's name retains the simplicity of Washington's, the accompanying FBI report and support documents from the White House, the Senate's own lengthy questionnaire responses from the nominee, and the

---

[3] Only the first withdrawal—of William Paterson by George Washington—is an exception. Washington had nominated the senator prior to the formal expiration of his first term as senator, a term in which Paterson participated in the establishment of the Supreme Court to which he was now appointed. Article 1 Section 6 of the Constitution prohibits such action. The nomination was withdrawn and resubmitted a few days later, after the expiration of Paterson's Senate term, at which point he was confirmed (Marcus and Perry 1985, 89–90).

[4] Whether to include Johnson in this list poses a slight problem. Chief Justice Earl Warren tied his 1968 retirement to the confirmation of a successor. Opponents to the confirmation of Abe Fortas as chief justice argued that no vacancy existed. When the Fortas nomination failed to come to a vote in the Senate and the nomination was subsequently withdrawn, Warren continued to serve until retiring unconditionally in 1969.

★ ★ ★ ★ ★   ★   ★   ★   ★   ★

BOX 1.3
Presidential Letters of Nomination to the Senate

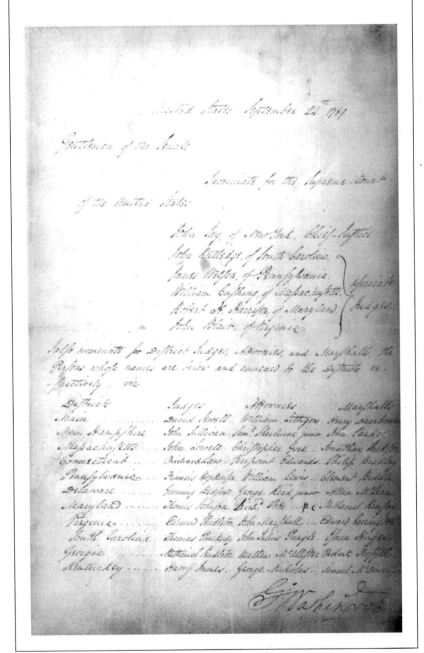

The White House,

July 8, 1991

To the

Senate of the United States.

I nominate Clarence Thomas, of Georgia, to be an Associate Justice of the Supreme Court of the United States, vice Thurgood Marshall, retired.

G Bush

"high camp" television production witnessed during the Bork and Thomas confirmation hearings in 1987 and 1991, respectively, all suggest a very different confirmation process from that which occurred 200 years earlier.

The Extra-Constitutional Role of the Senate

Told by the Constitution to render "advice and consent" to presidential nominations, the Senate has evolved a set of extra-constitutional procedures over the years with respect to how that terse command is implemented. At first, the Senate operated under a rule that nominations would lay over one day before being considered by the whole Senate in closed session. There was no such thing as a confirmation hearing, and the president's nominations were handled quickly. We shall cover the Senate procedures in much more detail in Chapters 5 and 6. For now, it is sufficient to recognize the key features of the modern confirmation process as

1. public hearings before the entire Senate Judiciary Committee (regularly since 1949);
2. an appearance by the nominee to testify (regularly since 1955);
3. prehearing visitations of the nominee to the Senate leadership and to senators on the Judiciary Committee (regularly since 1969); and
4. the testimony of the nominee broadcast on live television (regularly since 1981).

While procedures have changed over time, the basic questions concerning how much deference should be given the president and what criteria should be used by the Senate in reaching its collective decision have remained with us from the beginning. As recently as the Souter nomination in 1990 there seemed to exist in the minds of most senators a presumption in favor of the president's nominees. The Clarence Thomas nomination of 1991 may have signaled a watershed regarding that belief. Such a presumption remains strong among members of the president's own political party and among those who more closely identify with the president's political ideology and policy goals. Proponents of such a presumption argue that the power of selection belongs to the president, and opponents to a president or a nominee carry the burden to establish legitimate grounds for opposing the nominee. In the absence of persuasive reasons to vote no, senators should vote to confirm. A contrary view gaining increasing acceptance is that the burden rests with the president and the nominee to establish the nominee's fitness. The failure to do so should result in rejection of the nominee.

The proper scope of the Senate's inquiry and what constitutes persuasive reasons to vote no have been the subject of considerable debate. The view that minimizes the Senate's role was first and perhaps best stated by Alexander Hamilton in the seventy-sixth Federalist paper. He asserted that the Senate should reject a nomination only when there are "special and strong reasons for the refusal" (Hamilton 1987, 76:6). In his view the advice and consent function should be narrowly defined, designed to serve as

> an excellent check upon a spirit of favoritism in the president, . . .
> to prevent the appointment of unfit characters from state preju-
> dice, from family connection, from personal attachment, or from
> a view to popularity. (Hamilton 1987, 76:9)

In the middle decades of the nineteenth century, many in the Senate expressed a contrary notion that the president should defer to the Senate in the selection of judicial nominees, especially for the federal district courts, but even for the Supreme Court (Harris 1953,

65–78; Haynes 1960, 2:736–749). In part, this Senate dominance perspective reflected the significance of geography for nominations. Through much of the nineteenth century, Supreme Court justices were burdened with circuit-riding duty in which they physically traveled throughout the states within their circuits. Senators within those circuits expected to have a strong say concerning the suitability of a nominee, particularly if he were from their home state.

A middle view between presidential or senatorial dominance has been expressed by a variety of presidents and senators over the years but, as usual, George Washington was there first when he told the Senate "As the President has a right to nominate without assigning his reasons, so has the Senate a right to dissent without giving theirs" (Harris 1953, 39). The middle view does not exclude political, ideological, or partisan factors from coming into play, but it does assert that it is the president's prerogative to choose, while the Senate's role is reactive, namely, to accept or reject the nomination. There is an underlying assumption that both the president and the Senate want justices who are well qualified and otherwise ethically and temperamentally fit for the office.

The Role of Nonconstitutional Actors

Neither the president nor the Senate operate in a vacuum. Their actions are affected by the political and legal climate of the day. Thus, the political composition of the Senate, the political party and ideological orientation of the president, the nature of the key issues of the day, and the direction and divisiveness of public opinion all shape the process. These factors create the setting in which a nomination occurs, and they bring into the process a wide variety of political actors who are outside the constitutional provisions of the process. Concerned citizens, the American Bar Association (ABA), advocacy group representatives, journalists, the FBI, and others have assumed an increasingly prominent role in influencing the behavior of both the president and the Senate. Much of this book is devoted to describing and analyzing how this extra-constitutional setting shapes the play and the outcome of this constitutional ritual.

Politics, Language, and Nomination Controversy

"It is hard to understand," professed Senator Hatch to Robert Bork, "why your nomination would generate controversy. The answer is found in one word, . . . and that word is 'politics'" (Senate 1989, 36). For Hatch, as for many of his senatorial colleagues, the controversy surrounding Bork was a function of narrow, partisan politics. They viewed the campaignlike actions of advocacy groups opposed to the nomination as an unhealthy intrusion of politics in the confirmation process designed to stir up controversy and defeat the nomination.

Senator Hatch's statement focuses on two constructs that are central to this book—controversy and politics. Just what is controversy and what are its sources and consequences? Moreover, what is politics and what are the various ways in which politics manifests itself in the appointment process? The answers to these questions involve one other important consideration: language. Controversy and politics are called "constructs" because they are indeed constructed realities. In a sense, controversy does not exist until a given set of actions and situations are labeled as controversial. Similarly, one person's "politics" is another's principled actions.

Controversy and Politics

While it may be argued that controversy must be recognized and identified as controversy in order to exist, certain conditions are generally accepted as the defining characteristics of controversy in Supreme Court appointment settings. First, controversy requires that there be opposition to the nomination. That there is opposition further assumes that there is also support for the nomination. We do not recognize controversy without disagreement. In that sense, then, controversy arose in the Bork nomination not only because of the opposition of Senator Kennedy and others but because of the support of Senator Hatch and others.

A second defining characteristic of controversy addresses the intensity of the opposing sides. The opposition between participants in the process must exhibit a contentious nature; there needs to be some feeling—some intensity—behind the opposition. In fact, intensity is such a key that if it is lacking, then any opposition to the nominee will likely collapse or simply remain dormant. The nomination of Harrold Carswell in 1970 on the heels of the rejection of Clement Haynsworth was not well received by liberal Democrats in the Senate, but there was considerable apathy in opposing the nomination. Active opposition requires commitment and effort. Some intensity must be generated, and it took a speech by the Republican Edward Brooke of Massachusetts, an African American, to fire some intensity into the opposition by challenging the sincerity of Carswell's repudiation of his racist past and of President Nixon's campaign promise to "bring us together" as a nation (Harris 1971, 14–21). The rest is history; the opposition mobilized and Carswell was defeated. On the other hand, negative feelings concerning the nomination of Antonin Scalia in 1986 simply never developed into overt opposition in part because there was insufficient intensity to spark the opposition.

A third defining characteristic of controversy is quantitative in nature. There must be sufficient opposition to the nomination to raise at least some possibility of defeating the nominee. There were five no votes in the Judiciary Committee against Thurgood Marshall, but his nomination never approached the controversial level of a Bork or Thomas because all opposition was centered among conservative southern Democrats, who produced only 11 negative votes in the Senate. Almost no nomination totally escapes any opposition. Even Sandra O'Connor's 1981 appointment that broke the Court's gender barrier encountered opposition from a few pro-life advocates outside of the Senate and from a few senators as well. Yet her nomination was never considered controversial, in part because the opposition lacked intensity but more so because opponents were so few in number that there was no thought that she might be rejected.

Senator Hatch's disparaging reference to politics as the source of controversy in the Bork nomination suggests a view of politics as one of groups, both within and outside the Senate, seeking partisan advantage without regard to the merits of the issue. Senator Grassley emphasized that point in his statement that intense lobbying "has transformed this nomination into the legislative equivalent of a pork barrel water project" (Senate 1989, 59). Such a definition of politics is limiting, and the notion that controversy is a function of such politics is similarly narrow.

We prefer a more encompassing view of politics, like Harold Lasswell's definition of politics as the process that determines "who gets what, when, and how" (Lasswell 1958). This broader definition of politics directs our attention to all nominations—controversial and noncontroversial, successful and unsuccessful. We can't understand why some nominations become controversial if we do not understand what keeps others noncontroversial. In addition, this broader definition of politics focuses our attention on all behaviors that play out in the nomination and confirmation process, not just those involved with opposing a nominee or directed at overt support of a nominee. This definition also includes those actions that are directed toward goals other than support of or opposition to a nominee.

The tendency of the media and of scholars to focus only on nominations that are deemed controversial stems from biases found in journalism and certain academic scholarship. Journalists are drawn by the confrontation that controversy brings, and it is certainly no accident that the televised hearings of Anita Hill's sexual allegations against Clarence Thomas drew the largest television audiences in the history of many public broadcasting stations around the country. It was American soap at its purest—sex and politics in a two-person showdown, a natural for television.

Scholars are not immune to the journalistic appetite for controversy. We are much more apt to be interested in issues on which there are differing points of view simply because they permit us to analyze these differences. However, there is also a methodological bias that drives our attention. The dominant mode of research on the confirmation process focuses on observable behaviors, particularly with those that are readily and reliably quantifiable like outcomes in confirmation votes. The use of statistical analysis with such behavioral data requires variation in that behavior, for example, both yes and no voting. With such data, we may then analyze which factors—such as political party and political ideology—are connected with voting one way or the other on a nominee. Controversial nominations ensure the necessary vote variation for behavioral social scientists to practice their craft.

But there is much more to politics than trying to influence the outcome of controversial nominations. While controversy may be a function of politics, so too is consensus. Indeed, the most successful outcome for political activity is consensus. President Gerald Ford was faced with one of the most highly politicized environments in modern appointment history. Having entered office through the resignation of Richard Nixon because of the Watergate scandal and himself tainted with a recent effort to impeach Justice Douglas, Ford very deftly named John Paul Stevens to replace the retiring Douglas. Ford chose the politics of consensus rather than the politics of controversy. But make no mistake: his decision was based on politics.

Consensus regarding a nomination does not remove politics from the process; consensus merely permits other forms of politics to occur. As we have noted elsewhere (Watson and Stookey 1988, 187–193) and shall cover in Chapter 5, the absence of controversy permits senators to shift away from partisan conflict and pursue other political goals through less controversial means. Freed from concern over the outcome of the nomination, senators in the O'Connor confirmation hearings used the opportunity to promote certain individual agendas—with the nominee, their fellow senators, and their constituents as the targets of their actions. Even in the absence of controversy, senators are always engaged in political behavior in their public lives.

Again, while controversy may be a function of politics, it is also true that politics is a function of controversy. Just as consensus permits and fosters different political behaviors, opposition to a nomination precipitates certain actions. Senator Kennedy's statement that introduced this chapter was carefully crafted to incite opposition and generate controversy. Once the controversy was ignited, the perception of a controversial nomination influenced and shaped the form of the political discourse and behaviors that followed. Thus, Senator Hatch's disparagement of politics as the source of controversy was itself a political act designed to seek advantage in the very controversy he disavowed.

Language and Politics

In the interplay of language and politics, language does not exist apart from the political settings and behaviors it describes. Language is used to generate a discourse that will create and shape political situations. In the words of Murray Edelman,

> Actions and interpretations hinge upon the social situation in which they begin, including the language that depicts a social situation. The language that interprets objects and actions also constitutes the subject. (Edelman 1988, 9)

In the political dueling that shapes nomination controversy, language is the weapon of choice. Whether it be the 1795 Federalist effort to declare chief justice designate John Rutledge "insane," the Boston Bar's attempt in 1916 to label Louis Brandeis a "radical," or Senator Kennedy's graphic depiction of "Robert Bork's America," a common theme in the use of language is to incite opposition to the nomination.

On the other hand, those who seek to support a nominee typically attempt to minimize the perception of controversy by characterizing the nominee as competent, as having a fine legal mind in the mainstream of American legal thought, and as possessing great integrity. Such characterizations often culminate in an appeal for consensus, to shun controversy over such a qualified nominee. By suggesting that politics has no place in the confirmation process, supporters of a nomination attempt to construct a narrow and negative view of politics, to define the opposition as engaging in that negative behavior, and to rally opinion in support of their "nonpolitical" position.

Throughout this book, we shall argue a simple but basic point: Presidents and senators are politically motivated in making decisions about who should be on the Supreme Court. Their dialogue, along with that of various actors involved in the nomination and confirmation process, will be referred to as the *nomination discourse*. This discourse involves discussions and commentaries on the nomination and the nominee, and it especially focuses on the use of language to construct particular views of "politics," "contro-versy," "qualifications," and other constructs. In the context of nomination discourse, language is

> not simply an instrument for describing events but itself a part of events, shaping their meaning and helping to shape the political roles officials and the general public play. In this sense, language, events, and self-conceptions are a part of the same transaction, mutually determining one another's meaning. (Edelman 1977, 4)

At no time has the constructivist use of language to create im-agery in the appointment process been more evident than in the Clarence Thomas nomination. Combining two of the most divisive social categorizations of our time, the appeals to racial and gender stereotypes to credit or discredit both Thomas and Anita Hill trau-matized the whole confirmation process (Brock 1993; Morrison 1992; Chrisman and Allen 1992). Was Thomas himself decrying that fact or taking the lead in its use when he railed against the hearings as a "high-tech lynching for uppity blacks who in any way deign to think for themselves" (Phelps and Winternitz 1992, 332)? Whatever else, it was an effective use of language that painted an image of "nominee as victim," and it worked.

Journalists and political activists speak of the need to *frame* the debate or the discussion of a controversy. Framing is defining a situ-ation or circumstance with language designed to give advantage to one's particular interest. Raising insanity as an issue in the Rutledge confirmation was designed to frame the confirmation debate in terms of his mental stability and divert attention from his qualifica-tions and from the partisan nature of the opposition—and it worked.

Spin is a term that designates an effort to attach a particular in-terpretation to events, activities, and statements. No recent event in American history demonstrates more clearly the efforts by op-posing sides to cast a particular spin to events and statements as does the nomination of Robert Bork to the Supreme Court. Indeed, it may be said that the rejection of Bork by the Senate came about because his opponents were more successful than his supporters in getting their spin on the nomination accepted by the public and by the Senate. For example, when Bork responded that he looked for-ward to service on the Court as an "intellectual feast," opponents were somewhat successful in putting a spin on the comment that made Bork appear to lack compassion and sensitivity to the fact that Court cases affect people in very real and personal ways.

There is simply no way around the fact that the appointment process is a political process not only in a broad sense but in a nar-rower sense of partisan politics. This realization should not be surprising. The constitutional process involving Court appointments was itself a political compromise. Appointment by the president with advice and consent of the Senate did not reveal the wisdom of the framers; it demonstrated the inability of either those who favored a strong executive or those who favored a strong legislature to dominate the other (Harris 1953, 17–24). To expect that two political branches of government could avoid politics in establishing and staffing the third branch is not only unrealistic, it was unintended. Our political system is designed to cope with competing interests through a system of checks and balances. It deals with politics not through the denial of the existence of politics but through the recognition and competition of opposing political forces.

The Nature of Confirmation Politics

While the nomination and confirmation process is a political one, it is not politics as usual. Confirmation politics is different. To understand how it differs requires some understanding about the "normal" politics of the legislative process. Woodrow Wilson's wonderful metaphor of "the dance of legislation" (1913, 297) alluded to two major features of the legislative process that remain relevant today. First, the legislative process is intricate. Legislation must struggle through a maze of committees and subcommittees, at the mercy of a number of power brokers both within and outside of the Congress. The fact that there are two legislative chambers through which legislation must pass adds a second layer of mazes on top of the first. Second, legislation begets even more legislation. Most legislation "has a long lineage of statutes behind it" and most likely will result in "numerous progeny" (Wilson 1913, 297). While much in American politics and in the Congress may have changed, accounts of the modern process do not dispute the complexity of the process.

By way of contrast, confirmation politics is distinguished by the fact that the initiative for appointment rests solely with the president. The legislative role is merely to respond by giving or withholding consent. Moreover, this advice and consent function involves only the Senate. There are no deals, no compromises, and no playing off the House of Representatives. More often than not, the confirmation process also anticipates a single vote—to confirm or reject the nominee. There are no amendments, no riders, and lately no voice votes; there is no place for the senators to hide. There are no outcomes where everybody gets a little bit of what they want. There are only winners and losers.

In addition to these structural distinctions, changes in the role of the Court, the media, and advocacy group politics uniquely shape the process. The Court has expanded the scope of its authority in the twentieth century by incorporating many rights in the first eight amendments to apply to state action. The willingness of the Court to involve itself in matters that affect the general citizenry has consequently expanded and diversified the number of persons and groups who want to play a role in the selection of the Court's personnel. Coupled with an unprecedented rise in the 1960s, 1970s, and 1980s of organizations to advocate the views of particular interests, the number of advocacy groups that involved themselves in the Bork nomination totaled in the hundreds, likely the most numerous and diverse collection of groups involved in any single issue before the Senate. The recent intrusion of television into the hearings room and an increased propensity for "investigative journalism" have publicized the appointment process as never before.

These political realities have considerable consequences for the nature of politics in the confirmation process. First, they raise the stakes of the game in the sense that more people and groups perceive that they have something to gain or lose in the outcome. The stakes are further raised by the recognition that there are no partial or moral victories. Higher stakes are more likely to produce a "no holds barred" effort to achieve victory, assuming that the potential for a victory is present. On the other hand, widespread acceptance of a president's nominee tends to suppress opposition efforts if little is to be gained from such opposition. A little opposition does not go a long way.

Second, the normal legislative process is designed to frustrate the passage of legislation. The burden rests with the proponents of legislation to establish the benefits of passing that legislation. In confirmation politics, however, the exclusive power of the president to appoint, combined with the stark visibility of the senators' votes, has historically placed the burden on those who would reject the nomination to establish that the president's nominee is somehow unfit to serve. To apply Wilson's dance metaphor, presidents and their supporters aim for a confirmation two-step in which the president leads with a nominee and the Senate, following that lead, confirms.

However, in situations where considerable opposition to the president exists, a third consequence of the nature of confirmation politics is that the president's control over the process is diminished. The two-step gives way to an improvisation, one in which there is often no real leadership, with the president's supporters, senators, and advocacy groups all engaged in uncoordinated actions. In the Clarence Thomas nomination, a conservative group supporting Thomas placed television and newspaper ads shortly after the nomination. These ads assaulted the chair of the Senate Judiciary Committee, Joseph Biden, and Democratic Senators Ted Kennedy and Alan Cranston as lacking legitimacy to evaluate Thomas and urging the public to rally behind Thomas and against the Democratic liberals on the Committee (Marcus 1991b). The White House, dismayed by the ads, sent word to the conservative group that such character assassination in support of Thomas was not helpful.

Typically, the opposition is even less well organized. In *Decision*, Richard Harris details the reluctance among different senators to assume a leadership role in opposition to the Carswell nomination. He also portrays how individualistic the initial efforts were to organize opposition to Carswell (Harris 1971). Michael Pertschuk and Wendy Schaetzel, chroniclers of the Bork opposition efforts, describe the considerable effort that it took for the anti-Bork coalition to resist the individualistic impulses to go in different directions (Pertschuk and Schaetzel 1989, 36–61).

A fourth consequence that today's political realities have for confirmation politics is that the public is more easily aroused to attention as a result of increased media coverage. Unlike the normal legislative process, which deals with various matters of public policy, Supreme Court nominations focus uniquely upon a person and the question of whether that person is fit to be a justice. It is no accident that the *Anita Hill* v. *Clarence Thomas* confrontation snared large television audiences. By this personification of issues in single individuals, the media, particularly television, can take a heretofore obscure part of the American political process and elevate it significantly in the public consciousness. A major consequence of such media coverage is to effectively introduce constituency opinion into a senator's decision-making calculus, a factor of considerable importance in controversial nominations.

Confirmation politics thus differs from normal politics in significant ways, but it is still politics. The choice of a Supreme Court nominee by the president is a political policy choice, and it is responded to by various political interests as a policy choice. Attempts to cover the nomination and confirmation process with a normative gloss, namely, that the president and Senate should be concerned only with the nominee's qualifications, which have been generally defined as integrity, competence, and temperament, are largely ploys to gain an advantage over the opposition by claiming that the opposition is playing politics with the Court. It is this paradox of attempting to portray politically driven motivations as concern over a nominee's qualifications that brings about the discrepancy between words and actions and can make the process appear as a sham. In reality, both sides are involved in what they scornfully attribute to the other—the "low road" of politics. There is a certain irony to that portrayal, given that the business of all of these participants is politics.

CHAPTER TWO

The Vacancy

> I heard Justice Harlan tell of the anxiety which the Court had felt because of the condition of Justice Field. It occurred to the other members of the Court that Justice Field had served on a committee which waited upon Justice Grier to suggest his retirement, and it was thought that recalling that to his memory might aid him to decide to retire. Justice Harlan was deputed to make the suggestion. He went over to Justice Field, who was sitting alone on a settee in the robing room apparently oblivious of his surroundings, and after arousing him gradually approached the question, asking if he did not recall how anxious the Court had become with respect to Justice Grier's condition and the feeling of the other Justices that in his own interest and in that of the Court he should give up his work. Justice Harlan asked if Justice Field did not remember what had been said to Justice Grier on that occasion. The old man listened, gradually became alert and finally, with his eyes blazing with the old fire of youth, he burst, "Yes! And a dirtier day's work I never did in my life!"
>
> *Charles Evans Hughes*

The story may be apocryphal (Hughes 1936, 75–76; Wright 1990), but it conveys with some humor that justices, as a rule, cherish their time on the Court and leave it only with great reluctance. Holding office "during good behavior," in the words of the Constitution, is in reality a lifetime appointment, meaning that a vacancy occurs only when a sitting justice has decided to step aside or has died. Indeed, dying was the principle way by which justices left the Court prior to the attractive retirement package—retirement at full pay—implemented in 1937. Designed to entice the "tired old men" off the Court, retirement has become the principal way of departing the Court, Robert Jackson being the last to die in office in 1954 (Box 2.1).

"Timing is everything," so the saying goes. As a political maxim, this means that whoever controls timing often controls the outcome. While it appears that the occurrence of a vacancy rests with the justices themselves or with fate, the political stakes of who sits on the Court are often too great to resist tampering. Presidents, senators, the public, and the justices themselves have all attempted

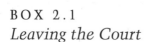

BOX 2.1
Leaving the Court

The Justice Marshall Press Conference, July 7, 1991

Reporter

Why did you decide to resign?

Marshall:

I didn't resign; I retired!

There are essentially four ways for justices to leave the Court: retirement, resignation, removal through the impeachment process, or death. In our earlier history, before full retirement options, three justices left through disability provisions, which we treat here as equivalent to retirement. Justice Whittaker also left the Court in 1962 under disability provisions but later resigned. As Justice Marshall vigorously pointed out to a reporter, retirement and resignation are not the same. Before 1869, there were no retirement benefits, hence no retirement. Resignation or death were the two ways to leave the Court. A retirement provision in 1869 permitted justices 70 years of age or over and with at least 10 years on the Court to leave the Court at their current pay, although that amount was susceptible to change, including a decrease. In the aftermath of the 1937 Court packing plan, a more attractive option permitted these "70/10" retiring justices to remain "on call" as Article 3 judges who, according to the Constitution, may not have their salaries diminished "during their continuance in office." Effectively, this permitted retirement at full pay. Resignations now occur when the sitting justice fails to meet the retirement criteria or chooses to forego the Article 3 retirement privileges. Below are data on the justices who have left the Court.

Year of Departure	Death	Resignation	Retirement	Removal
Through 1868	22	9	0	0
1869–1899	10	1	6	0
1900–1936	9	2	8	0
1937–1994	7	4	22	0
Totals	48	16	36	0

Methods of Departure

Note

The total number of departures (100) is one more than the total number of people who have left the Court (99) because Charles Evans Hughes served at two different times, resigning in 1916 to run for the presidency and then returning to the Court in 1930 and retiring in 1941. Moreover, the numbers here do not reflect the interim appointment and service of John Rutledge during his second time on the Court. Having resigned in 1791 from his initial appointment to the Court, Rutledge was subsequently given a recess appointment by George Washington and actually presided as chief justice in 1795, only to be rejected by the Senate when it returned to session and Rutledge's name was formally submitted for confirmation.

at various times to influence the timing of vacancies to promote their political agendas. This may mean seeking to create a vacancy immediately in order to change the current direction of court decisions. Alternatively, it may mean seeking to delay a vacancy until the timing is more favorable to appointing and confirming a justice presumed to possess a particular ideological or jurisprudential bent.

This chapter deals with the timing of vacancies and, therefore, the timing of appointments. We shall pay particular attention to two significant aspects of the appointment process that are influenced by the timing of a vacancy. First, a vacancy occurs within the context of a given political setting. It occurs within the term of a particular president and with a particular partisan and ideological division in the Senate. Second, the vacancy occurs amidst particular concerns and issues of the day. Those concerns inevitably serve to define the issues that will motivate the debate about the nominee and preliminarily establish the factors that will encourage or discourage controversy concerning the nomination.

The Politics of Timing

The Constitution provides that the president, with the advice and consent of the Senate, shall appoint Supreme Court justices. However, the timing of a vacancy will determine which president and which senators play these constitutional roles. One need not reach far back into history to find significant examples of timing that influenced outcomes. When Chief Justice Earl Warren announced his retirement in 1968, the president was the liberal Democrat Lyndon Johnson. However, when Johnson's nomination of Abe Fortas to fill that seat was blocked by the Senate, the vacancy was effectively postponed until Johnson's successor, Republican Richard Nixon, took office. Nixon's appointment of the conservative Warren Burger, compared to Johnson's nomination of the liberal Fortas, amply demonstrates that which president has the opportunity to fill a vacancy is of great importance (Abraham 1985, 286–287, 296–298).

The composition of the Senate can also be a factor. When President Reagan appointed Antonin Scalia to the Court in 1986, the Senate was controlled by the Republican party and the nomination sailed through. However, by the time of the next vacancy, scarcely one year later, the Senate was controlled by a more liberal set of Democrats. While many factors contributed to the Senate's rejection of Reagan's nominee, Judge Robert Bork, one significant factor was the timing of this vacancy, which led to a different cast of characters in the Senate.

Given what is at stake, it is not surprising that Supreme Court history is replete with attempts to manipulate the timing of a vacancy or the subsequent appointment. There are at least four constitutionally permissible methods by which such manipulation may occur to (1) impeach and remove a sitting justice, (2) change the size of the Court, (3) deny or postpone consideration of a nominee in order to extend the duration of the vacancy, and (4) time the departure of a sitting justice.

Impeachment

A Supreme Court justice serves during good behavior but may be impeached and removed from office for "high crimes and misdemeanors." To be impeached is, in effect, to be indicted. The consequence of being impeached, which can be performed only by the House of Representatives, is to face a trial in the Senate. Approval of the bill(s) of indictment by the Senate removes the justice from office. Rejection of the bill(s) leaves the justice in place. No sitting justice has ever been removed from office, and only one has been impeached, but a few justices have been the target of impeachment threats. While such attempts are usually cloaked in claims of unethical behavior, the motivation is invariably political— based on the desire to remove a politically offensive justice, thus creating a vacancy to which a more acceptable person might be appointed.

ARTICLE 2, SECTION 4

All civil officers of the United States, shall be removed from office on impeachment for, and conviction of, treason, bribery, or other high crimes and misdemeanors.

THE CONSTITUTION

It didn't take long for the impeachment process to be invoked. In 1804, Justice Samuel Chase was accused of conducting partisan activities and partisan diatribes from the bench that amounted to "high crimes and misdemeanors." In reality, his main "crime" was being an active Federalist at a time when the Jeffersonians had gained control of the presidency and Congress. It was well understood at the time that the impeachment was a partisan action, consistent with a Jeffersonian notion of using impeachment to "keep the Courts in reasonable harmony with the will of the Nation" (Warren 1935, 1:293). Although impeached by the House, Chase was acquitted by the Senate. Failing in this political purge, Jefferson lamented that impeachment was impracticable, "a farce which will not be tried again" (quoted in Warren 1935, 1:295).

Despite the precedent-setting acquittal of Chase there have been calls from time to time to impeach politically unpopular justices. The most visible call for such action came in the form of numerous road signs in the 1950s and 1960s to "Impeach Earl Warren," presumably because of the liberal direction the Court pursued under his tenure as chief justice (Schwartz 1983, 280–282). Another liberal justice, William O. Douglas, was pursued more seriously in the 1960s by then-House Minority Leader Gerald Ford. Again, while couched in terms of ethical impropriety, these attempts were primarily a result of liberal decisions by the justices, particularly in the areas of the rights of minorities and the accused (Simon 1980, 391–411). While vehement in spirit, these efforts could not surmount the Chase precedent.

Although direct attempts at impeachment have not been successful, the threat of impeachment may have led in one modern instance to the resignation of a justice. In 1969 Justice Abe Fortas was threatened with impeachment as a result of alleged improper financial dealings (Murphy 1988, 566). While there was some truth to the accusations against him, the primary motive seemed to have been to remove a liberal member of the Court and create a vacancy for the newly elected Richard Nixon to fill. The pressure on Fortas ultimately led to his resignation. In explaining his decision, Fortas admitted "no wrongdoing," but concluded that "the public controversy [concerning his alleged unethical behavior] is likely to continue and adversely affect the work and position of the Court." (Shogan 1972, 282).

Changing the Size of the Court

Article 3 of the Constitution simply says that there shall be a Supreme Court; it does not specify the size of that Court; the size is left for the Congress to legislate. During the first 70 or so years of the republic, the size of the Court was changed no fewer than seven times and proposals for change were defeated several other times. The Court has remained with nine justices since 1869, however, and as President Franklin Roosevelt would discover later, the days of tampering with the size of the Court are probably over.

Court membership was initially set at six by the Judiciary Act of 1789. That the Court was considered ripe for political picking, however, was evident with the first switch in partisan control of the Congress. In 1801, as the Federalists were about to lose both the presidency (from John Adams to Thomas Jefferson) and the House of Representatives, they reduced the size of the Court from six to five, even though no seat was presently vacant. Had the reduction in size stuck, Jefferson would not have been able to make an appointment even when one of the six justices left the Court! But the Federalist effort did not stick. In 1802, the Jeffersonian Congress repealed the 1801 law, and Jefferson made his first appointment in 1804.

As Box 2.2 illustrates, the size of the Court has been reduced with the intent to deny appointments to presidents on two different occasions, and it has been increased to provide or restore appointments for presidents five times. However, increases in the size of the Court were not solely motivated by a desire to give a president more appointments. The Judiciary Act of 1789 had created a system

---

★ ★ ★ ★ ★ ★ ★ ★ ★

BOX 2.2
Changes in the Size of the Court

Court Size	Congressional Action	Politics Involved
6	Judiciary Act of 1789	
5	Circuit Court Act of 1801	Federalists attempt to secure the Court against Jeffersonian encroachment by reducing its size to prevent Jefferson from replacing the next vacancy on the Court.
6	Repeal of the 1801 Act	Jeffersonians repeal the Circuit Court Act and restore the Court size to six. No vacancy occurs between the passage of the act and its repeal.
7	Act of February 24, 1807	Presumably necessitated by the growth of Kentucky, Tennessee, and Ohio, the Western Circuit is created and Jefferson gains an appointment. An amendment to postpone the effective date of the act in order to qualify one of the bill's congressional sponsors for the Court appointment is defeated (Warren 1935, 1:300–301).

Court Size	Congressional Action	Politics Involved
9	Act of March 3, 1837	Presidents Madison, Monroe, Adams, and Jackson are all unsuccessful in urging Congress to increase the size of the Court. Finally, on Jackson's last day in office, two new seats are created and Jackson immediately submits nominations. One nominee, however, declines, giving the vacancy to President Van Buren. The commission of the other appointee (Justice Catron) is issued by Van Buren (Warren, 1935, 2:39–41—note that Warren's statement that the Court was increased from six to eight seats is incorrect; it went from seven to nine).
10	Act of March 3, 1863	A circuit is created for California and Oregon to recognize and solidify their attachment to the Union during the Civil War.
7	Act of July 23, 1866	The vacancy created by the death of Justice Catron gives President Andrew Johnson an appointment. An antagonistic Congress moves quickly to reduce the size of the Court to seven to eliminate that vacancy and any other likely to occur during Johnson's term.
9	Act of April 10, 1869	The size of the Court actually reached eight under Johnson. As part of a broader overhaul of the Court system, a ninth justice is added, providing President Grant with a vacancy to fill.

of regional circuits for the handling of federal court business, and justices were responsible for literally riding the circuit to conduct that business. As the size of the country increased, circuit riding became an increasingly onerous responsibility, one in fact that led to considerable ill-health among the justices. If Congress wished to maintain these circuit-riding responsibilities, then more justices were needed to keep the task manageable and to ensure that new states were adequately covered. Efforts to increase the size of the Court, however, were typically defeated during the years between presidents Jefferson and Jackson by those who wished to avoid giving the president additional vacancies to fill.

Most of these changes in the Court's size involved a difference of only one or two justices. Therefore, when Franklin Roosevelt proposed a plan in 1937 that would permit the Court to increase from nine to fifteen members, even his allies gave pause. Roosevelt was confronted with the most severe challenge to the political system since the Civil War. Congress had given Lincoln one new position to fill, in part, to ensure that the Court did not interfere with the exigencies brought on by the war. Combined with three vacancies that came about naturally at the beginning of his term, Lincoln had four appointments within the first two years of office (Warren 1935, 2:374–380). Roosevelt, on the other hand, had no vacancies arise during his first term. He became increasingly frustrated with a conservative Court that seemed intent on striking down piece after piece of his New Deal for economic recovery.

After his landslide reelection in 1936, Roosevelt embarked on the infamous "court-packing" plan of 1937. As he saw it, his problem resulted from the Court being controlled by Republican-appointed justices, who opposed the abandonment of traditional free-market policies. He further assumed that if he could have the opportunity to appoint some of his own justices, the Court-imposed barrier to his New Deal would disappear. The problem was that there were no vacancies, and while the five anti–New Deal justices were over 70, they steadfastly refused to retire.

Though couched in terms of concern for the Court's workload, Roosevelt's plan was blatantly political in nature, though no more so than earlier changes in the Court's size. His initial plan—there were actually two (Leuchtenburg 1985)—would permit a president to appoint an additional justice to the Court for each justice on the Court who was over 70 and had served at least 10 years on the court. The Court would be permitted to increase to no more than fifteen members (Alsop and Catledge 1938, 54–55). The immediate effect would have been six new appointments.

Roosevelt's proposal ultimately failed because of a growing concern that to permit such explicit political manipulation of the

Court would forever destroy the independence of the Court. However, while Roosevelt lost the battles, he won the war. Two of the justices on the Court who previously had opposed the New Deal programs, Hughes and especially Roberts, began to uphold them against constitutional challenges. Whether this so-called "switch in time that saved nine" (Alsop and Catledge 1938, 135) came about by the pressure exerted on the Court, a concern about the independence and integrity of the Court, or an improved retirement option that did get enacted (see Box 2.1) will likely never be known (Stern 1988, 94–96). In the final analysis, the Court had weathered the strongest challenge to executive hegemony since Thomas Jefferson fomented the impeachment of Samuel Chase.

Senate Attempts to Delay Vacancies

Impeachment and modifying the size of the Court are rare almost to the point of nonexistence. A much more common method of influencing the timing of a vacancy for the Senate is to extend the vacancy until a situation or a nominee more favorable to the dominant group in the Senate presents itself. This is most easily done in a president's last year of office, with the argument that the new president should make the appointment. Of course, delays may also be achieved by rejecting a nominee or by other delaying tactics, such as prolonging the consideration of a nomination in an effort to extort the president into withdrawing it.

To do battle in the hope that the president will come forward with a nominee more suitable to the Senate is a risky proposition. Presidents carry the initiative and the Senate risks their ire by delaying or rejecting a nominee. When the Senate supported Daniel Webster's motion to postpone indefinitely the nomination of Roger Taney to the Court just moments before Senate adjournment, an angry President Jackson left the Capitol, noting that it was past midnight and he would accept no further messages from "the damned scoundrels" (Warren 1935, 2:802). However, Senate opponents had outsmarted themselves. Four months later, Chief Justice John Marshall died, and the president stuck Taney right back in the Senate's face, only this time as a nominee for chief justice. In an acrimonious debate, much more so than we are accustomed to today, Taney was approved (Warren 1935, 2:10–15).

The president's power to appoint usually provides him with the advantage in struggles with the Senate. Thus, when an angry Richard Nixon followed up the rejection of Clement Haynsworth with orders to find "almost any southerner" who fit his profile of a conservative, strict constructionist without the financial holdings that doomed Haynsworth (Massaro 1990, 106), the Senate at first seem predisposed to go along. Nonetheless, despite fatigue and little desire to do battle on another nomination, the Senate refused to acquiesce and rejected the new nominee, Harrold Carswell. This second rejection resulted in Harry Blackmun being appointed to the Court, a true victory for those in the Senate opposed to the first two nominees.

Such Senate "victories" are rare, and few senators are eager to battle a president over the prerogative to name the nominee. On occasion, arguments are heard that a nominee should be accepted because the alternative may be worse. For example, among the comments regarding President Grant's appointment of Morrison Waite was "Considering what the President might have done..., we ought to be very thankful and give Mr. Waite a cordial welcome" (Warren 1935, 2:561).

More common than direct and continuing confrontation with the president is the use of delays by the Senate to provide a new president with an immediate Court vacancy to fill. Abe Fortas's nomination to be Chief Justice was blocked by a minifilibuster, resulting in his eventual withdrawal and the gift of a Court vacancy for Richard Nixon in his first year as president, courtesy of a coalition of Republicans and southern Democrats. In a much earlier battle, the ill-fated Millard Fillmore failed to gain Senate action on three consecutive nominees for a particular vacancy over a period of seven months in 1852 and 1853, and the vacancy was passed on to Franklin Pierce (Warren 1935, 2:242–245). Much more recently, the Democratic chair of the Senate Judiciary Committee, Joseph Biden, didn't even wait for a vacancy to occur when he announced in the spring of what would be the last year of George Bush's presidency in 1992 that the Committee would not hold confirmation hearings even if a vacancy and nomination did arise!

Delaying tactics by the Senate do carry some peril. The Whigs in 1844 were determined to frustrate John Tyler's effort to fill a vacancy on the Court in anticipation of a Henry Clay presidential election victory. One of the leaders in rejecting and postponing Tyler nominations was John J. Crittenden, who expected to be Clay's first nominee to the Court. However, when Clay lost the election, the Whigs discovered they had succeeded instead in giving a nomination to the incoming Democrat, James K. Polk.

Timing Departures from the Court

While the Senate may prolong a vacancy once it has occurred, the timing of the initial vacancy is more susceptible to influence by the president or, of course, by the departing justice. Lyndon Johnson in 1965 engineered one of the most blatant manipulations of Court personnel when he was confronted with the need to appoint a new ambassador to the United Nations. Johnson saw this as an opportunity to place his friend and advisor, Abe Fortas, on the Court. There were only two obstacles to overcome: Fortas didn't want to be on the Court and there was no vacancy to be filled. Not bothered by such trifles, Johnson persuaded a reluctant Arthur Goldberg, who had cheerfully accepted an appointment to the Court only three years prior, to resign from the Court and take the position of ambassador to the United Nations (Abraham 1985, 282–283). All that remained was for Johnson to refuse to take no for an answer, a response that Fortas was giving even as Johnson, unbeknownst to Fortas, walked him into the press conference where the nomination was announced (Murphy 1988, 179–180).

More common than presidential attempts to induce a court departure is the behavior of sitting justices who attempt to use their departure in such a way as to influence a nomination. Justices try to hang on during periods in which the presidency is in hands they deem hostile to their vision of the Court, and they may step aside more easily if they perceive the presidency is in friendly hands. After the reelection of Andrew Jackson in 1832, Chief Justice John Marshall and Justice Duvall were intent on outlasting Jackson, despite their failing health. Duvall left the Court early in 1835 after assurances that Jackson would appoint Roger Taney, of whom Duvall approved (Swisher 1974, 22–23). As we saw, however, Taney was initially rejected by the Senate, but in a touch of irony was later that year nominated and eventually confirmed as the replacement for the legendary Marshall, who died in July, unable to outlast Jackson.

Justice Story, Marshall's ally on the Court, continued to hold out through Jackson's successor, Martin Van Buren (Newmeyer 1985, 221). Story was prepared to resign to give the newly elected Whig, William Henry Harrison, a Court vacancy when fate intervened. Harrison's untimely death brought John Tyler to the presidency. Tyler was an anti-Jackson Democrat, not a Whig, who had been put on the Whig ticket with Harrison to draw voters from the Democratic party. A rift developed quickly between the new president and the Whigs, which stayed Story's resignation until at least 1845. Now anticipating a Whig victory with the legendary Henry Clay as its presidential candidate, Story was stunned by Clay's defeat at the hands of the Democrat James K. Polk. Depressed over the future of the Court, he could hold out no longer (Dunne 1970, 424–425). But having decided to resign, Justice Story died before he could do so, unable to place his vacancy in the hands of a president he could trust.

A different tack of a sitting justice attempting to control the destiny of his own vacancy was the announced retirement in 1967 of Chief Justice Earl Warren, a retirement that he made contingent upon the confirmation of his replacement. Warren hoped to have President Lyndon Johnson name a successor, presumably one compatible with the constitutional views of the sitting chief justice. The contingency apparently was based upon Warren's recognition that Johnson, who had already announced he would not seek reelection and whose support in Congress was waning, might have difficulties in appointing a successor.

As the saying goes, "The best laid plans. . . ." Southern conservatives and Republicans teamed to thwart the Fortas nomination, arguing in part that no vacancy existed. That Warren continued to serve enabled the conservative coalition to discourage any further effort by Johnson to name a replacement. Warren had no desire to continue for another four years and with the election of Richard Nixon, Warren retired, permitting his old political rival to fill the chief justiceship with Warren Burger—someone that Warren may have respected but with whom he no doubt did not agree on many issues of constitutional interpretation.

Other recent justices who hoped to outlast presidents they perceived as inimical to their own constitutional views were William O. Douglas and Thurgood Marshall. Douglas made it past Nixon but not Gerald Ford, who years earlier had spearheaded attempts to impeach Douglas. Had he held out another year and a half, he would have given the more ideologically compatible Jimmy Carter an opportunity that evaded his presidency—the chance to appoint a Supreme Court justice. Thurgood Marshall was reputed to have said that he would outlast the conservatives and retire when a more liberal Democratic president was elected. Little did he know that the decade of the 1980s would be dominated by conservative Republicans. With small hope that George Bush would be defeated in 1992, in declining health ("I'm falling apart," he said), and increasingly a mere dissenting voice in a diminishing minority, Marshall retired in 1991, giving the Republican Bush an opportunity to appoint a presumably more conservative Clarence Thomas to the Court. As it turned out, of course, George Bush was defeated by the Democrat Bill Clinton. Had Marshall not retired and remained on the Court until his death in early 1993, Clinton would have had the opportunity to fill the vacancy—almost certainly with someone who would have been closer to the ideological leaning of Marshall than was Clarence Thomas.

Timing and the Nomination Discourse

The timing of a vacancy not only affects which president and which Senate will fill the vacancy, it also shapes the issues and concerns that will animate the discourse surrounding the nomination. Thus, as reaction to the Court's decision in *Roe* v. *Wade* swelled into a national debate on abortion through the 1970s, the major issue in the nomination of Sandra O'Connor to the Court in 1981 became her position on abortion. All through the 1980s and again with the nomination of Clarence Thomas in 1991, the major opposition to a nominee was led by one side or the other on the abortion issue (pro-life opposition to O'Connor, pro-choice in the remaining instances). In the case of O'Connor, who had an ambiguous record on this issue, pro-life senators on the Judiciary Committee (Denton, East, and Grassley) immediately began to question her feelings about *Roe* and her willingness to overturn that decision. Before 1981, the words *abortion, birth control,* or even *privacy* were not a part of the language in Supreme Court nominations. Now they dominate the discourse and likely will continue to do so until the legacy of *Roe* v. *Wade* is settled.

One way to anticipate the discourse that will dominate a nomination is to ask what decisions of the Court have stirred public controversy during the period immediately before the vacancy. While there are a variety of ways to determine this, one that seems particularly useful is to look to the issues in Court cases that Congress has attempted to overturn through legislation or constitutional amendments. These actions should reflect issues before the Court that are of concern to the Congress and, therefore, likely to surface in the Senate's investigation of a nominee.

Issues Across the Decades

In 1954 the Court's decision in *Brown* v. *the Board of Education*, which declared racially separate public schools unconstitutional, caused a flurry of congressional actions. For example, on March 12, 1956, 19 senators and 74 representatives signed the "Southern Manifesto" protesting the "decisions of the Supreme Court in the school cases as a clear abuse of judicial discretion" (Congressional Quarterly 1956, 416–417). During the same period of time, the Court was taking a pro civil-libertarian stance in cases involving internal security, contempt of Congress, the federal loyalty-security program, and antisubversive statutes. In response, Congress in 1958 considered, but eventually rejected, legislation that would have deprived the Supreme Court of authority to review many of these types of cases.

These congressional actions during the 1950s should be reflected in the nomination discourse of that decade, and they are. For example, every nominee was questioned by southern senators about segregation and related "code words" like states' rights. Potter Stewart was perhaps the most straightforward in his response to these concerns. "I would not like you to vote for me on the assumption that I am dedicated to the cause of overturning [the Court's 1954 segregation] decision. Because I am not" (Congressional Quarterly 1959, 664). In a different and extraordinary action, the Senate Judiciary Committee permitted noncommittee member Joseph McCarthy to participate in the confirmation hearings of William Brennan. With the Court prepared to hear cases that would consider the constitutionality of congressional actions that would, among other things, define communism as a conspiracy to overthrow the government of the United States, McCarthy confronted Brennan:

> It is important before we vote on your confirmation that we know [whether] you consider communism merely as a political party or do you consider it as a conspiracy to overthrow this country? (Senate 1957, 19).

During the 1960s Congress acted upon a constitutional amendment that would have overturned the Supreme Court's decision in *Engel* v. *Vitale* (1962), which struck down mandatory prayer in public schools. Similarly, a constitutional amendment was introduced to overturn the Court's decisions in *Baker* v. *Carr* (1962) and *Reynolds* v. *Sims* (1964), which had mandated reapportionment for both chambers in state legislatures. Later in the decade, anti-Court sentiment found expression in the Omnibus Crime and Safe Streets Act of 1968, portions of which attempted, with limited success, to reverse three decisions of the Supreme Court dealing with defendant rights.[1]

The issues of religion, reapportionment, and criminal defendant rights did in fact shape much of the nomination discourse during the 1960s. A particularly dramatic example is Senator Strom Thurmond's pillorying of chief justice–designate Abe Fortas regarding decisions of the Court, especially *Mallory* v. *U.S.* (1957).

> Why did he go free? Do you believe in that kind of justice? Mallory, Mallory. I want that word to ring in your ears. He raped a woman and confessed it in court and the Supreme Court turned him loose on a technicality—free to commit other crimes. Can you condone such a decision? I ask you to answer this question. (*Congressional Quarterly* 1968, 534)

---

[1] *Mallory* v. *U.S.* (1957) restricted the use of confessions where there was unnecessary delay in bringing the suspect before a judge for arraignment. *Miranda* v. *Arizona* (1966) required police to advise suspects of their constitutional rights before conducting an interrogation or obtaining a confession. *U.S.* v. *Wade* (1967) established a right to counsel for suspects placed in a pretrial lineup in front of identifying witnesses.

The 1970s, of course, witnessed the infamous *Roe* v. *Wade* (1973) decision. Congressional actions in 1976 showed the salience and controversy of this issue. For example, while the Senate blocked an antiabortion constitutional amendment that year, Congress did pass the first Hyde Amendment, which prohibited federal funding for any nontherapeutic abortions. A similar funding prohibition has been attached annually to each Medicaid funding authorization since then. The Supreme Court declared these prohibitions constitutional in *Harris* v. *McRae* (1980).

The 1970s also saw Congress continue to wrestle with Court cases involving desegregation. This time, the issue was often busing. For example, in 1979 the House defeated an antibusing constitutional amendment. Failing with the amendment route, opponènts of Court rulings proposed legislation to remove the Court's authority to rule in these areas, as well as on the persistent school prayer issue. All such attempts failed, but their initiation marked these as issues likely to arise in a Court nomination. Of course, there was only one vacancy in the 1970s after *Roe* v. *Wade,* and the easy consensus with which John Paul Stevens was accepted preempted any serious questioning.

Confirmation issues do not rise and fall with the beginning and ending of decades. The abortion battle touched off by *Roe* v. *Wade* and the reaction that precipitated the Hyde amendment would carry into the 1980s and 1990s, driven by additional Court cases and Congressional and presidential responses.[2] The only serious questioning of Sandra Day O'Connor in 1981 came from pro-life senators Denton, East, and Grassley and concerned her stance on a woman's right to choose. Similarly, the abortion issue, along with the related question of privacy, was central to the Bork nomination discourse in 1987. More recently, if the Anita Hill charges are set aside, a dominant aspect of the Clarence Thomas discourse was his views on privacy and abortion. For example, Judiciary Committee Chair Joseph Biden led off the Thomas hearings with a series of questions concerning natural law and the nominee's view of the relationship between such "higher" law and the Constitution. These questions were clearly motivated at least in part by Biden's concern about whether abortion violated Thomas's conception of natural law and whether as a justice he would act upon such conceptions.

---

[2] Although in the 1992 Casey decision the Supreme Court by a vote of five to four explicitly reaffirmed a woman's constitutional right to an abortion, the closeness of that vote assures that nomination discourse well into the 1990s will continue to focus on the nominee's views on abortion and the Roe decision (see *Planned Parenthood of Southeastern Pennsylvania* v. *Casey,* 60 U.S.L.W. 4795 [1992]).

While speech issues have been an aspect of nomination discourse for much of this century, they took on a new dimension in the late 1980s when the Supreme Court ruled unconstitutional a Texas law that prohibited the desecration of an American flag (*Texas* v. *Johnson,* 1989). In response Congress quickly passed and the president immediately signed the Flag Protection Act of 1989, which explicitly overruled *Texas* v. *Johnson,* only to be declared unconstitutional itself in 1990 (*U.S.* v. *Eichman*). A further attempt to overrule Johnson through a constitutional amendment failed, although it gained presidential support and favorable votes from 254 members of the House of Representatives. Both David Souter and Clarence Thomas were questioned on their views of the First Amendment and flag burning.

The 1990s will witness the linkage between abortion and freedom of speech as that linkage relates to the constitutional right of antiabortion groups such as Operation Rescue to protest in front of and often block access to abortion clinics. In January 1993 the Supreme Court reaffirmed on statutory grounds the rights of these protesters in *Bray* v. *Alexandria Women's Health Clinic* (1993). However, as the issue becomes more inflamed and perhaps even violent, there will be increasingly strident calls for the government to act and for the Court to rule on those actions. The obvious salience of the flag-burning question, the continuing question of antiabortion protesters' rights, and the Court's 1992 decision declaring unconstitutional St. Paul, Minnesota's attempt to prohibit cross burning (*R.A.V.* v. *St. Paul,* 1992) indicate that the issue of symbolic and protest speech will continue to be part of the 1990s nomination discourse.

A final aspect of 1980s' nomination discourse, which will surely extend into the 1990s, is the question of affirmative action. First ruled on by the Court in 1978 in *Regents* v. *Bakke* (1978), the question has often appeared before the Court (*Richmond* v. *Croson,* 1989). Congressional conflict over this issue is reflected in the debates about the Civil Rights Act of 1990, which reversed several key affirmative action–related decisions by the Supreme Court. Every nominee in recent times has been questioned about affirmative action. The controversy associated with this issue, combined with the Court's consistent failure to articulate a clear majority position, suggest that it will continue to play an important role in nomination discourse.

Litmus Tests as Nomination Discourse

When an issue becomes so critical that acceptance or rejection of the nominee is based solely on that issue, a litmus test has been created. The use of a litmus test in the appointment process is almost universally decried by presidents and senators, though not of course by advocacy groups. An advocacy group is likely to see its interest as critical, enough so that its support should be a necessary condition for confirmation to the Supreme Court or at least that its opposition should be a sufficient condition for rejecting a nominee.

The conventional view is that litmus tests have no place in the appointment of justices. It is to the advantage of both the president and the Senate to maintain that justices are selected on the basis of legal and judicial qualifications and not because of political ideology or because of some view on a particular issue. This belief constitutes one of the splendid myths of American politics. Claiming an overriding concern with legal and judicial qualifications can help either side claim the higher moral ground while charging the other side with baser political motivations. In the 1980s and 1990s, however, charges that abortion is a litmus test for both pro-life and pro-choice forces have become common—and not without some justification.

Both Presidents Reagan and Bush are thought to have selected justices with a view to overturning *Roe* v. *Wade*. The rejection of any potential nominee believed sympathetic to *Roe* means that it has been used as a litmus test. In 1981, it became clear that Judiciary Committee members East, Denton, and—perhaps—Grassley would vote no on O'Connor if they determined that she would likely support *Roe*. In Thomas's 1991 confirmation hearings, Senator Metzenbaum stated, "I will not support yet another Reagan-Bush Supreme Court nominee who remains silent" on abortion (Woodward 1991, A9). During his campaign for the presidency, Bill Clinton hinted that a willingness to uphold *Roe* v. *Wade* might be important in his selection of a justice.

The opprobrium directed at litmus tests is somewhat curious, however, because selection to the Court actually involves a series of litmus tests. It is an irony of political language that the more universally accepted a particular litmus test, the less likely it is to be recognized and labeled as a litmus test. For example, acceptance of the result in *Brown* v. *Board* (1954) in desegregating public schools is today effectively a necessary condition for a Supreme Court appointment. Similarly, accepting that the "equal protection" clause of the Fourteenth Amendment applies to classifications other than race or that the First Amendment's free speech guarantee extends beyond political speech are two other litmus tests in the minds of a sufficient number of senators to disqualify nominees who would oppose such views.

In the vocabulary of nomination politics, litmus tests that are universally accepted define the legal mainstream. Opponents of Robert Bork were able to frame his confirmation debate around the issue of whether he was outside the mainstream of American legal and constitutional thought on precisely those issues just mentioned. Bork's supporters could not justify his earlier published opinions, which violated those liberal litmus tests now enshrined as mainstream; they could argue only that he either never did or did not now believe that way. Thus was born the "confirmation conversion" label that stuck to Bork and did so much to bring about his rejection. He was damned if he did adhere to his earlier positions and, as it turned out, damned if he didn't.

One strategy employed by players in the confirmation game is to define their particular litmus test as rightfully belonging within the mainstream of legal and constitutional thought. An example of that effort has been to wrap the controversial term *abortion* in a package of "privacy" and then declare that privacy is a fundamental right, with those who believe otherwise labeled as outside the mainstream. That tactic has likely helped pro-choice forces gain added public support for their cause, but it has not worked in the confirmation process. That abortion raises issues other than privacy and generates considerable controversy will prevent it from being successfully included within the notion that privacy is constitutionally protected.

Recent Confirmation History as a Source of Nomination Discourse

In addition to looking to the major criticisms of the current Court as a source of nomination vocabulary, the more recent nominations also play a role. This is particularly true if a recent nomination has received considerable opposition or has been defeated. For example, while a conservative coalition succeeded in stopping the Fortas nomination and even forced his eventual resignation, they unwittingly sowed the seeds for the defeat of Clement Haynsworth, Nixon's nominee for the 1969 Fortas vacancy (Massaro 1990, 79–86).

As opponents of Fortas looked for ways to nail him, they focused on allegations of financial impropriety and conflict of interest. Consequently, Senate liberals retaliated in the Haynsworth nomination by incorporating financial and ethical concerns into the vocabulary of that nomination. As several senators stated, given what had happened to Fortas it was impossible simply to ignore the financial record and ethical issues regarding Clement Haynsworth (Massaro 1990, 80–81). Certain Republicans like Robert Griffin, the minority whip who had led the fight against Fortas, found it impossible to escape the trap set by the Haynsworth opposition. Since that nomination, terms like *financial dealings, conflict of interest,* and *unethical behavior* have been on the lips and minds of all participants in subsequent nominations. For its part, the Senate Judiciary Committee now requests extensive documentation concerning the nominee's financial dealings and professional associations.

Other issues that have been brought into the discourse of Supreme Court nominations are memberships in clubs that exclude minorities or women (Carswell in 1970), whether the nominee is within or outside the "mainstream" of American legal thought (Bork in 1987), and the previous use of marijuana or other drugs (Ginsburg in 1987). Attention to these issues is now a standard part of the nomination process. Of course, issues may come and go over time, although perhaps not as frequently as one might expect. Louis Brandeis' nomination in 1916 actually foreshadowed more recent ones in many ways, particularly with its allegations of financial misconduct, conflict of interest, and the characterization of Brandeis as lacking judicial temperament and being outside the mainstream of American legal thought (Mason 1946, 465–508).

Nomination Setting

The timing of a vacancy is critical to a nomination because of the political context or setting within which the vacancy arises. While the qualifications and character of a particular nominee to the Court also significantly affect the extent to which a nomination will be controversial, the seeds of controversy lay in the setting at the time of the nomination. If the setting is quite favorable for the president, then the likelihood of a nomination becoming controversial is considerably diminished. On the other hand, if the setting is not so favorable for the president, then the likelihood of opposition developing about the nomination is increased. It is worth emphasizing again that the favorableness of the setting for the president's nomination exists at the time of the vacancy. It precedes any controversy that might arise in response to a particular nominee or to the nomination itself. It is the presumption of favor that would attach to any nominee at the time of the president's announcement.

There are several elements that contribute to the nomination setting. We identify four that seem to be particularly important: (1) the political composition of the Senate, (2) the level of support in the Senate for the president's programs, (3) public opinion regarding the president, and (4) attributes of the vacancy itself, such as the influence of previous recent nominations and the status of the departing justice. The first three of these elements relate to the effectiveness of a president more generally to achieve programmatic success in Congress (Brace and Hinckley 1992, 79–83).

The fourth relates specifically to the nature of Supreme Court nominations.

Political Composition of the Senate

The presumption in favor of a president's nominee is probably greatest when the Senate is dominated by members of the president's party and by senators who are ideologically compatible with the president. The partisan and ideological composition of the Senate is not only relevant to the actual voting on the nominee but also as a cue to opposition advocacy groups. The greater the split be-

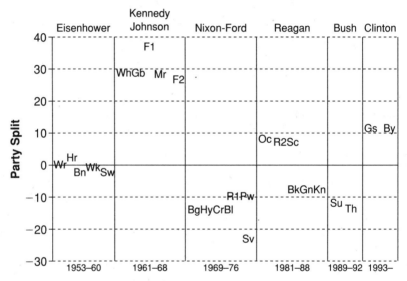

Figure 2.1 Party Split in the Senate Across Six Presidential Eras
Party split is measured as the seat advantage in the Senate for the president's party. Plus scores indicate the president's party is in the majority. Negative scores reflect the minority status of the president's party. Party split data were gathered from issues of the Congressional Quarterly Weekly Report as close as available to the time that the nomination was announced. The placement of the nominees in this space indicates how party split favored the president at the time of their nomination. The abbreviations for the nominees are:

Bg	Burger	Gn	Ginsburg, D	R2	Rehnquist 2nd
Bk	Bork	Gs	Ginsburg, R	Sc	Scalia
Bl	Blackmun	Hr	Harlan	Su	Souter
Bn	Brennan	Hy	Haynsworth	Sv	Stevens
By	Breyer	Kn	Kennedy	Sw	Stewart
Cr	Carswell	Mr	Marshall	Th	Thomas
F1	Fortas 1st	Oc	O'Connor	Wh	White
F2	Fortas 2nd	Pw	Powell	Wk	Whittaker
Gb	Goldberg	R1	Rehnquist 1st	Wr	Warren

tween the Senate and the president, the greater potential such groups will see for an effective campaign against the nominee.

Figure 2.1 shows the party split facing the president at each vacancy from 1953 to the present. One of the clearest examples of party split as a factor in confirmation is the consecutive nominations by Ronald Reagan of Antonin Scalia and Robert Bork in 1986 and 1987 respectively. With Scalia, the president was comforted with a 53 to 47 advantage in the Senate for his own Republican party, and Scalia was easily confirmed. That partisan edge had been gained in 1980 when Reagan was elected and markedly conservative Republicans defeated several long-time and more-liberal Democratic members of the Senate.[3] In 1986, the Democrats rebounded and defeated many of those first-term Republicans, resulting in a 54 to 46 edge for the Democrats by the time of the Bork nomination.[4]

In addition, the newly elected 1987 Senate was distinctly more liberal than its 1986 counterpart. Ideology is more difficult to observe than party affiliation, but it is very closely connected with political party. The generalization that Democrats are liberal and Republicans are conservative gained increasing validity during the Reagan and Bush presidencies. A commonly used indicator of political ideology is the senator voting scores developed by the Americans for Democratic Action (ADA), a liberal advocacy group. A senator's percentage of votes in agreement with the positions articulated by the ADA is taken as a measure of "liberalness." Scores range from 100 (a liberal vote on every issue) to 0 (the failure to vote on the ADA-defined liberal position on any issue). The median ADA score for the 14 new senators who arrived in 1987 for the Bork nomination ended up at 82.5 for the year compared to 12.5 for the departing senators in 1986. These two sets of scores are quite representative of the parties more generally.

All of the votes in favor of Bork's confirmation came from the president's Republican party with the exception of two conservative Democrats. All opposition to Bork came from Democrats plus the five most liberal Republicans. Only senator Warner, a Republican from Virginia, voted contrary to both party and ideology—

---

[3] In 1980, concurrent with Ronald Reagan's election to the presidency, the Democrats lost 12 seats to Republicans, while the Republicans did not lose any to the Democrats. Among the losses were four seats in the South as well as veterans such as George McGovern, Birch Bayh, Warren Magnuson, Gaylord Nelson, Mike Gravel, Adlai Stevenson, and Herman Talmadge (*Congressional Quarterly* 1986, 7B).

[4] In 1986, Republicans lost nine seats to the Democrats while gaining only one. The Democrats regained all four seats lost in the South in 1980 (*Congressional Quarterly* 1986, 7B).

although a conservative Republican, he voted against confirmation. The defeat of Bork can be attributed rather directly to these partisan and ideological variables.

Senate Support for the President

One quick measure of how strong the presumption in favor of the president's nominee might be in the Senate is how successful the president has been in moving a legislative program through the Senate, which can be calculated by taking the total number of bills on which the president took a stance and dividing that into the number of Senate voting outcomes consistent with the president's position. The percentage for each year since 1953 in which a nomination has occurred is reported in Figure 2.2.[5] In 1981, for example, Reagan's support score was 88, indicating the Senate votes concurred with President Reagan's preferences on 88 percent of the roll-call issues. While Reagan's early success rate was substantial, it was still not as high as the amazing 93 percent success rate achieved by Lyndon Johnson in 1965, the year he appointed Abe Fortas an associate justice.

A president's success rate in the Senate is not necessarily constant across the years. Often as a president's term winds down support decreases. This is particularly true during the "lame duck" period, that time between the mid-term election of a president's last term in office and the end of the president's term. Figure 2.2 reveals fairly consistent declines in Senate support from the beginning to the end of particular presidential administrations. Thus, by 1987 and the Bork nomination, Reagan's support had dropped from 88 percent to only 56 percent. Similarly, in 1968 when Johnson attempted to elevate Fortas to the Chief Justiceship, his support was down to 69 percent.

The lame duck period is an open invitation to opponents of the president to seek a rejection or delay regarding any nominee. As the 1992 presidential race heated up, the Democratic chair of the Senate Judiciary Committee made it clear that if there were to be a vacancy on the Court during this closing period of President Bush's term, the Committee would not consider the nomination until after the election and then not at all if Bush lost. Some scholars build

---

[5] We report support scores for all roll-call issues on which the president took a definite stand. We would prefer to measure Senate support only for the president's domestic issues, excluding foreign policy issues. However, data were not consistently available for that breakdown. Support levels for all issues average almost 10 percentage points higher than for domestic issues only. Support scores were taken from the annual editions of the *Congressional Quarterly Almanac.*

in the lame duck period as one of automatic decline in how well the setting favors the president's nomination. We think such a decline is not automatic. Some presidents remain strong. The greatest achievement in this regard has to be Andrew Jackson, who was able to submit two nominations on his last day in office and have them confirmed after he had left office (Warren 1935, 2:39). With support like this, the lame duck period need not be an obstacle. For this reason, we believe that the presidential support variable is a better indicator than is lame duck status in assessing the nomination setting.

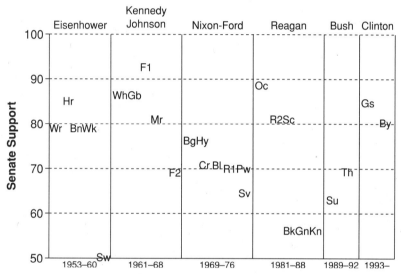

Figure 2.2 Senate Support Across Six Presidential Eras
Support scores represent the percentage of votes on bills in the Senate in which the outcome was in accordance with a position taken by the president during the session of the Senate in which a Supreme Court nomination occurred. Data were taken from the relevant *Congressional Quarterly Almanacs*. The 1994 score for Clinton was estimated on the basis of the analysis of Senate votes as reported through the *Congressional Quarterly Weekly* listings of votes. The placement of the nominees in this space indicates the Senate support level of the president at the time of their nomination. The abbreviations for the nominees are:

Bg	Burger	Gn	Ginsburg, D	R2	Rehnquist 2nd
Bk	Bork	Gs	Ginsburg, R	Sc	Scalia
Bl	Blackmun	Hr	Harlan	Su	Souter
Bn	Brennan	Hy	Haynsworth	Sv	Stevens
By	Breyer	Kn	Kennedy	Sw	Stewart
Cr	Carswell	Mr	Marshall	Th	Thomas
F1	Fortas 1st	Oc	O'Connor	Wh	White
F2	Fortas 2nd	Pw	Powell	Wk	Whittaker
Gb	Goldberg	R1	Rehnquist 1st	Wr	Warren

Public Opinion Regarding the President

When a president enjoys high public support, the setting is more favorable for the president and presidential nominations. Any opposition that does emerge at that time is vulnerable to the president's mobilization of favorable public opinion. Senators are not oblivious to the president's popular standing. As Senator Simpson argued during the Rehnquist hearings in 1986,

> President Reagan was elected by a large majority. . . . He has the right and the obligation to nominate qualified men and women who share the philosophy of this president. (Senate 1987, 30)

Figure 2.3 traces the public opinion support of presidents since Eisenhower at the times of their Court nominations. They range from a high of 79 for President Kennedy at the time of Byron White's nomination to a low of 37 for President Clinton at the appointment of Ruth Ginsburg. Clinton's choice of Ginsburg illustrates that a low public approval rating need not automatically generate opposition. That point is further illustrated with Gerald Ford's appointment of John Paul Stevens at a time when Ford's approval rating stood at only 41. However, the only opposition of any consequence with Eisenhower nominees occurred during periods of relatively low public approval. The same is true for the Kennedy-Johnson years and to some extent for Reagan. Presidential weakness in the polls can only encourage those who might wish to mount a campaign against the nomination.

In contrast to what might be called *diffuse* support for or opposition to a president, *specific* issues arise that may jeopardize a favorable setting for the president. Widespread opposition to a president's stance on a particular issue, particularly one deemed relevant for protection or adjudication by the Court, can diminish the president's favorable situation. President Bush's overall popularity in the first three years of his term was offset in part by opposition engendered by his pro-life antiabortion views. Despite denials that he did not take potential nominees' views on abortion into account, pro-choice forces increased the level of controversy by their adamant assertion that a woman's right to choose was cloaked within fundamental privacy rights and should serve as a virtual litmus test for nominees.

Measuring such opposition requires contextual understanding of when an issue has reached the status of diminishing the favorableness of the setting for a president's appointments. One contextual factor is the salience of the issue to the business of the Supreme Court, the likelihood that the Court would adjudicate the issue. Another is the intensity with which feelings about the issue are held. Quantitatively, the president's favorable status diminishes as the issue polarizes significant numbers into opposing camps. Once again, the issue of abortion has dominated confirmation assessments in the 1980s and early 1990s precisely because of its salience (*Roe, Webster, Rust, Casey*), its intensity, and its polarization of significant numbers of people (Hugick and Hueber 1991, 36–37).

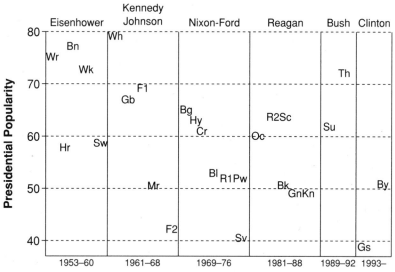

Figure 2.3
Presidential Popularity Across Six Presidential Eras
Presidential popularity scores were taken from Gallup Poll results, as close as possible to the nomination date, as reported in *Public Opinion* (Lipset and Wattenberg 1989, 40) except for the Bush and Clinton data. Bush figures were Gallup Poll results reported in *American Enterprise* (Keene and Ladd 1991, 92). The Clinton figure for the Ginsburg nomination was taken from the *Gallup Poll Monthly* (Moore 1993, 7) and the Breyer figure was provided in conversation with the Gallup Poll organization. The placement of the nominees in this space indicates the public opinion support level of the president at the time of their nomination. The abbreviations for the nominees are:

Bg	Burger	Gn	Ginsburg, D	R2	Rehnquist 2nd
Bk	Bork	Gs	Ginsburg, R	Sc	Scalia
Bl	Blackmun	Hr	Harlan	Su	Souter
Bn	Brennan	Hy	Haynsworth	Sv	Stevens
By	Breyer	Kn	Kennedy	Sw	Stewart
Cr	Carswell	Mr	Marshall	Th	Thomas
F1	Fortas 1st	Oc	O'Connor	Wh	White
F2	Fortas 2nd	Pw	Powell	Wk	Whittaker
Gb	Goldberg	R1	Rehnquist 1st	Wr	Warren

Vacancy Attributes

The attributes of a particular vacancy also structure the nomination setting. More specifically, the immediate past nomination history and the significance of the departing justice can both affect how favorable the setting is for the president and the nominee. Strong opposition to a nominee, especially if it results in the nominee's rejection, has an interesting bipolar effect on the subsequent nomination. On the one hand, if the opposition has injected new language into the nomination discourse then scrutiny involving those issues will carry over, adversely affecting the setting for the president. For example, the ability of those opposed to Abe Fortas to legitimize their opposition in terms of financial, ethical, and conflict of interest issues meant that such issues would inevitably be investigated by the political opposition to the next nominee, who in this instance was Clement Haynsworth.

It didn't help Haynsworth that Fortas was defeated and eventually driven from the Court by Republican and Democratic conservative opposition. This only heightened liberal scrutiny of Haynsworth for the potential of political payback and as an assertion of liberals' political resolve not to let President Nixon create a Court in his own image. When Haynsworth opponents found some blemishes relating to finances, ethics, and conflict of interest, they were able to exploit those same arguments that had been used against Fortas, forcing some senators who had opposed Fortas and had been expected to support Haynsworth to oppose Haynsworth as well.

While recent history can increase the potential for controversy, a countervailing force is also at work. Rejection of a nominee takes considerable effort and expends much political capital among both senators and the advocacy groups who supply the "ground troops" for the confirmation battle. After a controversial nomination, there may be a natural letdown, especially if the next nomination is immediately forthcoming. The initial response to the nomination of Judge Carswell in the wake of the Haynsworth rejection was to let the president have his way. Only the insistence of a few lobbyists and a couple of senators permitted an opposition to build slowly in the wake of increasing evidence that Carswell was not someone that many people wished to see on the Court (Harris 1971). By shifting from his "southern strategy" and selecting Harry Blackmun in the wake of the Carswell defeat, Nixon avoided further difficulties by finding someone who was clear of the problems that plagued Fortas, Haynsworth, and Carswell.

In further support of this notion that the Senate has only a finite amount of energy to oppose nominations is the 1986 nomination of Antonin Scalia, which came forward at the same time as Justice

Rehnquist's chief justice nomination. This dual scrutiny occurred as a result of Justice Rehnquist being named to fill the vacancy created by the retirement of Chief Justice Burger and Scalia then being nominated for the Rehnquist vacancy. Those who opposed both nominees settled for a strategy that would direct their energies only toward Rehnquist. There is no doubt that Scalia's seemingly noncontroversial status was facilitated by Rehnquist being the target of liberal opposition that might otherwise have been directed at Scalia. Opposition forces thought it would make them look too obstructionist to oppose both. They also knew how difficult it would be to carry on a battle along two fronts. Perceiving Rehnquist as the more vulnerable of the two, opponents also reasoned that a Rehnquist defeat would forestall the Scalia nomination as well.

To the extent that the departing justice has played a unique or crucial role on the Court, the president may find the nomination setting somewhat unsettling. The quintessential example of a role-generated controversy resulted from the 1987 retirement of Justice Lewis Powell, the archetypal swing vote on a divided Court. In one view, a justice serves as a swing vote to the extent that he or she alternately joins enduring opposing blocs of four justices to create a five-justice majority. Not only had Powell been the major swing vote on the Court for the three terms preceding his retirement (Harvard Law Review 1985, 325; 1986, 307; 1987, 365), he had played the crucial swing role in the significant issues of the day, including privacy, abortion, criminal justice, and affirmative action. The Powell vacancy created a volatile situation no matter who the nominee would be. For either side to secure an appointee who would align solidly with only one bloc rather than swing back and forth would be to gain the upper hand in the shaping of America.

Being a swing vote is not the only characteristic of a departing justice that can adversely affect the nomination setting for the president. Any special or unique characteristic of the departing justice may do so. For example, the fact that Thurgood Marshall was the only person of color on the Court and was the strongest defender of minority rights there made the setting surrounding his vacancy potentially more controversial because of the attention focused on whether or how those unique contributions might be replaced. Presidents can ignore such situations only at their peril.

There are those who argue that the replacement of a chief justice may be grounds for diminishing the presumption in favor of the president. Certain senators on the Judiciary Committee have articulated that view (Senate 1987, 4, 14). However, the appointment of the chief justice is such a rarity, it is difficult to say whether the level of nominee scrutiny is really higher or whether it is a rhetorical ruse to diminish the presumption in favor of the nominee. The examples of Fortas and Rehnquist do suggest that when a *sitting* justice is elevated to the position of chief justice, the potential for controversy increases. Unlike most other nominees to the Court, the justice's views on the critical issues that have come before the Court are now well-known. Thus, associate justices quite literally are sitting targets, certain to draw the fire of opponents if proposed as candidates for chief justice.

Figure 2.4 summarizes vacancy attributes by cumulating the number of unique characteristics present from among those just listed. If there is nothing particularly significant about the recent

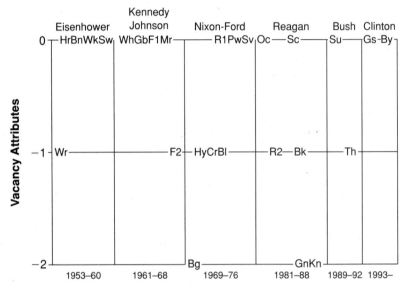

Figure 2.4 Vacancy Attributes Across Six Presidential Eras
The vacancy attributes score is a sum of the number of special attributes present for the vacancy confronting the nominee. Potential attributes are: chief justice vacancy; vacancy was not successfully filled with an earlier nominee; swing-vote status of the vacating justice; and special representative status of vacating justice (e.g., race with respect to the Thurgood Marshall vacancy that confronted Clarence Thomas). Attributes are summed in a negative direction to indicate how these factors work to decrease the favorableness of the setting for the president. The abbreviations for the nominees are:

Bg	Burger	Gn	Ginsburg, D	R2	Rehnquist 2nd
Bk	Bork	Gs	Ginsburg, R	Sc	Scalia
Bl	Blackmun	Hr	Harlan	Su	Souter
Bn	Brennan	Hy	Haynsworth	Sv	Stevens
By	Breyer	Kn	Kennedy	Sw	Stewart
Cr	Carswell	Mr	Marshall	Th	Thomas
F1	Fortas 1st	Oc	O'Connor	Wh	White
F2	Fortas 2nd	Pw	Powell	Wk	Whittaker
Gb	Goldberg	R1	Rehnquist 1st	Wr	Warren

nomination history or about the departing justice, the attributes are considered to be inconsequential, promoting neither controversy nor consensus. Figure 2.4 reflects chief justice vacancies for Eisenhower's first, Johnson's last, Nixon's first, and Reagan's second appointment opportunities. On occasion, the vacancy attributes cumulate. The vacancy to which Warren Burger was appointed in 1969 was that of the retiring Chief Justice Earl Warren, and it came on the heels of the blocked confirmation of Abe Fortas to that position. Similarly, the setting was potentially more troublesome for Douglas Ginsburg and Anthony Kennedy in 1987 due to the twin attributes of a recent defeat of a nominee (Bork) and a special vacancy (Powell). It is conceivable that the "fatigue" factor set in with Anthony Kennedy, negating the potentially more controversial situation caused by the Bork defeat and Douglas Ginsburg's withdrawal, but we are inclined to maintain a description of the setting as one that was ripe for controversy, quieted by the selection of a relatively noncontroversial nominee.

Putting It All Together

The more indicators of controversy that characterize a particular time in which a vacancy occurs, the less favorable the setting is for the president and the less likely a nominee will be presumed to be suitable. This general rule can be seen most clearly with some comparisons. Using data from Table 2.1, we can observe that when Johnson persuaded Arthur Goldberg to step off the Court in 1965, the president's support level in the Senate was at an all-time high of 93 and he enjoyed a whopping 36-seat Democratic majority. In addition, his public popularity was a personal best of 69. The vacancy was not unique; the Court was solidly liberal; and the chief justiceship was not at stake. The setting for the president and his nominee was quite favorable.

Only three years later, the president was hopelessly mired in the Vietnam War, and he had already announced that he would not seek reelection. He had entered his lame duck period. Public support had dropped to 43 percent. While the Democrats still retained a 32-seat advantage in the Senate, his support level had dropped to 69, still high but certainly down from 93. In addition, the chief justice position was at stake and the outgoing justice was Earl Warren, the symbol of Court liberalism and activism. To nominate Fortas, a sitting justice and the president's close friend and advisor, was tantamount to pinning a large target on him and inviting all opposed to a liberal activist Court to fire away.

President Reagan seemed intent on showing that history can repeat itself. In 1981 when Justice Potter Stewart resigned, Reagan en-

TABLE 2.1

Nomination Setting Factors for Nominations from 1953 to 1994

President	Vacancy	Nominee	Party Split	Senate Support	Public Support	Vacancy Attributes	Nomination Setting
1. Eisenhower	Vinson	Warren	0	78	75	−1	1.1
2.	Jackson	Harlan	3	85	57	0	1.7
3.	Byrnes	Brennan	−2	79	77	0	2.5
4.	Reed	Whittaker	−1	79	72	0	2.2
5.	Burton	Stewart	−2	50	58	0	−1.7
6. Kennedy	Whittaker	White	28	86	79	0	5.3
7.	Frankfurter	Goldberg	28	86	66	0	4.1
8. Johnson	Goldberg	Fortas	36	93	69	0	5.5
9.	Clark	Marshall	28	81	51	0	2.3
10.	Warren	Fortas	26	69	43	−1	−1.1
11. Nixon	Warren	Burger	−14	76	65	−2	−2.3
12.	Fortas	Haynsworth	−14	76	62	−1	−1.2
13.	Fortas	Carswell	−14	71	61	−1	−1.7
14.	Fortas	Blackmun	−14	71	53	−1	−2.4
15.	Harlan	Rehnquist	−10	70	52	0	−1.0
16.	Black	Powell	−10	70	52	0	−1.0
17. Ford	Douglas	Stevens	−24	64	41	0	−3.4
18. Reagan	Stewart	O'Connor	7	88	60	0	2.4
19.	Burger	Rehnquist	6	81	64	−1	0.7
20.	Rehnquist	Scalia	6	81	64	0	2.1
21.	Powell	Bork	−8	56	51	−1	−3.6
22.	Powell	Ginsburg, D.	−8	56	49	−2	−5.2
23.	Powell	Kennedy	−8	56	49	−2	−5.2
24. Bush	Brennan	Souter	−12	63	62	0	0.8
25.	Marshall	Thomas	−14	69	72	−1	−0.9
26. Clinton	White	Ginsburg, R.	12	60	37	0	0.4
27.	Blackmun	Breyer	12	80	51	0	1.2
	Mean		1.37	74.04	58.89	0.52	−0.04
	Standard Deviation			16.16	11.12	10.92	0.70

Notes

1. *Party split* is the seat advantage in the Senate for the president's party.

2. *Senate support* is the percentage of votes recorded in the Senate in which the outcome was in accordance with the president's announced position during that session in which the nomination was made.

3. *Public support* is the percentage of respondents who report a favorable view of the president's job performance in the Gallup public opinion poll closest to the nomination date.

4. *Vacancy attributes* sums the number of factors attributable to the vacating justice that reduce the favorableness of the setting for the president, as indicated by the use of negative numbers. See Figure 2.4 for the list of attributes.

5. *Nomination setting* is the sum of standardized scores across the four setting variables. Standardizing a score is accomplished by subtracting the mean of the distribution from the score and dividing that difference by the standard deviation.

joyed a seven-seat advantage in the Senate and a Senate support level of 87 percent. Public opinion was a warm 60 percent. Moreover, the Stewart vacancy was not particularly a key one, and Reagan was only in his first year of office. It was a setting high on presumption in favor of the president's nominee, whoever it might be. The fact that he took the opportunity to appoint the first woman to the Court only reinforced the ease with which this nomination would be confirmed.

By 1987, however, the Democrats had regained the Senate by a solid eight-vote margin. Reagan's support level in the Senate had dropped to 56 percent, the lowest of any president in this modern era of appointments. The so-called Iran-Contra scandal had cut his public approval rating to 51 percent. If the situation weren't already bleak enough, the vacancy was created by Lewis Powell, as we have noted, the quintessential swing vote. In the eyes of Reagan opponents, what was at stake was nothing less than the future of the country. The situation was potentially a political firestorm and Reagan responded by throwing gasoline on it. The nomination of Robert Bork, who had articulated controversial stances on many of the major issues of the day—abortion, affirmative action, and minority rights—virtually insured the most rancorous confirmation battle since that of Louis Brandeis in 1916 (Stookey and Watson 1988, 194–195).

Figure 2.5 summarizes the nomination setting confronting the various nominees to the Court across six presidential eras. The summary is obtained by standardizing the data on party split, Senate support, presidential popularity, and vacancy attributes in terms of their arithmetic means and standard deviations.[6] By then summing across the different indicators, it permits a somewhat oversimplified but nonetheless effective way of visualizing the nomination setting. The higher the number the more favorable the setting for the president and a nominee. Conversely, the lower the number the less favorable the setting for the president, and the greater care the president must take in naming a nominee to the Court to avoid controversy.

---

[6] A score is standardized by subtracting the mean (average) of all scores and dividing by their standard deviation, a measure of how much the scores differ from the mean. The effect is to alter the scores so that their mean is now zero and their standard deviation is one. For example, a president with a presidential popularity score of 70 has a standardized score of +1, by virtue of being 11 points above the average presidential popularity score of 59. Being 11 points above the average and dividing that deviation from the mean by the standard deviation, which is 11 for presidential popularity, produces the standardized score of 1. Consequently, positive scores indicate being above average and negative scores indicate being below average. Standardizing the scores for all four nomination setting factors permits us to combine them to produce a composite measure for nomination setting.

We can distinguish four different levels of favorableness for the president in terms of the nomination setting. The first level includes vacancies in which the setting is so favorable for the president that the absence of controversy and easy confirmation of a nominee is virtually insured. Without a doubt, the John Kennedy and Lyndon Johnson years from 1962 to 1965 exhibit the most favorable settings for a president. Experience suggests that this highest favorable level can extend even somewhat lower to any setting over a score of 2, which would also capture a couple of Eisenhower

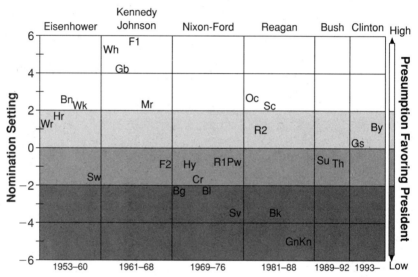

Figure 2.5 Nomination Setting Across Six Presidential Eras
The nomination setting constitutes a sum of the standardized scores for each of the four setting variables appearing in Figures 2.1 through 2.4, namely, party split, Senate support, presidential popularity, and vacancy attributes. While there are reasons to be concerned about the methodology of such a summation, it does permit us to visualize the cumulative effect of these four factors in establishing the setting in which a nomination takes place. As scores move away from 0 towards 6, the setting becomes more and more favorable for the president and, consequently, the nominee. As scores move away from 0 in a negative direction, the setting becomes increasingly unfavorable for the president. The abbreviations for the nominees are:

Bg	Burger	Gn	Ginsburg, D	R2	Rehnquist 2nd
Bk	Bork	Gs	Ginsburg, R	Sc	Scalia
Bl	Blackmun	Hr	Harlan	Su	Souter
Bn	Brennan	Hy	Haynsworth	Sv	Stevens
By	Breyer	Kn	Kennedy	Sw	Stewart
Cr	Carswell	Mr	Marshall	Th	Thomas
F1	Fortas 1st	Oc	O'Connor	Wh	White
F2	Fortas 2nd	Pw	Powell	Wk	Whittaker
Gb	Goldberg	R1	Rehnquist 1st	Wr	Warren

and Reagan vacancies, as well as one more during the Johnson administration. At this level, the president enjoys broad latitude in choosing a nominee. Scrutiny of the nominee will be more relaxed, perceptions will be more positive, the likelihood of controversy is quite remote, and confirmation is assured.

A second level, ranging from scores of 0 to 2, constitutes a nomination setting that is still favorable to the president but is sufficiently less stable for opposition to a nominee to be expected. The likelihood of a nominee being defeated in this setting remains rather remote, but presidents must exercise somewhat more discretion in nominee selection if they wish to avoid controversy. President Reagan's twin appointments of Rehnquist to the chief justice vacancy and Scalia to the Rehnquist vacancy in 1986 illustrate how nominee selection can make a difference. The less favorable setting for Rehnquist compared with Scalia was due solely to the chief justice position being at stake. Nonetheless, Scalia was widely accepted as a strong nominee despite his anticipated conservatism, and no opposition developed. Rehnquist, on the other hand, was a bit of a lightning rod. The combination of a weaker nominee in a somewhat less favorable setting provoked considerable and powerful opposition. Had the setting been on the negative side for the president, Rehnquist might well have been defeated. As it was, the positive setting for the president helped ensure Rehnquist's confirmation.

When crossing into negative territory on the nomination setting, the president's situation continues to deteriorate in the third level. There is no longer a presumption in favor of the president and a nominee. The particular nominee becomes much more critical to the outcome of the nomination. Even in the most negative setting, the "right" nominee can always keep controversy from erupting. Indeed, only one of the four rejections by the Senate during this period of time occurred in the fourth level of settings least favorable to the president—settings with scores lower than –2. The other rejections occurred in the range of 0 to –2.

Presidents are more acutely aware of the potential for rejection in settings that are least favorable, and they are more likely to respond with nominees that can command bipartisan support. Ford's appointment of John Paul Stevens, Nixon's appointments of Warren Burger and Harry Blackmun, and Reagan's appointment of Anthony Kennedy all illustrate this point. However, it is when the setting is not quite so negative, in that 0 to –2 range, that presidents are more likely to assume a "business as usual" approach and exercise less care than the political setting really requires. In this range, opposition to a nominee is quite likely and only Justice Powell avoided it. What distinguishes this setting from the more positive one above it (the 0 to +2 range) is that there is typically sufficient political opposition in the Senate in this more negative setting to actually defeat the nominee.

By combining this continuum of nomination setting with the language of the nomination discourse illustrated earlier, we not only can suggest that certain vacancies are likely to engender opposition but also predict what that controversy will be about. For example, vacancies during the controversial period of the late 1960s could have been expected to focus on issues such as school prayer, racial issues, and criminal defendant rights. In addition, the Fortas rejection inserted other nominee issues involving conflict of interest and financial considerations. The somewhat negative setting for the Bush vacancies not surprisingly developed a discourse involving abortion, affirmative action, and the unique characteristics of race and minority rights represented in the Marshall vacancy.

The nomination setting, however, is only one-half of the controversy equation, and not the controlling half at that. Confronted with either a potentially controversial or noncontroversial setting and being aware of the discourse-defining context in which the vacancy exists, the president must now choose what type of nominee to select. The choice may dampen the controversy; it may fuel even higher levels of contention; or it may pass as it were and leave the level of controversy engendered up to the opposition. It is a key decision for a president, a decision that Lyndon Johnson, Richard Nixon, and Ronald Reagan all made incorrectly at least once. It is to this presidential decisional calculus that we now turn.

CHAPTER THREE

Presidential Nominations

> Regarding the due administration of Justice as the strongest cement of good government, I have considered the first organization of the Judicial Department as essential to the happiness of our Citizens, and to the stability of our political system. Under this impression it has been an invariable object of anxious solicitude with me to select the fittest Characters to expound the laws and dispense justice.
>
> *George Washington*

Like most of his successors, George Washington considered the appointment of Supreme Court justices one of the more significant decisions of his service as president (Marcus and Perry 1985, 20). They understand that appointments to the Court will most assuredly have a tenure that extends beyond the end of the their terms, frequently beyond their lifetimes. Only five presidents have lived beyond the service of their appointees to the Court: John Quincy Adams, Martin Van Buren, Millard Fillmore, Herbert Hoover, and Harry Truman. All presidents are cognizant that a vacancy represents an obligation and an opportunity to shape the future of the nation.

In discussing the type of person a president is likely to appoint to the Supreme Court, we start with a simple, though perhaps arguable, assumption that presidents seek to reproduce themselves. The biological metaphor may overstate the case, but there is little doubt that presidents seek nominees who share their views on the role of the Court and on the appropriate behavior of a justice, certainly with respect to the interpretation of the Constitution and hopefully concerning public policy. Theodore Roosevelt's assessment in a letter to friend and Senator Henry Cabot Lodge concerning a candidate for appointment is typical of how presidents think, even with respect to some specifics:

> He is right on the negro question; he is right on the power of the Federal Government; he is right on the insular business; he is right about corporations; and he is right about labor. (Lodge 1925, 2:228)

This underlying premise is based upon the presidents' recognition of what has been called "realistic jurisprudence." This philosophy of law holds that a judge does not simply apply the law to the facts. Rather, law and facts are abstractions that require each individual judge to define them. While the plain meaning of statutory or constitutional language or precedent may delineate the law, it does not determine it. A Court decision is a human process. In exercising this human process a judge inevitably interjects personal attitudes and values. Thus, an "unreasonable" search and seizure may mean one thing to one judge and something else to another. As we noted in Chapter 1, this is why who is selected for the Supreme Court is so important. It is also why the president expects to find a nominee who will make "my type of decision."

While vacancies present obvious opportunities, a president is not unconstrained in his choice of nominees. As we have seen, the timing of a vacancy can serve to expand or contract the options for a president. A controversial time period may require that a president accept something less than an ideal choice or risk the possibility of Senate defeat. The retirement of Thurgood Marshall, the first and only nonwhite on the Court, brought irresistible pressure on President Bush to appoint another minority person, albeit within the parameters of Republican conservatism. His assertion that Clarence Thomas represented "the best person at the right time" was true enough, the time being the Marshall vacancy and the best person being a respected conservative African American.

In this chapter, we shall address the motivations that drive presidents in their selection of nominees. Regardless of what motivations are dominant, however, any president must also pay attention to the qualifications of the nominee. In trying to find a qualified nominee who also fits the typically broad political and ideological parameters imposed by the president and by the nomination setting, the president also hopes to avoid selecting a nominee whose decisions will bring surprise and dismay. To do all of this, the president has the advantage of considerable advice from a number of different sources. Once the selection is made, the president initiates the nomination discourse by announcing the appointment and making the case for confirmation. We close the chapter by analyzing the relationship between the nomination setting and the construction of nominee qualifications, along with the implications of that relationship for the appointing president.

Motivations in Nominee Selection

Presidents are, for the most part, results oriented. This means that they want justices on the Court who will vote to decide cases consistent with the president's policy preferences. The Roosevelt quote given earlier is illustrative, but one need only look to the recent history of Supreme Court nominations to see the primacy of policy considerations in presidential appointments. While preferring to appoint a justice consistent with their own philosophy, most presidents would rather be safe than sorry, so there is also some concern about avoiding surprises by picking a justice who makes decisions contrary to what the president would want.

The Primacy of Policy and Ideology

Lyndon Johnson's appointment of Thurgood Marshall clearly represented that president's commitment to civil rights. Richard Nixon's appointment of William Rehnquist and Reagan's elevation of him to chief justice reflected these presidents' desire to appoint a conservative justice to the Court. Franklin Roosevelt's policy-driven appointments of justices who would support the New Deal was quite explicit. Finally, George Bush's appointments of Souter and Thomas demonstrated his desire to consolidate a conservative Court, in spite of constraints imposed by the settings in which those vacancies occurred. Though denied by the Reagan and Bush administrations, it seems probable that no little consideration was given to selecting nominees with an eye to those who would likely vote to overturn *Roe* v. *Wade.*

This is not to say that presidents use some sort of policy checklist. Often they are more attentive to somewhat broader ideological orientations than to any one particular policy issue. But most would agree with George Washington that to ignore the loyalty of potential nominees to basic principles for which the president stands would be "a sort of political suicide" (Fitzpatrick 1940, 34:315). There are occasions when political considerations may force a president to make appointments without regard to anticipated policy outcomes (O'Brien 1989, 23, 28). Even those appointments, however, are made as a choice among alternatives and with regard to the political consequences of each.

The desire to appoint justices sympathetic to their own ideological and policy views may drive most presidents in selecting justices, but that goal does little to narrow the field of potentially acceptable nominees. Other subsidiary motivations must serve to narrow the search. The history of Supreme Court appointments reveals at least five such factors. These factors are (1) rewarding personal or political support; (2) representing certain interests; (3) cultivating political support; (4) ensuring a safe nominee; and (5) picking the most qualified nominee.

Rewarding Personal or Political Friends

There are few better examples of a president systematically using Supreme Court vacancies to reward personal and political friends than that of Harry Truman. His four appointments were all of this type—Harold Burton, an earlier senatorial colleague of Truman's whose service on Truman's War Investigation Committee helped bring Truman to national prominence; Fred Vinson, Truman's political and personal friend and his secretary of the treasury; Tom Clark, a personal confidant who had served as Truman's attorney general; and Sherman Minton, another confidant from earlier days in the Senate (Heller 1980, 29–31). Our earlier example of Johnson's appointment of Abe Fortas is also very much a case of the appointment of a personal and political friend (see page p. 33).

Whether to appoint friends, associates, or other political loyalists to the Court is predominantly a personal characteristic of a president's style (MacKenzie 1981, 11–12). It is one way that a president attempts to secure justices who will perform predictably and reliably, from the perspective of the president's own policy views. For Lyndon Johnson, an affirmative response to the simple question "Will he be an all-out J-man?" provided a quick reference to whether one candidate was worth appointing to the federal bench (McFeeley 1987, 84). As we shall observe shortly, however, such a basis for appointing justices may imperil the selection of a quality justice and does not even guarantee a reliable ally of the president.

Ensuring Interest Representation

A second factor that often surfaces in the selection of nominees is representation. George Washington established a precedent of ensuring geographic representation. The first six justices on the Court included three northerners and three southerners, all from different states. Of course, regional loyalties played an extremely significant role in our country during its first 100 years. Indeed, the Civil War would reveal these loyalties to be a matter of life and death.

The significance of region was reinforced by the division of the country into judicial circuits and the responsibility of justices for riding those circuits to conduct the business of the federal courts. It was common, though by no means required, to select a justice who was from one of the states in the circuit and familiar with life in the region. The relief from circuit-riding duties for the justices in 1869 and the blurring of regional differences through increased mobility and national media have eliminated most concerns for geographical representation. However, in an effort to secure the vote of independently minded Republican Senator Margaret Chase Smith of Maine against Harrold Carswell in 1970, opponents called to her attention the fact that this southern jurist, accused of incompetence and racism, would have responsibility for the federal circuit that included Maine (Harris 1971, 182).

Other representational concerns have arisen to take the place of geography. More recently, representation considerations have focused on certain group characteristics such as religion, sex, and race or ethnicity. The retirement of Thurgood Marshall immediately raised questions of whether Marshall's seat constituted an African-American seat or, more generally, a racial or ethnic minority seat. President Bush's rhetoric denied such a proposition, but the focus on Emilio Garza and Ricardo Hinojosa, either of whom would have been the first Hispanic American on the Court, along with the eventual African-American nominee, Clarence Thomas, spoke more forthrightly than did the president.

In the same vein, we may fully expect never again to see a Supreme Court that does not have at least one woman justice. Sandra O'Connor was named to the Court as the result of an intensive search, initially by the Nixon and then Ford administrations, to find a woman with whom conservative Republicans could feel comfortable. For Ronald Reagan, the Republican president with a reputed gender gap (with women being less likely than men to support him), the opportunity to appoint the first female justice was a political coup. The fact that President Clinton took his first nomination opportunity to appoint a woman to the Court was especially significant, removing the onus that would have befallen a president and a nominee had the only female seat on the Court become vacant. For now, at least, there is no "female seat" on the Court, and we may anticipate a time in which a majority of the Court may even be women. The day will come when we may also say that there is no racial or ethnic minority seat.

Presidents generally prefer not to acknowledge representational constraints on their appointments to the Court. They typically assert that appointments are based solely on qualifications and that they are selecting the most qualified person for the job. At the same time, presidents often observe that we have a diverse society and it is desirable for the Court to reflect such diversity. It is all part of a not-so-elaborate game in which a president perpetuates the myth of appointing the best person while simultaneously attending to significant group representational demands.

Cultivating Political Support
A third subsidiary motivation that may drive a president's decisional calculus in selecting a nominee is the desire to garner political support. This factor is somewhat related to the previous one of representational interests. However, demands and expectations for the representation of interests are essentially nonpartisan; they are

directed at both parties. Thus, regardless of who is president or which party dominates the political scene, there is now an expectation that the Court will never be without a female justice. With the Thomas nomination, the same expectation may have been created for African-American representation.

In a more narrowly partisan mode, presidents have attempted to induce or reward support from a group by selecting a Court nominee whose appointment will be recognized as a reward. For President Andrew Jackson, architect of the so-called spoils system, even Court appointments were a "means of liquidating political debts or purchasing political aid" (Jackson quoted in Remini 1984, 268). In his 1968 presidential campaign, Richard Nixon pursued a "southern strategy," designed to secure inroads into the "solid South's" Democratic vote. This strategy was based on the assumption that it no longer made political sense for the conservative South to continue its traditional support for Democratic candidates, who typically were much more liberal than the region. By naming a southern jurist to the Court, Nixon intended to reward white southerners for their support and to solidify that support while simultaneously achieving his policy objectives for a more conservative Court. The Haynsworth and Carswell nominations were the result of that motivation (Massaro 1990, 106; Frank 1991, 135).

Whether the initial appointments of Thurgood Marshall or of Sandra O'Connor were motivated by external pressures for representation or by presidential desires to reward or gain support is largely inconsequential. The point is that either or both of these motivations may lie behind Court appointments. It is worth suggesting, however, that appointments initially motivated by rewarding or seeking political support may produce subsequent expectations for continued representation on the Court.

Securing a Safe Nominee

A fourth factor that may intrude upon a president's screening of potential nominees is whether there is a need to appoint a "safe" nominee, that is, one who is a virtual shoo-in for confirmation. The rationale for such a choice is simple. A president may perceive that the setting is too controversial to permit the appointment of a nominee who would offend a major segment of the political spectrum. Nixon's appointment of Harry Blackmun, a distinctly more moderate conservative with more impeccable legal and judicial credentials than either Haynsworth or Carswell, was motivated in part by the need to find a nominee who could pass easily through the Senate in light of the back-to-back rejections. Blackmun's consideration was quick—only three hours in the Judiciary Committee—and his confirmation unanimous.

One impact of the 1987 Bork nomination for the Republican presidents facing a Democratic Senate was the development of a presidential strategy designed to appoint nominees who appeared "safe." In the first few appointments since Bork, both Reagan (with Douglas Ginsburg and Kennedy) and then Bush (with Souter, though perhaps not Thomas) seemed to seek nominees whose written record was sparse, who were relatively obscure (at least in comparison to a Bork), and whose backgrounds and professional careers revealed little about how they stood on the key issues of the day. Yet, such nominees must have solid legal or judicial credentials sufficient to ward off questions of competence.

For President Bush, David Souter was such a nominee. Dubbed the "stealth nominee" because so few people knew anything about him and having virtually no paper trail to link him one way or another to key issues, Souter represented a reasonably safe nominee in a setting not particularly favorable for the president. At the same time, the Bush administration felt confident that they knew their nominee on the strength of some New Hampshire insiders, most notably Bush's Chief of Staff John Sununu and Republican Senator Warren Rudman. They achieved the best of both worlds—a nominee who likely would fulfill the policy aspirations of the Bush team and a safe nominee who would be hard to oppose because so little was known about him.

As a Democrat with a Democratic Senate, President Clinton could presumably feel more confident about naming a nominee. However, the Clinton administration did not get off to a particularly good start. The president seemed to move from one controversy to another, never gaining strong ratings in the public opinion polls. He faced a Senate whose minority opposition was fairly united, but one with a comfortable Democratic advantage that supported him regularly. For whatever reason, Clinton felt the need for a safe nominee—to the point that the names of potential nominees were often run up the flagpole to see who saluted. Nearly unprecedented communication between the White House and members of the Judiciary Committee transpired in an effort to produce a nominee that would be assured of confirmation without a fight.

In nominating Stephen Breyer to the Court in 1994, Clinton abandoned his preferred choice, Interior Secretary Bruce Babbitt, because Babbitt's anticipated nomination produced public opposition from key western Republican Judiciary Committee members Hatch and Simpson. They promised to garner bipartisan western opposition based on Babbitt's unpopular stance on increasing grazing fees paid by ranchers on government lands. Despite the fact that Babbitt would likely have gained a fairly easy confirmation, the president opted for the nominee who was assured of strong bipartisan support from the Judiciary Committee. Breyer had served as chief counsel to the Committee when it was chaired by Senator Kennedy and when Hatch, Simpson, and other senior Republicans were in their early years of service. He had impressed them then, and the opportunity now to replace the most liberal member of the Court, Blackmun, with the more moderate Breyer rather than the more liberal Babbitt, sat well with the Republicans.

The Clinton administration framed their decision to avoid controversy in a Supreme Court nomination by suggesting that the president was giving life to the "advice" portion of the constitutional clause requiring the president to seek the "advice and consent of the Senate" in making nominations. The effect of avoiding controversy, however, is to empower one's opposition. There is little doubt that Bruce Babbitt could have been confirmed by the Senate, but those who opposed him sensed that by threatening a battle over his nomination they could prevent it from happening, which was exactly the case. In such instances, presidents may wish to consider the advantages of taking on a battle they are nearly certain to win with those of avoiding a battle altogether.

Seeking the Most Qualified Nominee

Listed intentionally last is the consideration of selecting the best person for the Court, largely disregarding the other factors. This factor is placed last because it is the motivation least likely to drive presidential considerations. Presidents simply cannot afford to disregard the other factors. For them, political considerations are part and parcel of any potential nominee's qualifications. More typically, then, a president seeks the best person from among a list of those who fulfill certain of these other criteria and, of course, who share a president's vision of the nation and the Court. Arguably, there is little that is wrong with that approach. Who is to say what qualities constitute some "best" set of criteria? There are literally hundreds of individuals who could perform acceptably on the Court, certainly as well as many of those who currently serve. To claim that any one individual is the best qualified is, more often than not, rhetorical overstatement.

There are a few individuals, however, who have achieved the status of "superstars" in the legal or judicial profession. John J. Crittenden was considered a leading contender for an appointment to the Court for more than three decades in the nineteenth century. He was initially nominated in 1828 by John Quincy Adams but became a victim of the Democrats' desire to hold the vacancy over until Andrew Jackson acceded the presidency. Box 3.1 details just how elusive a position on the Supreme Court can be, even for someone widely recognized as eminently qualified. In the twenti-

★ ★ ★ ★   ★   ★   ★   ★   ★

BOX 3.1

The Elusiveness of a Supreme Court Nomination: John J. Crittenden

John J. Crittenden was a politician and lawyer with considerable respect and a national reputation. For over thirty-two years, Crittenden's name was prominent among potential nominees to the Court. He served in the U.S. Senate on four different occasions between 1817 and 1861. He also served as attorney general under William Henry Harrison and Millard Fillmore (Jacob and Ragsdale 1989, 847). The Supreme Court, however, remained beyond his grasp. His brushes with appointment were the following:

1829 Nominated by John Q. Adams, the Democratic Senate refused to act on the nomination, carrying it over for the incoming Jackson (who nominated McLean) (Warren 1935, 1:701–704).
1841 A "midnight appointment" was made by Van Buren to fill the Barbour vacancy with Peter Daniel, a nomination opposed by the Whigs, who would save the nomination (presumably of Crittenden) for the incoming president, William Henry Harrison. Nonetheless, the Senate confirmed, literally after midnight before adjourning, with less than a majority present (22 to 5) (Warren 1935, 2:82).
1844 Nominations by John Tyler (elected on the Whig ticket with Harrison but adamantly opposed by Clay Whigs) were held up by the Senate in anticipation of a presidential victory by Henry Clay. There was little doubt that Crittenden, a Clay protégé, would receive a nomination. However, James K. Polk was a surprise winner over Clay in the 1844 election (Warren 1935, 2:116).
1852 Millard Fillmore considered appointing Crittenden, but the vacancy occurred in the wrong circuit, geography being important in Supreme Court nominations then. Although Fillmore eventually did go outside the circuit for a nomination, it was to a Senator (Badger), Crittenden having left the Senate to become Fillmore's attorney general. The common wisdom was that a Crittenden nomination would run into trouble in the Democratic Senate. In fact, Badger's nomination was "postponed" and this vacancy was carried over to Franklin Pierce's administration (Warren 1935, 2:242).
1861 Abraham Lincoln was reported to favor Crittenden, a nomination favorably regarded by many, in part as recognition for Crittenden's work in helping to avoid war through the Crittenden Compromise. Apparently, nomination papers were even drawn up, but the nomination was never sent forward. Opposition from the more radical antislavery elements of the Republican party and from the Democratic party prompted a delay, prolonged by Lincoln's reluctance to fill the vacancy. Ultimately, it went to Samuel Miller, from Iowa (Warren 1935, 2:365).

eth century, Judge Learned Hand established a reputation through nearly three decades as a distinguished jurist that outshone most of the Supreme Court justices during his lifetime. More recently, Paul Freund, an eminent law professor, rated highly with the Kennedy and Johnson administrations. But neither Crittenden, Hand, nor Freund was destined to sit on the high court. As Justice O'Connor knowingly pointed out to us, it also takes considerable luck to receive an appointment.

A superstar who did make it to the Court was Benjamin Cardozo. In a remarkable sequence of events really unique in the Court's history, President Hoover was subjected to a groundswell of support and bipartisan pressure in 1932 to name Cardozo to the vacancy created by the retirement of Oliver Wendell Holmes. Using the stature of Holmes as a springboard, Cardozo supporters pressed the necessity of appointing a justice of preeminent stature (Kaufman 1979, 30, 45). Cardozo, by then 62 years old, had made his mark as a jurist in New York and with his classic work, *The Nature of the Judicial Process* (Cardozo 1922). Hoover, in part for representational reasons (two New Yorkers and a Jew already served on the Court) and because Cardozo did not match Hoover's brand of moderately conservative Republicanism, persisted in seeking another nominee (Kaufman 1979, 44–45). Eventually, however, Hoover yielded to pressure and nominated "the best person for the job," an appointment that he later pointed to with pride.

Despite his initial resistance to Cardozo, Herbert Hoover stands as an example of a president who showed great concern with the quality of his nominees. His nominations of Cardozo, Charles Evans Hughes as chief justice, Owen Roberts, and even John J. Parker (whose rejection is generally regarded as denying the Court a valuable member) are among the best crop of any president. Even for Hoover, however, the foremost concern was finding qualified justices who shared his political views. So it is with most presidents. There is an implicit caveat that whenever they state their nominee is the best qualified they mean the best qualified, consistent with those political views, representational interests, reward or support necessities, and any other constraints that may be imposed by the setting.

Surprises

Presidents, justices, and scholars are fond of pointing out the futility of trying to appoint justices on the basis of predicting how they might decide issues. Inevitably, they point to justices who have disappointed the presidents who appointed them. The presidential quotes are legendary. Harry Truman had entrusted Tom Clark with the Justice Department and then elevated him to the Supreme Court, only to find Clark frustrating his former boss. "It isn't so much that he's a bad man," the plain speaking Truman would say. "It's just that he's such a dumb son of a bitch" (Miller 1973, 225). A little less graphically, President Eisenhower reportedly told of how he made two major mistakes in his presidency and "they are both on the Supreme Court," referring to Earl Warren and William Brennan (Richardson 1979, 108).

There are good reasons why presidents may fail to predict how their appointees will perform on the Court. First of all, the Constitution and the law do constrain the latitude that any justice might have to pursue personal policy preferences or biases, even if there were an inclination to do so. Justices cannot always "do the right thing" with respect to policy outcomes. Before coming to the Supreme Court, Justice Blackmun wrote an appeals court opinion upholding capital punishment in which he lamented that the decision was "particularly excruciating" for one "who is not personally convinced of the rightness of capital punishment and who questions it as an effective deterrent" (*Maxwell* v. *Bishop* 1968, 153–154). Conversely, Blackmun also recognized that the Constitution and the law are considerably more restrained for lower-court judges than for Supreme Court justices. He was simply unwilling to make decisions as an appeals court judge that he would in fact deal with as a justice. Such a view can surprise a president who relies too heavily on a judge's previous record.

Second, cases that reach the Court present a specifically delineated set of facts and a situation that may prove inadequate as a vehicle to achieve a particular outcome that a president, or even a justice, might like to see. A justice who wishes to overturn *Roe* has to find the right case that permits *Roe* to be overthrown. Justice O'Connor has felt constrained in reconsidering the ruling in *Roe* v. *Wade* because she argues that cases like *Webster* do not permit one to address *Roe*. If President Reagan did expect O'Connor to seek to overturn Roe, then she has not delivered. On the other hand, Justice Scalia exhibits no such constraint, dismissing O'Connor's reasoning as something that "cannot be taken seriously" (*Webster* v. *Reproductive Health* 1990, 532).

Third, cases and issues will arise during the lifetime of the justice that were not anticipated by an appointing president. Abortion was not an especially salient issue for the Republicans and Richard Nixon at the time of Justice Blackmun's appointment. Yet, with Nixon still in the White House, Blackmun wrote the *Roe* v. *Wade* opinion, one that was destined to precipitate a political and moral debate that shaped the American political landscape for the next 20 years. It is also true that as the issues change and evolve over the years, justices who may be perfectly consistent appear to move in their positions. Justice Hugo Black's credentials as a civil libertarian and absolutist on the First Amendment's protection of free speech seemed unimpeachable in the 1950s and early 1960s. However, his failure to leap with fellow liberals to First Amendment protection for the symbolic speech that confronted the Court in the 1960s made him appear increasingly conservative during his later years.

Fourth, presidents and their advisors will misjudge their appointees or underestimate their potential for "mischief" on the Court. Eisenhower's selection of Earl Warren as chief justice seems to fall into this classification. The appointment of individuals from the political arena can always be a risky proposition because politicians and lawyers are adept at taking positions with which they do not personally agree, to which they have little commitment, or that would simply represent changes from existing laws or constitutional interpretation. The insulation of a Court seat permits justices to follow the dictates of their consciences rather than those of a political constituency.

Finally, justices may themselves evolve in their jurisprudence and views concerning constitutional interpretation. Not too many would have predicted in 1939 that the New Deal liberal, Felix Frankfurter, would become a virtual icon to conservatives and those who called for judicial restraint in the 1950s and early 1960s. To think that Justices Blackmun and Stevens, appointed by Nixon and Ford, respectively, would be the two most liberal members of the Court in the early 1990s was never imagined at the time of their appointments (Wasby 1991; Canon 1991). Sometimes it is difficult to know whether a justice has evolved or whether the changing landscape of cases and Court personnel simply shift the relative position of the justice. In our examples, the appointing presidents would probably be justified in thinking that these justices did indeed move away from their initial jurisprudence.

Despite these many reasons why justices may not fulfill the expectations of their appointing presidents, the notion that justices' behaviors on the Court are unpredictable and that they are as likely as not to deviate from appointing presidents' expectations is overstated. We agree with Laurence Tribe, who argues that presidents who take the time to choose justices carefully will usually get what they are looking for (Tribe 1985, 50). Presidents Reagan and Bush seem to have done just that, although the most recent Court term to the writing of this book has raised some interesting questions about Justices Kennedy and Souter. Our assessment of how the 1991–1992 and 1992–1993 Courts would be evaluated by their appointing presidents is presented in Box 3.2.

BOX 3.2

Hypothetical Grades for the Justices from Their Appointing Presidents

There are a variety of factors that might influence presidents' evaluations of their appointees to the Court. Given our assumption that presidents generally attempt to appoint justices perceived to be ideologically compatible and a further assumption that presidents are as results oriented as a considerable portion of the population, we might expect presidential evaluations to consider the policy direction of the justices' votes.

What follows is our perception of how the appointing presidents would evaluate their appointees with respect to their performances on all nonunanimous cases during the 1990–1991, 1991–1992, and 1992–1993 terms that involved civil rights or civil liberties claims. The scores reported in the grade cards are the percentage of cases in which the justice voted in favor of the individual's claim to a right or liberty. Such a vote is conventionally considered liberal. Thus, high scores are considered liberal, such as Blackmun's 85. Low scores are considered conservative, such as Rehnquist's 4. Our first-person evaluations by the president are our own hypothetical "best guesses" about how the appointing president might evaluate the justice's performance. They do not represent actual evaluations given by the presidents.

How to Read This Report Card

Subject - Evaluation is based on decisions of the Supreme Court during the 1990, 1991, and 1992 terms that dealt with civil rights and liberties issues.

Name - Name of the justice

Teacher - Appointing president

Score - Percentage of nonunanimous cases in which the justice voted in favor of the rights and liberties claim. The left score is for 1990; the middle for 1991, and the right for 1992.

Grade - Likely evaluation of score by appointing president. High scores are considered more liberal; low scores more conservative. Presidents will evaluate accordingly.

Report Card

Subject: <u>Civil Rights & Liberties</u>
Name: <u>Byron White</u>
Teacher: <u>John Kennedy</u>

Scores	Grade
37 - 36 - 23	C+

Comments

Byron scores high in the civil rights area. He would have an A if it were graded separately. However, he is fairly consistently conservative on civil liberties issues. He can swing liberal on certain First Amendment issues, but given those overall scores in the 30's and 20's I can only give him a C+.

Report Card

Subject: <u>Civil Rights & Liberties</u>
Name: <u>Harry Blackmun</u>
Teacher: <u>Richard Nixon</u>

Scores	Grade
85 - 76 - 89	D

Comments

Quite frankly, I did not expect
Harry to score so liberal on a
civil rights and liberties scale.
He came to the Court with
solid conservative credentials
and the highest recommendation
from Chief Justice Burger. At
first, he and Burger were thought
of as the Minnesota Twins. I'm
disappointed with Harry's turn.

Report Card

Subject: <u>Civil Rights & Liberties</u>
Name: <u>William Rehnquist</u>
Teacher: <u>Richard Nixon</u>

Scores	Grade
4 - 32 - 9	A-

Comments

Bill is my prize appointee. Not
only his decisions, but his
opinion writing expresses those
conservative views that I have
tried to expound. --RN
I too am pleased with Bill's
performance, as evident from
my elevating him to Chief
Justice. That was both a reward
and hope for the future. --RR

Report Card

Subject: <u>Civil Rights & Liberties</u>
Name: <u>John Paul Stevens</u>
Teacher: <u>Gerald Ford</u>

Scores	Grade
82 - 83 - 89	D

Comments

While I did not appoint John
with any considerations of
ideology, nonetheless I am
disappointed in his performance.
To think that I appointed
someone whose performance
in 1991 would be the most
liberal on the Court is not
what I prefer.

Report Card

Subject: <u>Civil Rights & Liberties</u>
Name: <u>Sandra O'Connor</u>
Teacher: <u>Ronald Reagan</u>

Scores	Grade
27 - 62 - 29	B+

Comments

In general, Sandra was doing
so well, as evident by her 1990
score. I am astounded by that
remarkable liberal shift in the
1991 term. Hopefully that was
simply an unusual term and
her 1992 score represents
a return to form. On that basis
I will give her a B+.

Report Card

Subject: <u>Civil Rights & Liberties</u>
Name: <u>Antonin Scalia</u>
Teacher: <u>Ronald Reagan</u>

Scores	Grade
15 - 19 - 14	A

Comments

Nino has brought to the Court exactly the philosophy and leadership that was expected of him. On occasion, his libertarian bent will show through, as it did in the one case in which he joined the liberals. Such instances are sufficiently rare to warrant a strong A.

Report Card

Subject: <u>Civil Rights & Liberties</u>
Name: <u>Anthony Kennedy</u>
Teacher: <u>Ronald Reagan</u>

Scores	Grade
28 - 48 - 23	B+

Comments

Until the 1991 term, Tony had been consistently a moderate conservative, who usually did the right thing in big cases. His 1991 score was unsettling and I feared he had begun running with the wrong crowd. However, upon his return to form in 1992, I can assign a B+.

Report Card

Subject: <u>Civil Rights & Liberties</u>
Name: <u>David Souter</u>
Teacher: <u>George Bush</u>

Scores	Grade
24 - 49 - 45	C+

Comments

David's first year on the Court was superb. He provided the 5th vote in no fewer than 5 cases to assure a conservative outcome. Like Kennedy and O'Connor, his distinct shift to the left in 1991 was disappointing. Unlike them, he has failed to return, and he has fallen from an A his first term to no more than a C+.

Report Card

Subject: <u>Civil Rights & Liberties</u>
Name: <u>Clarence Thomas</u>
Teacher: <u>George Bush</u>

Scores	Grade
-- - 19 - 11	A

Comments

Clarence has been everything I hoped for during his first two terms. Not only has he voted the right way in almost every case, but he has also established the right kind of friends, as shown by his close association with Nino Scalia.

Nominee Qualifications

Presidents may be driven largely by partisan and ideological concerns in nominating justices, but presidents also appreciate the solemn responsibility of appointing justices who are qualified to serve on the Court. Exactly what qualifies one to be a justice, however, is very much in the eye of the beholder. With Clarence Thomas, for example, there were disputes not only over the relevance to the Court of his experience as chair of the Equal Employment Opportunity Commission (EEOC), but on whether his performance in that position was exemplary or substandard.

Unlike the nomination setting, which is defined in terms of relatively concrete indicators, nominee qualifications are fluid and abstract characteristics that depend upon constructions of the nominee and the nomination by supporters and opponents. By "constructing" a nominee, we mean establishing the manner in which the nominee is described and portrayed. The outcome of the confirmation process can depend upon whose construction of the nominee, the supporters or the opponents, carries the day.

This was exactly the situation in the Clarence Thomas nomination. Not well known outside of the capitol, Thomas would be confirmed or rejected on the perceptions of senators concerning who Clarence Thomas was. Senator Howell Heflin articulated that very point in his opening statement.

> To some you are the very embodiment of the American dream.
> You have overcome the bonds of poverty and racial segregation
> and deprivation and have risen to the top. To others you have suc-
> ceeded but forgotten your past and turned your back on others
> less fortunate than you. I and my colleagues will attempt to look
> into your heart and mind. (Senate 1991b, 39)

It is the nature of the discourse developed about the nominee that determines what level of consensus or controversy will emerge in the nomination. Significantly, however, that discourse is constrained by the widespread acceptance of language by most participants in the process that identifies suitable norms that qualify one to serve on the highest court in the land.

Various scholars (e.g., Abraham 1983, 286; Goldman 1982, 113–114), politicians (Nixon 1969, 727; Senate 1989, 29–101), and others (ABA 1991, 3–4, 8) have described their views of what constitute the qualifying norms for Supreme Court justices. Taking our lead from the American Bar Association (ABA), those norms assert that a justice should possess the highest standards of integrity, professional competence, and judicial temperament. From the very first rejection of a Supreme Court nominee—John Rutledge in 1795—to the near defeat of Clarence Thomas in 1991, opposition to a nominee inevitably is articulated in terms of deficiencies in one or more of these criteria.

Integrity

The ABA calls *integrity* "self-defining." A slight elaboration says the word deals with the "nominee's character and general reputation in the legal community" and also with "industry and diligence" (ABA 1991, 3). That integrity is self-defining should be taken quite literally. However, contrary to implications intended by the ABA, "self-defining" does not mean that everybody understands what constitutes integrity but rather that different individuals will define it in different ways. That is the lesson of history concerning Supreme Court confirmation battles.

The susceptibility of a term like *integrity* to different constructions makes it a common means by which opponents of a nominee will attack a nomination. All it takes is one person to make an allegation or a single event revealed from a person's past to raise disqualifying concerns where a nominee's integrity is involved. Anita Hill's allegation of sexual harassment concerning Clarence Thomas is only the most recent example of the vulnerability of a nominee to a charge of lack of integrity. Concerted challenges to the integrity of Louis Brandeis almost derailed his confirmation. In 1925 Harlan F. Stone, generally regarded as possessing the highest integrity, became the first nominee in history to testify before the Senate Judiciary Committee as he attempted to fend off allegations of unethical practices. The charges against Stone were generally dismissed as stemming from narrow political motives, and only six senators voted against his confirmation (Harris 1953, 117–118). Nonetheless, that experience indicates how only one or two opponents can attempt to generate controversy, particularly with a charge impugning one's integrity.

In recent years and dating back to the Fortas nomination as chief justice in 1968, several integrity factors have made their way into the confirmation discourse:

conflict of interest (Fortas, Haynsworth)

racial or ethnic bias (Haynsworth, Carswell, Rehnquist, Kennedy, Thomas)

drug use (D. Ginsburg and, to a lesser extent, Thomas)

sexual harassment (Thomas)

The conflict of interest charges were instrumental in the defeats of Fortas and Haynsworth, as was the racial bias charge against

Carswell and the drug use by Douglas Ginsburg. Of all the nominee rejections in the twentieth century, only the Bork nomination was untainted by a challenge to one's integrity. Even then, it was not for lack of some effort by Bork opponents to find such an issue. Attacking the character and integrity of a nominee has become a fairly standard method of opposing a nominee.

Professional Competence

There are no constitutional or statutory professional qualifications to be a justice of the Supreme Court. In practice, all have had legal training—legal apprenticeships in our earlier history, law school in this century. However, one need not have been a judge; John Marshall was not, nor were Louis Brandeis, Felix Frankfurter, Earl Warren, William Rehnquist, and many others. Yet while one cannot list any particular trait that serves as a necessary condition for becoming a justice, we can say what training, experience, and competencies strengthen or weaken the perception of a nominee's qualifications.

With respect to training, nominees who come from the nation's most prestigious law schools are likely to be more highly regarded than those who do not. Moreover, one's performance in law school may add credibility. While Justice O'Connor was not well-known outside of Arizona at the time of her nomination, her graduation from Stanford Law School, presumably near the top of her graduating class, did much to alleviate concerns about her competence. Hugo Black graduated from Alabama—not among the nation's elite—but he did so impressively, entering without even an undergraduate degree but graduating with honors. On the other hand, Harrold Carswell's graduation from law school at Mercer University did little to mitigate questions about his competence. Honors and legal training at a top school are not necessary conditions— Warren Burger's graduation from St. Paul in Minnesota is an example of that. However, a distinguished background does help to create an image of a qualified nominee.

A variety of backgrounds may serve to distinguish the credentials of nominees. Naturally, judicial experience rates as one of the more straightforward qualifiers. David Souter's 12 years of judicial experience helped to establish his credentials, especially in the absence of particularly distinguishing achievements in other areas. The same was true for Warren Burger, who served 13 years on the federal bench before coming to the Supreme Court. Benjamin Cardozo's 18 years as a distinguished state court judge prompted strong bipartisan pressure and acceptance of his nomination by Herbert Hoover. Ruth Ginsburg's judgeship allowed her to distinguish her judicial from her political philosophy, alleviating potential opposition from conservative senators. Of course, being a judge can also bring trouble. John Parker's defeat in 1930 and Clement Haynsworth's in 1969 came, in part, because of cases that produced antilabor outcomes, which brought the enmity of certain labor groups upon them. Harrold Carswell's service as a judge brought forth complaints about his competence. Generally, however, those with judicial experience are likely to be considered more qualified than those without such experience.

Next to judicial experience, a distinguished career in the law or in public service serve to qualify an individual for the Court. Felix Frankfurter and Robert Bork were distinguished law professors. Frankfurter was challenged and Bork defeated, in part, because of their public writings, but no one challenged their basic legal qualifications to sit on the Court. Lewis Powell's distinguished private practice of law and status as a former president of the ABA boosted his qualifications to serve. Earl Warren's extensive public service in elective and appointive offices brought a familiarity and experience with public issues that served as a qualifier. Even Sandra O'Connor's varied service in the executive, legislative, and judicial branches of state government was viewed as a unique and positive experience to bring to the Court. On the other hand, questions were raised with respect to the qualifications of Clarence Thomas, who had served little more than one year as a circuit court judge and whose work during the 1980s in the Reagan administration was the subject of controversy. Thomas' disavowal of public writings and statements as reflecting views that he might bring to the Court served only to fuel concern about his qualifications.

Judicial Temperament

Judicial temperament is an ideal term for the nomination and confirmation process. It can mean virtually anything to anybody, making it particularly susceptible to manipulation by actors in the appointment process. Clearly the term encompasses a number of characteristics, but there is considerable disagreement about what those characteristics are. The ABA offers "compassion, decisiveness, open mindedness, sensitivity, courtesy, patience, freedom from bias, and commitment to equal justice" as characterizing temperament (ABA 1991, 4). Quite a different view of this concept is provided by Senator Strom Thurmond, a conservative Republican, for whom judicial temperament "prevents pressures of the moment from overpowering composure and self-discipline" (Senate 1989, 29).

It was precisely the construct of judicial temperament that spelled trouble both for Robert Bork and the ABA when four members of the ABA's Committee on Federal Judiciary evaluated Bork as lacking proper judicial temperament, a perception largely based on his critiques of equal protection decisions. They apparently construed compassion, open mindedness, and fairness to refer to beliefs about equality or to prejudices concerning the roles of women, ethnic groups, races, or people with varying sexual orientations. Bork opponents put a spin on his earlier writings that expressed a narrow view of the Fourteenth Amendment's "equal protection" clause as evidence of a lack of judicial temperament.

In retaliation, conservatives on the Judiciary Committee attacked the ABA for permitting political or ideological issues to enter their considerations regarding Bork via the construct of judicial temperament. However, temperament seems precisely the door through which concerns about a nominee's commitment to equal justice might enter the nomination discourse. As with Brandeis in 1916, those who opposed Bork generated the claim that the nominee was "outside the mainstream" of American legal thought and then attached this mainstream requirement to the presumably legitimate qualification of judicial temperament. To do so is a stretch, but then again, that's the way the game is played.

Presidential Decision Making

Presidents have taken different approaches in seeking to determine which person should be entrusted with fulfilling their agenda on the Court. In the beginning George Washington did most of his own work to secure names and evaluate potential nominees to the Court. In more recent times, presidents like Lyndon Johnson have also preferred to be personally involved in the evaluation and selection process, often reserving the choice for friends (Abe Fortas), political allies (Homer Thornberry), or someone who otherwise is known personally and is expected to be faithful to the president's policy views (Thurgood Marshall). Interestingly, other presidents of the modern era who have tended toward this model, namely, Roosevelt, Truman, and Kennedy, were also Democrats.

Republican presidents of the modern era have been more likely to trust advisors with the responsibility for developing and winnowing the candidate list. Presidents Eisenhower, Nixon, Ford, Reagan, and Bush have all followed this style more often than not. With Eisenhower and Reagan, there was considerable reliance on staff to run the presidency, partly because of the lack of Washington experience in the president. Presidents Bush and Nixon were both much more interested in foreign than domestic policy, trusting aides for domestic issues, including Court appointments. President Ford was too constrained by the fallout from Watergate and Nixon's resignation. His immediate need was to take the politics out of the presidency, not infuse it with his own.

In his first two appointments, President Clinton exhibited a blend of these contrasting styles. Following the Republican model, presidential aides developed and winnowed the list for this Democratic president, but then Clinton took an intense look at the short list and did not hesitate to ask for something different. In his first nomination, the president's decision came down to the greater interpersonal rapport he established with Ruth Ginsburg rather than with Stephen Breyer. In the second, the president ultimately opted to avoid any controversy by selecting Breyer over Bruce Babbitt and Richard Arnold, both of whom were likely to draw some opposition.

Washington life can be cruel. Breyer's interview with the president for the first nomination went fine, and the president seemed ready to name him to the Court, asking him to stay over to the next day in anticipation of receiving the nomination. But after meeting with Ginsburg the next morning, Clinton decided that she, not Breyer, would be the nominee. Babbitt suffered a similar experience, talking late into the night with the president and leaving the White House with a sense that his name would be forwarded by the president. However, as the press reported the impending Babbitt nomination and as opposition surfaced in the Senate, Babbitt had to content himself with the honor of being seriously considered—twice, no less.

Regardless of presidential style, there is no doubt that the scrutiny of potential nominees has become more intense in recent years. Liberals might argue that Nixon, Reagan, and Bush have placed more emphasis on the importance of the Courts in achieving their political agenda, which then spurs opposition efforts by advocates within and outside the Senate opposed to that agenda. Conservatives could respond that the closer scrutiny is prompted by liberal efforts to frustrate these more conservative presidents from replacing retiring liberal justices, appointed by liberal presidents, with appointees more in line with the president's—and the country's—own conservatism.

In a sense, there has been a return to the early years of the nation when the Federalists recognized the importance of the courts in sustaining the Federalist view of the constitution against the rising tide of Jeffersonian and, eventually, Jacksonian democracy. Partisan and ideological differences between the president and the Senate meant that appointments and confirmation decisions were often made on openly partisan and ideological grounds. A president preparing for such a battle must now scrutinize potential nominees very carefully. Any surprises from the nominee's background, such as occurred with Harrold Carswell, Douglas Ginsburg, or even Clarence Thomas, can prove fatal to the nomination.

Regardless, then, of whether a president's style is highly personalized or more reliant on advisors, presidents must now seek assistance in the scrutiny of potential nominees. Such assistance in recent years has typically come from four different sources: political allies and advisors, the Justice Department, the FBI, and the ABA.

Political Allies and Advisors

The cliché "It's who you know, not what you know that counts" holds for Supreme Court appointments. For the Democratic administrations of Roosevelt, Truman, Kennedy, and Johnson, it meant that you had better be known by the president himself. For the Republican presidents—Eisenhower, Nixon, Ford, Reagan, and Bush—and now for the Democrat Clinton, this has not been as true, but you still must be well known and respected by the people that the president listens to. Fortunately for President Nixon and William Rehnquist, "Renchburg" had his backers in the attorney general's office who kept his name straight and helped the future chief justice become Nixon's prize appointee.[1]

Political connections are almost always a prerequisite to nomination. To a certain extent, presidents have always looked to the Senate for recommendations and subsequently relied on a nominee's backers there to help move the nomination through the Senate. Both Senators Goldwater and DeConcini, as well as Justice Rehnquist, all from Arizona, were quite instrumental in Sandra O'Connor being identified and then selected from among her competitors as the first female justice on the Court. No other president has gone quite as far as Thomas Jefferson when he invited members of Congress from states in the newly created Seventh Circuit to submit names to him of first and second choices for a justiceship that Jefferson intended to fill from that circuit. On the other hand, senator sponsorship took on a new look and a new significance in the Bush administration. By attaining the vigorous sponsorship and intense lobbying of Warren

[1] *Renchburg* refers to President Nixon's effort to recall Rehnquist's name as a leading advisor in the Justice Department. An agitated Nixon, speaking with his White House domestic advisor, John Ehrlichman, said "Nobody follows up on a . . . thing. You remember the meeting we had when I told that group of clowns we had around here—Renchburg and that group. What's his name?" Scarcely three months later, Rehnquist was a Court nominee who, in Nixon's words, would "add distinction and excellence" to the Court (*Washington Post* 1974, A12).

Rudman for David Souter and of John Danforth for Clarence Thomas, President Bush did much to ensure their confirmation.

There are, of course, other allies and advisors to the president besides senators. Among them are sitting justices. Justices have a vested interest in who sits on the Court, and there are numerous instances of their trying to influence presidential appointments, not to mention some instances of trying to generate a vacancy in the first place. A 1976 study documented at least 94 efforts of justice interventions dating back to 1798 (Abraham and Murphy 1976, 40–49). Their efforts took a variety of forms, with simple letters of recommendation being the most common. While most of the efforts (roughly three-fourths) were in behalf of a desired candidate, justices have been much more successful in their opposition efforts—60 percent successful in support and 83 percent successful when in opposition (Abraham and Murphy 1976, 63). One of the more successful efforts was the letter from the first former justice, John Rutledge, to George Washington in 1795 upon hearing of the imminent departure of Chief Justice John Jay to be governor of New York, in which he "humbly" offered himself for the position, "I have no Objection to take the place which he holds" (Marcus and Perry 1985, 94). His ill-fated nomination came shortly thereafter.

Probably few individuals have had as much influence on as many presidential Court appointments as William Howard Taft, at first as president, then as a former president and jurist, and finally from his position as chief justice to which he ascended in 1921. Taft actively opposed Woodrow Wilson's nomination of Louis Brandeis, and once the Republicans regained control of the White House with the presidency of Warren Harding, Taft sought immediately to influence the appointment of judges at all levels but with particular attention to the Supreme Court. He did not hesitate to press for his own candidacy as well (Mason 1965, 77–84). Not content to be a "mere" associate justice, Taft had yearned for the chief justiceship even in his youth, and his presidential appointment of Edward White to that position in 1910—the first time a sitting associate justice had been elevated to that position—was in part motivated by the thought that Taft himself would then be available for the position upon White's future departure from the Court (Mason 1965, 39–40). As fate would have it, that was the first vacancy during Harding's administration, brought about by White's death. As chief justice, Taft continued to exercise considerable influence over nominations and played greater or lesser roles in the selections of Sutherland, Butler, Sanford, and Stone, although he was more successful at blocking (Benjamin Cardozo and Learned Hand, among others) than at securing his first choices (Mason 1965, 157–176).

As a former president, Taft had direct access to the president, at least after the presidency of Woodrow Wilson. Few people are in that position, but a great number are in positions that give them access to the president's advisors. In addition to letters from justices, the White House is the recipient of letters from many other people who would advise the president about how to fill a vacancy. David Danelski's documentation of who knew whom and who wrote to whom leading to the nomination of Pierce Butler is particularly instructive. One of the more interesting recent stories in that regard is the apparent effort that Martin Ginsburg made in behalf of his spouse, Ruth Bader Ginsburg. To push her candidacy and at the suggestion of a sympathetic Clinton administration official, Martin persuaded some well-regarded academics and friends to write the White House encouraging her nomination. To counter some rumblings that some women's advocacy groups were not supporting her candidacy, he also arranged to have letters submitted from prominent women in the legal profession who would support her nomination (Randolph 1993).

A final classification of advisor to the president is of more recent vintage. The growth of the executive office of the president, that is, advisors who work within or adjacent to the White House itself, has diminished in some instances the role of the attorney general (discussed later). Presidents differ with respect to which advisors are trusted to help in the selection process. Lower federal court appointments are almost always handled through the Justice Department, under the ultimate—though not immediate—supervision of the attorney general. However, the political significance of a Supreme Court nomination often means that the White House, typically someone in the legal counsel's office, will become seriously involved in every phase of the appointment process. The nomination of David Souter was influenced heavily by President Bush's chief of staff, John Sununu, who is a former governor of Souter's home state, New Hampshire. Similarly, much of the extensive searching for a nominee in President Clinton's appointments has been conducted by staff in the White House.

On occasion, this overlap of responsibility between the White House and the Justice Department causes problems. The Reagan administration's handling of the Bork nomination revealed differences of opinion between White House and Justice Department staff, both with respect to whom the nominee should be and how to handle the nomination once the choice had been made (McGuigan and Weyrich 1988, 215–220). More typically, there is cooperation if not agreement as White House staff advise on the political questions and the Justice Department advises concerning legal and judicial questions.

The Justice Department

Most presidents in the modern era have come to rely on their attorneys general to identify prospective nominees to the federal bench, including the Supreme Court. In turn, most attorneys general create or designate a unit within the Justice Department to prepare in advance for nominations by preparing lists of potential Court nominees. The lists are based on recommendations from various friends of the administration, typically with strong reliance on the attorney general. Thus, John Mitchell, Edward Levi, William French Smith, Edwin Meese, and Brad Reynolds have all exercised considerable influence with their respective Republican presidents.

One of the more prominent examples of such influence is President Ford and his attorney general, Edward Levi, who was given the power to select federal judges and recommend a Supreme Court nominee. Levi assembled a knowledgeable and impressive staff to handle the nominations. In the case of Ford's appointment of John Paul Stevens, Levi's description and recommendation of Stevens left little doubt he was Levi's choice, and Ford did not hesitate to follow the recommendation of his trusted attorney general (O'Brien 1989, 23, 31–32).

The particular emphasis of recent Republican administrations on selecting nominees with previous judicial experience has meant that Justice Department personnel must pore over opinions and writings of potential nominees to ensure that they meet the requirements of the administration and that there is little grist for the opposition mill. These people are kept very busy with the screening process for judges of the appeals and district courts. There were 327 appointments to Article 3 courts during the Reagan administration (Goldman 1989, 318). Nonetheless, they find the time to prepare analyses of potential Supreme Court nominees, analyses that will prove important not only in selecting a nominee but in subsequent preparation by the nominee for the Senate confirmation process.

Often there may be a need to find individuals with a particular trait in mind. Edward Levi had prepared a list of potential female nominees with the expectation that President Ford might appoint the first woman to the Court. Ford did not, but the Reagan people later plucked Sandra O'Connor from that list in a historic appointment. More recently, the Bush team compiled a list specifically designed to maintain a member of the Court from a racial or ethnic minority, in this instance Clarence Thomas. Almost surely, however, the list also contained the name of the first Latino to be named to the Court had Bush won reelection in 1992. Bill Clinton's victory undoubtedly ensured a different list, one not likely to exhibit much overlap with that of the Bush administration.

The Federal Bureau of Investigation

While the Justice Department team examines the legal and political qualifications of potential nominees, the FBI has come to be used as an investigative arm in checking candidate backgrounds and reputations. The first use of the FBI to check the background of a Supreme Court nominee created a stir. That the character of a nominee should be subject to such scrutiny was viewed as an insult to one's honor. Today, the background check is accepted as essential for all federal judicial nominees. The checklist of items has expanded over the years from simple character checks to details concerning the finances, the club memberships, the clients, and even the personal life of a potential nominee.

Indeed, it is precisely when presidents fail to require thorough checks that trouble is likely to arise. In 1969, President Nixon's attorney general, John Mitchell, and J. Edgar Hoover, director of the FBI, agreed to conduct "a quiet check" of Fourth Circuit Judge Clement Haynsworth, whom Nixon intended to appoint. The check, which purposely avoided making any outside inquiries, simply consisted of submitting materials collected during the 1957 check of Haynsworth in conjunction with his appointment to the circuit court and the observation by the special agent in charge in Columbia, South Carolina, that Haynsworth was regarded as

> the foremost jurist in the area, very conservative and definitely in
> favor of law and order. [He] has [a] slight lisp, but is considered to
> have [a] brilliant mind. [I] know of no derogatory information. (FBI
> 1969a)

Unfortunately for both Haynsworth and the president, the cursory FBI check left unrevealed questions of financial dealings and conflicts of interest that would eventually doom the nomination. Without learning from the first mistake, the Nixon Administration rushed headlong into another hurried selection, Harrold Carswell, without full knowledge of flaws that would prove fatal in his background. A similar failure occurred as the Reagan administration rushed to bring forth a nominee in the wake of the Bork defeat. In this instance, the rushed investigation failed to uncover the marijuana episodes of Douglas Ginsburg, which led to another presidential setback in the appointment process.

The use of the FBI by presidents has not always been limited to simple checks of proposed nominees. The systematic use of J. Edgar

Hoover's FBI for political intelligence by presidents from Herbert Hoover through Richard Nixon had outcomes that occasionally influenced the composition of the Court. For example, it has been suggested that wiretaps of conversations between Justice Douglas and Democratic activist Tommy Corcoran dissuaded President Truman from elevating Douglas to chief justice in 1946 (Charns 1989, C4). Libertarian decisions of the Court in the 1950s led Hoover to seek intelligence from Court employees concerning "leftist" law clerks and liberal justices. The Nixon administration asked Hoover to collect information on Justice Douglas that might be used to support the impeachment effort being headed by Congressman Gerald Ford. Moreover, during the Haynsworth confirmation battle, the White House requested that information be gathered on the D.C. property of Senator Birch Bayh, a leader of the opposition to Haynsworth, presumably in an effort to gain intelligence that might undermine Bayh's legitimacy[2] (FBI 1969b).

It is also true that J. Edgar Hoover did not always act on orders from the White House or the attorney general. He had his own political agenda. On his own initiative he reportedly compiled information on potential nominees and specifically worked to push the nominations of Potter Stewart and of Warren Burger[3] (Theoharis and Cox 1988, 303). He gathered information on Abe Fortas to be used by those opposing his elevation to chief justice (Theoharis and Cox 1988, 403–405). It has also been alleged that he worked with Warren Burger in an effort to staff support positions in the federal judiciary with those loyal to the conservative agenda they shared (Theoharis and Cox 1988, 407). We still do not know the full extent of Hoover's activities with respect to the Court, but it certainly represents an extra-constitutional effort to influence the composition and output of the Court.

The American Bar Association

Unlike the Justice Department and the FBI, the ABA is not a government entity. Nonetheless, it has achieved a status from time to

---

[2] Whether the FBI actually carried out this request is not known to us. The memo communicating the request contains the handwritten comment, "I don't think we should do this."

[3] Ironically, Potter Stewart may have owed his Court appointment in part to an earlier negative by Hoover over Stewart's application to become an FBI agent in 1941. Stewart's association with an isolationist group while at Yale and the activity of his mother in the Peace League led to Hoover's rejection of Stewart's application. Stewart then turned to the practice of law and a public life that eventually brought him to the Court (Theoharis and Cox 1988, 202).

time as an important advisory group to the president and to the Senate. Here we shall consider only its role in the president's selection of a nominee. In the next chapter, we expand the assessment of the ABA's role in the confirmation process more generally.

Founded in 1878, the ABA has always purported to be a nonpartisan group interested only in furthering the administration of justice. From the beginning, however, the ABA has been perceived by progressive and liberal groups as an association of establishment conservative lawyers and very much biased by their political values (Grossman 1965, 52–55; Rees 1981, 281–285). Nowhere was this more evident in its early history than by its strident opposition to the Brandeis nomination, highlighted by a letter from seven former ABA presidents to the Senate Judiciary Committee saying that Brandeis was "not fit" to serve on the Court. More recently, the ABA has been rapped by conservative groups and senators, who have been alienated by certain liberal public-policy stands of the ABA and by some public opposition within the ABA to the confirmation of Robert Bork (Rees 1981, 281, 285–286; Legal Times 1990, 21; Senate 1990).

In 1947, the ABA created a Committee on Federal Judiciary and charged it with promoting the selection of competent judges for the federal courts and opposing the confirmation of unfit ones. Beginning late in the Truman administration, the committee has secured working relationships with the attorneys general of the various presidential administrations to help assess the qualifications of nominees or potential nominees to the Court. These relationships have taken three different forms. Most preferred by the committee is one in which the attorney general consults the committee in advance of selecting a nominee, receiving both suggestions and reactions from the committee regarding potential nominees. This procedure has also proven to be the least common, occurring twice under Eisenhower (Brennan and Whittaker), once with Nixon,[4] and for Ford's single nomination (Stevens).

A second format has given the committee the name of the nominee in advance of a public announcement. In this arrangement, the committee is requested to provide feedback, presumably favorable, before the nomination is announced. So it was under Kennedy and Johnson and for certain Nixon appointments. More recently, Presi-

---

[4] The lone Nixon episode was rather bizarre. Attorney General John Mitchell provided the Committee with six names to investigate in little more than a week, with a special focus on two—Mildred Lillie and Herschel Friday. While the committee focused on the two, both of whom were piling up not qualified ratings from committee members, Nixon and Mitchell had already settled on nominations for Lewis Powell and William Rehnquist, names that had not appeared among the six given the committee (Simon 1973, 220–226).

dents Reagan and Bush have adopted a third format, actually used by Nixon in the Powell and Rehnquist nominations. Least supportive of an ABA role, this procedure does not provide the committee with the name of the nominee in advance. The committee's role is thereby limited to the confirmation phase of the process, affecting only the Senate's consideration of the nominee.

In their first nomination, the Clinton administration conducted a very protracted and public perusal of potential candidates. Byron White announced his retirement shortly after the presidential election in 1992, effective at the end of the Court's term in the summer of 1993. With more advance notice of a specific vacancy than is customarily accorded a president, the Clinton team went through several iterations with the president, typically ending with a request to bring in some new names fulfilling particular characteristics. Ultimately, they followed the Reagan/Bush model of announcing the nominee before informing the ABA, once again limiting the activity of the ABA to a postannouncement evaluation that can be used by the Senate but not by the White House. However, their public assessment of potential nominees permitted them more effective feedback on the strengths and weaknesses of making a particular nomination.

Presidents are reluctant to share any aspect of their appointment power. Only the most nonpartisan of the recent presidents, Eisenhower, seemed genuinely willing to listen to the ABA and to feel its approval was significant. The unique circumstances of Ford's brief presidency also fostered a nonpartisan strategy. For the other presidents, however, partisan motivations have ruled out any significant preselection participation by the ABA committee. Indeed, to do otherwise might precipitate unnecessary criticism of the president as relinquishing constitutional authority. In addition, such use of the ABA would only shift the politics of the appointment process to the ABA. While presidents need not and probably should not give up any control over this initial stage of the process, they must still consider how their nominees will fare in the investigation by the committee after the selection. A finding of "not qualified" by a committee majority could well mean the death knell for a nomination. In this sense, the committee retains a presence, even in presidential administrations that do not work with it.

Initiating the Nomination Discourse

All that remains at this point is for the president to make the selection and initiate the discourse that he or she hopes will frame the nomination. As we noted in Chapter 2, however, both the selection and the discourse are constrained to some extent by the setting in which the nomination takes place.

Framing the Nomination

Because presidents have the constitutional duty to appoint nominees to the Supreme Court, they also have the first opportunity to structure the political discourse about the suitability of the nominee. To hear the president tell it, nothing but the best qualified person is selected for the Court. Thus, President Clinton characterized Stephen Breyer as "one of the outstanding jurists of our age" (Clinton 1994) and Ruth Ginsburg was "one of our nation's best judges [with a] historic record of achievement" (Clinton 1993, 1074). Clarence Thomas was "the best qualified at this time" (Bush 1991a, 870). David Souter was "the very best" (Bush 1990, 1144). Sandra O'Connor was "the most qualified woman,. . . [one] who meets the very high standards I demand of all court appointees" (Reagan 1981, 729). For Richard Nixon, Warren Burger was "superbly qualified" (Nixon 1969, 727) and Clement Haynsworth as an "eminently qualified jurist, scholar, and intellect" (Nixon 1969, 1164). However, it was his relatively lukewarm support for Harrold Carswell as one who would be "fair and . . . a very competent judge" (Nixon 1970, 94) that attracted attention because of the very absence of those superlatives that are the norm when nominating a justice.

These positive characterizations of nominees are significant not only because they appeal to the general public's views of the importance of qualifications but also because they inhibit successful opposition to a nominee, which requires serious challenges to the nominee's qualifications. Mere political opposition to a nominee is not widely perceived as legitimate unless it can be successfully packaged as an attack upon the nominee's qualifications. For this reason, presidents usually initiate the nomination discourse by ignoring the likely political reasons for selecting the nominee and by emphasizing instead the nominee's "unique" and "impeccable" qualifications.

To the extent that presidents are forthcoming about appointing justices who share their policy views, they typically direct the nomination discourse to those issues of significance to them, though often in very general terms. President Nixon's desire to appoint justices who favored the "peace forces" against the "criminal forces" was an attempt to rally support on the basis of his nominees' anticipated opposition to earlier Warren Court decisions on the rights of the accused. President Reagan expressed support for the Republican party platform, which called for the appointment of justices who favored the "sanctity of life," a reference to antiabortion views.

Those who support the appointment of more liberal justices will often use vocabulary rich in references to the First Amendment and to the rights of minorities and women under the "equal protection" clause of the Fourteenth Amendment, as Clinton did with Ginsburg. In addition to drawing an analogy between her work on gender equality with that of Thurgood Marshall on behalf of racial equality, Clinton said,

> [Judge Ginsburg] has repeatedly stood for the individual, the person less well-off, the outsider in society, and has given them a sense that the Constitution and the laws protect all of the American people, not simply the powerful (Clinton 1993, 1074).

While the assumption that presidents seek to appoint nominees who share their policy views seems evident, many presidents prefer to direct the discourse not so much with policy terms but with a vocabulary rich in what might be called "role" labels. A *role label* is a characterization of a judge in terms that reflect a personal philosophy of constitutional interpretation or that depict a perception of the appropriate role of the Court in our society. For example, Richard Nixon revived the term *strict constructionist* as he campaigned in 1968 about the type of justices he would appoint to the Supreme Court (Simon 1973, 5–8). More than 120 years earlier, President James K. Polk, as had Andrew Jackson before him, wrote of his resolve to appoint only those persons who were "strict constructionist" in their constitutional interpretations (Polk 1952, 37).

By the use of this term, both Nixon and Polk perceived that they were making reference to a constitutional interpretation of original intent, that is, an interpretation consistent with the intentions of the framers, or perhaps the ratifiers, of the Constitution. The problem is that "strict construction" establishes no reliable or objective standard (Tribe and Dorf 1991; for an opposing view, see also Bork 1990). It all depends on how one views the Constitution in the first place. Nixon wanted to curb the expansion of individual civil rights and liberties that characterized the Warren Court. Polk, on the other hand, saw the Marshall Court as limiting the individualism of Jacksonian democracy with wide-ranging decisions that gave the national government too much power. Polk's Constitution was a constitution of the democrat; Nixon's Constitution was a constitution of the republican. Both saw what they wanted to see because the framers had used the language of democracy to create a federal republic.

A companion though more encompassing term that Republican presidents of the modern era have given considerable play is *judicial restraint,* which has as its antithesis *judicial activism.* These terms are ideal for nomination discourse because they are multidimensional constructs, sufficiently fluid to mean different things to different people. Such multidimensionality means it is possible to be activist on one dimension and restraintist on another (Canon 1982; Lamb 1982). In a general sense, *judicial restraint* refers to the tendency of a justice to limit the scope of personal judicial decision making. Activism asserts a more expansive scope of appropriate judicial jurisdiction and action. The Warren Court—from 1954 through 1968—was identified as the archetypal activist Court. Opponents of the liberal policy outcomes of that era often couched their arguments for a more conservative court in the vocabulary of judicial restraint. Their attachment of liberalism to activism on the Court was so successful that the two terms became virtual synonyms, along with their counterparts of conservatism and judicial restraint.

For conservative presidents, the vocabulary of restraint has proved an effective tool in the framing of judicial qualifications. It has been easier to attack activism than liberalism and to defend judicial restraint rather than conservatism. Seizing on the public sense that courts should be above politics, the Republican presidents have been able to attack activism on the Court and argue for judicial restraint without appearing to be attacking the liberal tenets of the Constitution, all the while seeking justices who read the constitution in a manner more consistent with conservative policies.

Now that conservative forces have gained the upper hand on the Court, some reversal is occurring. As Justices Rehnquist, Scalia, and other conservatives on the Court lay the foundation for reexamining previous decisions by a more liberal Court,[5] there are decreasing references to judicial restraint by conservative voices. Liberals, on the other hand, increasingly decry the activism of the conservatives on the Court.

Constraints on Presidential Control of the Discourse

While presidents may seek to control the style and content of the discourse, their ability to do so tends to vary directly with the political situation at the time of the nomination. The less favorable the setting for the president, the more difficult it is to prevent the emergence of negative discourse designed to depict the nominee as lacking in qualifications and, therefore, not suitable for the Court.

[5] See especially the exchange between Rehnquist and Marshall in *Payne* v. *Tennessee* (1991).

An unfavorable setting leads to greater negative discourse and increases the likelihood that such discourse will control the general perception of the nominee. While we reserve for the next chapter a discussion of how the nomination discourse is ultimately shaped not only by the president but also by advocacy groups, the media, public opinion, and congressional participants, it is important now to consider briefly the relationship between nomination setting and the perception of nominee qualifications. This relationship suggests an important moral for appointing presidents.

In Figure 2.5, we arrayed the various Court vacancies from 1953 to 1993 according to the nomination setting at the time. In Figure 3.1 we relate that information to a measure of the perceived qualifications of the nominees who were appointed to fill those vacancies. This measure of qualifications was derived from the work of Charles Cameron, Albert Cover, and Jeffrey Segal, who carried out a content analysis of four of the nation's leading newspapers, two "liberal" and two "conservative," concerning their evaluations of the nominees.[6]

While the authors of the qualifications measure used the scores to help predict the confirmation vote on the nominees (Cameron, Cover, and Segal 1990), we believe that by showing the relationship between the qualifications measure and nomination setting we can make a much more important point about nomination discourse and perceived nominee qualifications. It is significant to note that all nominees who have been defeated during this time period (i.e., Fortas for chief justice, Haynsworth, Carswell, and Bork—their data omitted Douglas Ginsburg) fall into the lower-left quadrant of the figure, which marks them as having been nominated when the setting was weighted against the president and as nominees who were perceived as relatively low on the qualifications dimension.

The simplistic message of these data is that if a president appoints a weak nominee at a time when the setting is not favorable for the president, that nominee is likely to be rejected. The more subtle and, we believe, more important point is that during periods less favorable to the president a nominee is more likely to be perceived and attacked as unqualified. The fact that all nominee rejec-

---

[6] The liberal papers were the *New York Times* and the *Washington Post*. The conservative ones were the *Wall Street Journal* and the *Chicago Tribune*. Each paragraph on a nominee was coded as positive, neutral, negative, or not applicable with regard to the nominee's qualifications. Statements relevant to qualifications included any that dealt with integrity, temperament, achievement, and education. The result was a composite measure that reports that percentage of applicable paragraphs that were coded positive (Cameron, Cover, and Segal 1989).

tions have involved the combination of an unfavorable setting for the president and low perceived nominee qualifications is a consequence of the fact that an unfavorable setting is virtually a necessary condition for the emergence of a negative perception about the nominee's qualifications.

This interpretation is supported both by the grouping of rejected nominees in the lower-left quadrant of Figure 3.1 and by the near absence of nominees in the lower-right quadrant, that area representing a more favorable setting for the president and a low perception of nominee qualifications. Nominations in the lower-right quadrant are rare not because presidents choose better nominees in such a situation but because the favorable setting for the president discourages attempts to cast doubt on the qualifications of a nominee. This allows the president's initial characterization to go largely unchallenged. Indeed, the data suggest such discouragement is reasonable. Even though some newspaper discontent managed to call the qualifications of Byron White into question, he was easily confirmed by a voice vote, reflecting the favorable setting for President Kennedy's appointments.

Arguing that perception of nominee qualifications and nomination setting are interrelated does not mean that they are totally interdependent. A certain independence is demonstrated by the nominees in the upper-left quadrant of Figure 3.1. These nominees were appointed during settings not favorable for the president yet they were perceived as highly qualified. In part, by downplaying partisan and ideological factors with the likes of Anthony Kennedy, John Paul Stevens, Harry Blackmun, and Warren Burger, it is possible to appoint nominees who are so incontestably qualified as to discourage the emergence of any successful negative discourse.

These observations lead to some interesting thoughts about nominees who have been easily confirmed. Those who were confirmed during periods in which the nomination setting was unfavorable for the president can be rather safely considered truly qualified because they were able to withstand the negative pressures of the setting in which they were appointed. On the other hand, nominees perceived as highly qualified during periods favorable to the president such as Brennan, Scalia, Whittaker, and O'Connor may, in fact, have been highly qualified, but we are less sure of that judgment because the setting tended to discourage negative discourse about these nominees. In a setting less favorable to the president, a negative discourse almost surely would have emerged, would have been taken more seriously, and might have diminished their perceived qualifications.

The Abe Fortas nominations are particularly instructive in this respect. What changed most for Abe Fortas between his nomination as an associate justice in 1965 and his nomination as chief justice in 1968 was not his own qualifications but the setting that confronted Lyndon Johnson. Had the setting in 1968 remained what it had been in 1965, Fortas likely would have been confirmed. Either the issues that were raised concerning his integrity would have been perceived as less serious, keeping his qualifications status higher, or the lower perceived qualifications simply would not have mattered to the outcome because the situation was favorable for confirmation.

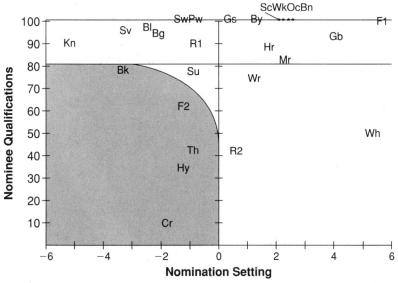

Figure 3.1 Nominee "Qualifications" by Nomination Setting
The qualifications measure is taken from Cameron, Cover, and Segal [1990, 530]. Scores for Souter, Thomas, and Ginsburg were communicated to us by Professor Segal. Breyer's score was estimated by the authors, following the methodology of Cameron, Cover, and Segal.
The nomination setting scores are taken from the sum of standardized setting factors presented in Table 2.1.
The quadrants are formed by intersecting the average (mean) scores for "qualifications" (.81) and nomination setting (0). The shaded area of the lower-left quadrant represents a situation almost certain to generate controversy.
Justice abbreviations in the body of the figure are:

Bg	Burger	Gs	Ginsburg, R	Sc	Scalia
Bk	Bork	Hr	Harlan	Su	Souter
Bl	Blackmun	Hy	Haynsworth	Sv	Stevens
Bn	Brennan	Kn	Kennedy	Sw	Stewart
By	Breyer	Mr	Marshall	Th	Thomas
Cr	Carswell	Oc	O'Connor	Wh	White
F1	Fortas 1st	Pw	Powell	Wk	Whitaker
F2	Fortas 2nd	R1	Rehnquist 1st	Wr	Warren
Gb	Goldberg	R2	Rehnquist 2nd		

Advice to the President

Having described in some detail the motivations that drive presidential appointments, the resources that support presidents, and the factors that constrain them, we can assemble a set of recommendations for presidents designed to produce a successful outcome for a nomination. First, assess the favorableness of the nomination setting for the president. The more the setting favors the president, the less likely controversy will arise. Therefore, consider what vacancy on the Court is being filled. What is the partisan division in the Senate? What is the ideological dispersion in the Senate? What is the strength of the president vis-a-vis the Senate? What level of popularity does the president enjoy with the public? Which term of the presidency is it and how early into the term is it? A president must anticipate a common feature of American politics: Most of the setting factors that favor nominations will tend to decrease throughout a tenure. By anticipating that the difficulty in securing nominations will only increase over time, a reasonable strategy for nominations may be worked out.

Second, given the setting, select an appropriate nominee. Put simply, the more positive the setting is for the president, the more controversial the nominee can be. In that sense, the Reagan administration put things exactly backwards. They began with their least controversial nominee in Sandra O'Connor and brought in the most controversial, Robert Bork, for the last Court vacancy. Of course, hindsight is 20/20. There were rational justifications for each nomination at each vacancy. Nonetheless, the situation into which Bork was thrust involved either a misreading of the setting or the nominee. The Bork nomination went forward despite warnings from Democratic senators that his nomination was highly controversial and would precipitate a considerable fight.

Even in a setting quite unfavorable for the president, however, a highly qualified and strong nominee can win confirmation. Millard Fillmore, the last Whig president, wrestled fairly unsuccessfully with a belligerent Democratic Senate, which rejected three of his nominees within the space of a year. Yet his nomination of Whig Benjamin Curtis sailed through with little opposition during this same period because of the universally acknowledged quality of the nominee.

It should go without saying that the president should require a most thorough background check and analysis of the writings and statements of any potential nominee. Given the hurried checks of Haynsworth, Carswell, and Douglas Ginsburg, however, such a warning bears repeating. Keep in mind that the opposition to the president will attempt to construct and sell their own view of the nominee's qualifications or lack thereof. The less favorable the setting for the president, the more these opponents will dig into the nominee's background, the more intense efforts will be to frame issues unfavorable to the nominee, and the greater will be attempts to weave an interpretation of the existing record that is inimical to the confirmation.

Third, seize the initiative in establishing the nomination discourse. President Nixon's occasional style of allowing his press secretary to announce the nomination was too weak. On the other hand, President Bush's hyperbole regarding Clarence Thomas as the best-qualified person he could find and his assertion that race was not a factor in his selection were certainly strong approaches, but they undermined the credibility of both the president and the nominee. Reagan's announcement of the O'Connor nomination was more masterful. He acknowledged the purposeful selection of a woman, though only from a pool of women who met the highest standards for selection to the Court. Other than the credibility problem, Bush's emphasis on Thomas's rise from poverty and discrimination is a classic example of a president framing the nomination discourse. To fail to take this initiative, especially with a nominee who may generate controversy, is to permit the opposition to frame the debate, much as Senator Kennedy did with his blistering portrayal of Robert Bork.

There are certain keynotes that engage the concerns of the public and the Senate. While the public is willing to accommodate considerable leeway on nominations, it is important with contemporary nominations to specify goals that ensure equal justice for all and a commitment to the fundamental civil rights and liberties of the American people. Being tough on crime still sells, but presidents simply have not done that well emphasizing judicial restraint at the level of the Supreme Court. All in all, a president must be aware of the discourse that surrounds a particular vacancy and of any new discourse that may emerge as the result of the specific nominee named to the vacancy.

How the characteristics of the setting and the characteristics of the nominee interact determines the level of consensus or controversy about a nomination. That determination has much to do with the way the nomination is accepted by the advocacy groups, the media, the public, and the Senate. Their reactions and interactions are the subject of Chapter 4.

CHAPTER FOUR

The Interim Period

Dear Senator:

I want to urge you in the strongest terms possible to ignore the special interest groups who are attempting to politicize the Senate's confirmation of Supreme Court nominees and return to your proper role of reviewing the nominee's qualifications.

The nomination of Clarence Thomas should be considered only on the basis of *his qualifications, and not whether Norman Lear and the organization People for the American Way or other like groups happen to agree with him.*

Are you going to hand over the selection of all future Supreme Court nominees to the heads of the biggest special interest groups, or are you going to keep faith with one of America's most cherished and important Constitutional principles? I'll be watching your vote with great interest.

Sincerely,
CCAGW Charter Member

Subtlety is hardly the hallmark of American politics, and the interim between the president's announcement of a nomination and the Senate vote on confirmation reveals American politics at its best—or is it at its worst? Let's drop the adjectives and simply say that the confirmation process reveals American politics at work. The postcard quoted above, apparently good for any senator, illustrates one advocacy group's effort (the Council for Citizens Against Government Waste) to mobilize its membership, agitating them to submit these preprinted cards in the hope that the recipient senator will be influenced. The irony of one advocacy group urging a senator to ignore the politicizing efforts of "special interest groups" opposing Thomas while simultaneously seeking to intimidate the senator into a consenting vote is perhaps lost only on the senders of the cards.

Despite the fact that the process has always been political, it also seems that the process is now more highly politicized than ever before. This is hardly surprising given changes in the way politics is conducted in the modern era. Several factors have contributed to increasing politicization, but certainly a major one is the length of time between the president's announcement of a nominee and the formal beginning of the Senate's evaluation of the nominee. Washington's nomination of the first six justices of the Court was transmitted to the Senate on September 24, 1789, and the confirmations came just two days later (Marcus 1985, 1:1, 9–10). In the early days, unless the Senate sought a purposeful delay, nominations were commonly considered within a couple of days of the president's announcement. Today it is typical for a nominee to wait two to three months before the Senate begins its formal considerations.

While this expansion of time may be explained in a variety of benign ways,[1] it nonetheless has fundamentally altered the nature of confirmation politics by expanding the opportunity for advocacy groups, the media, the public, and individual political actors to participate actively in creating the views and establishing the discourse that will inform the hearings of the Senate Judiciary Committee, the first step in the Senate's formal consideration of the nomination. Whether a nomination will be controversial or noncontroversial when it finally is considered by the Senate is determined in large measure by the political activities that occur in this interim between the presidential nomination and Senate consideration.

In this chapter we examine the roles of four major groups of actors: advocacy groups, the ABA, the media, and the American public. Each plays an increasingly important role in the modern confirmation process. Of particular importance is their contribution to the nomination discourse and how that discourse affects perceptions of the nominee's qualifications and character. Finally, we model how the nomination setting affects the development of the discourse and produces a perception of nominee qualifications.

Actors in the Confirmation Drama

The Constitution anticipates an appointment process that involves only the president and the Senate. Given the significance of Supreme Court appointments, however, it is not surprising that several nonconstitutional actors have involved themselves in the process. Their involvement constitutes the democratizing of the appointment process because it is only with their participation

---

[1] Many recent nominations have occurred in the middle of the summer, after the Supreme Court's adjournment in June or July and prior to the Senate's customary August recess. The Senate recess provides a "natural" layover time for the nomination and places the beginning of the Senate's confirmation activity in the middle of September. Moreover, the extensiveness of background checks on a nomiee now required takes at least six weeks.

that citizens formulate and articulate opinions regarding Supreme Court nominees.

Advocacy Groups

Whether you know them as interest groups, political action committees, or by some other label, *advocacy group* refers to a group of people organized to promote some particular set of interests. The active participation of advocacy groups in the confirmation process is one of the more prominent features of modern-day nominations. Supporters of recent nominations are particularly fond of attributing the acrimony that has surfaced in those nominations to the activities of these advocacy groups. It is a mistake, however, to assume that advocacy by special interests is a recent phenomenon. Those whose interests have been affected by the Court have always been there to attempt to exercise influence in support of their position.

When the "radical" Louis Brandeis was nominated to a Court in 1916 that carefully guarded businesses from government interference, business interests worked hard to defeat the nomination. The efforts to defame the character of Brandeis, to question his veracity, to challenge his integrity and temperament were persistent and intense although ultimately unsuccessful (Mason 1946, 465–508). David Danelski's analysis of Pierce Butler's nomination in 1922 revealed efforts by various labor, progressive, and regressive anti-Catholic groups to derail the confirmation, effort that once again fell short (Danelski 1964). As the labor movement and the fledgling National Association for the Advancement of Colored People (NAACP) began to find the Court more and more a venue for their policy agendas, they successfully battled the nomination of John Parker in 1930.

Despite the activities of interests in earlier nominations, however, it seems generally accepted that groups play a more prominent role today than ever before. What distinguishes the role of advocacy groups today in the confirmation process compared even to the pre-1980s is what distinguishes advocacy groups more generally in the political process: There are more of them. They have stronger financial backing. They are more likely to maintain professional staffs in Washington to pursue their goals. They effectively utilize modern technologies and behavioral science techniques to secure their policy objectives (Knoke 1990; Schlozman and Tierney 1986; Salisbury 1990).

Major Players

Prior to the 1980s, Supreme Court nominations were simply one additional policy issue to be handled by an advocacy group, and nominations to the lower federal courts were virtually ignored altogether. The formation of a number of public-interest groups in the 1970s (Berry 1977, 34) signaled the emergence of a more formal politicization of the judicial selection process that occurred in the 1980s.

On the conservative side, overt politicization was presaged by Richard Nixon's rhetoric in 1968 for the need to appoint "strict constructionists" to the Court and became more formal with a 1980 Republican party platform plank advocating the appointment of judges and justices

> whose judicial philosophy is characterized by the highest regard
> for protecting the rights of law-abiding citizen, . . . is consistent
> with the belief in the decentralization of the federal government
> and efforts to return decision-making power to state and local-
> elected officials. . . . [and] who respect traditional family values
> and the sanctity of innocent human life. (*Congressional Quarterly*
> 1980, 74B)

Shortly after the Republican victories for the presidency and the Senate, conservative activists conducted a symposium that brought forth *Blueprint for Judicial Reform* (McGuigan and Rader 1981). At the same time, the Reagan administration was recruiting lawyers who had been actively involved in public-interest law, conservative style (O'Connor and McFall 1992, 273–275). It was clear that the federal judiciary was a major target of opportunity and—before the Reagan administration was through—Reagan would appoint more than half of the federal judiciary and, in combination with President Bush's first two appointments, a majority of the Supreme Court (Box 4.1).

Liberals, already stung by some retrenchment of the Burger Court in the areas of civil rights and civil liberties, were dismayed by the onslaught of conservative nominations coming from the Reagan administration. In 1984, a meeting of liberal activists produced the Judicial Selection Project, which would operate within the existing Alliance for Justice. This represented a commitment of resources that would facilitate communication and presumably stronger advocacy and action concerning nominations to the federal courts.

When push came to shove in the 1987 Bork nomination, the conservatives found they had had it too easy. The previous six years of Republican presidential and Senate control had not required them to establish an apparatus that was prepared to gear up for a major fight in a nomination. The liberals, on the other hand, were now experienced in the coalition formation that would facilitate the coordination of resources, strategy, and tactics needed to mount their massive anti-Bork campaign.

★ ★ ★ ★ ★   ★   ★   ★   ★

BOX 4.1
*Major Advocacy Group Players
in the Appointment Process*

Most of the advocacy groups that contribute to the nomination discourse and supply the human resources to work the confirmation
process are organized as tax-exempt bodies under section 501(c)(3)
of the Internal Revenue Code. This section permits the groups to receive tax-deductible charitable donations. Because the groups are
not permitted to engage in "substantial" lobbying, they all establish high profiles with respect to an educational and social scien-
tific research agenda, which permits them to pursue their efforts to
"educate" the public and the Senate with respect to judicial nominations.

Conservative Groups

Free Congress Research and Education Foundation (Founded 1977)
One of a number of conservative think tanks, the Free Congress
Foundation consists of about 40 staff members. One of its divisions,
the Institute for Government and Politics, is particularly active in
support of conservative judicial appointments.

Washington Legal Foundation (Founded 1976)
The Washington Legal Foundation conducts extensive research and
publication activities involving corporate civil liberties and economic rights. Sporting a staff of about 15 and claiming 200,000 members and supporters, the group is home to conservatives who have
spearheaded efforts for a more conservative judiciary.

Heritage Foundation (Founded 1973)
The largest of the conservative think tanks that devotes considerable attention to Supreme Court nominations consists of well over 100 staff
members. Like the other conservative organizations listed here, the
Heritage Foundation pursues an active research and publication agenda.

Coalitions for America (Founded 1977)
Coalitions for America is registered as a (c)(4) organization, which
permits it to engage in lobbying activities more overtly than (c)(3)
groups. Serving as an umbrella for a number of different groups with
diverse policy interests, Coalitions for America was particularly active in developing and disseminating detailed analyses in support of
the Court nominees of Reagan and Bush.

continued

---

continued

Liberal Groups

Alliance for Justice (Founded 1975)
Exerting influence beyond its meager staff of fewer than a half-dozen, the Alliance is prototypical of the coalition-building entities that characterize liberal efforts. The Alliance became home for the Judicial Selection Project, a liberal coalition effort to monitor and influence judicial appointments.

Leadership Conference on Civil Rights (Founded 1950)
One of the oldest organizations to consistently maintain a major role in judicial nominations, the Leadership Conference on Civil Rights is a coalition of almost 200 minority, labor, religious, disabled, aged, and civic organizations.

People for the American Way (Founded 1981)
While one of the newer public interest advocacy groups, People for the American Way (PFAW) immediately established itself as a major player as a result of its sheer size (over 250,000 members and nearly 60 professional staff). PFAW's main contribution to the liberal cause is its strong grassroots organization.

The Nation Institute's Supreme Court Watch (Founded 1980)
The Supreme Court Watch publishes material on the Court at periodic intervals. With only one full-time staff member, the Watch relies heavily on a network of lawyers and scholars around the country to help formulate its position on nominees.

NAACP Legal Defense and Educational Fund (Founded 1939)
The NAACP is one the oldest organizations to have lobbied effectively in the defeat of a Supreme Court nominee, namely, that of John Parker in 1930. The Legal Defense and Educational Fund was subsequently created to utilize the courts on behalf of the organization's goals. Part of that effort is directed at securing judicial appointments desired by the NAACP.

Networks

A major key to success in politics, as with the business and academic worlds, is networking. This is hardly news. Danelski's analysis of Pierce Butler's seemingly bland nomination literally becomes a textbook analysis of networking among prominent individuals (Danelski 1964, 153–166). What advocacy groups like the Alliance for Justice and Coalitions for America have achieved is the expansion of networks horizontally into coalitions of a variety of groups and the individuals who constitute them. Meanwhile, other groups like People for the American Way have expanded networks vertically to empower those who live quite remotely from the center of power in Washington but whose input is never further away than the nearest telephone, fax, or computer network (Abrahamson, Arterton, and Orren 1988, 185–186).

Ultimately, what makes a network effective is that it brings people together. It is the story of the anti-Bork coalition that most vividly illustrates how individuals, connecting with and trusting each other, actually overcame the counterproductive tendency of organizations to pursue their own agendas rather than collaborate in a common cause with their peer organizations. Witness this brief portrayal of an anti-Bork effort.

> Kate Michelman of NARAL [the National Abortion Rights Action League] had early offered to hire a full-time grassroots coordinator for the coalition. She was not pleased to learn that [Ralph] Neas, without consultation, had seized the initiative and hired a coordinator for the Leadership Conference. The fact that he chose [Mimi] Mager, who was so widely seasoned and trusted, eased the resentment.
>
> When Nan Aron, for the Alliance [for Justice], engaged Carol Foreman and Nikki Heidepriem, in part to develop themes for guiding the grassroots movement, there arose potential rivalry or conflict between the roles of the Alliance and Leadership Conference. But that threat evaporated because Heidepriem and Mager had worked closely and happily together on women's issues in the Mondale/Ferraro campaign; they readily worked together again on the anti-Bork campaign. (Pertschuk and Schaetzel 1989, 82–83)

In just two paragraphs, the description mentioned six activists and four separate organizations coming together to work in yet a fifth cause.

Networking is not that difficult in the nation's capitol. In perhaps the most interconnected city in the nation, hardly anyone is more distant than a single intermediary (Salisbury et al. 1992, 135–136). As we interviewed one leading conservative activist in his office, we were first interrupted by a phone caller from North Carolina seeking support for a federal judgeship position. Our activist relayed the good news/bad news scenarios (the caller was apparently on the list that Senator Jesse Helms submitted to the Justice Department but not at the top), schmoozed the unhappy caller ("I'd really like to see you get an appointment"), and indicated he would check further with his sources at the Justice Department. Somewhat later in the interview, a call came through from a *New York Times* reporter seeking insider information on the status of a nomination. For those in the Washington political culture, if there is someone you don't know personally, you probably do know someone who does who know that person.

Motivations

Advocacy groups arise from a desire to affect public policy. To the extent that the Court influences public policy, groups will exhibit concern over the composition of the Court (O'Connor and Epstein 1989). As we have noted already, it is no accident that the Bork nomination generated intense opposition. The retirement of Lewis Powell signaled a true turning point in the types of decisions that could be expected from the Court. As conservative forces appeared to consolidate their hold on the Court with Reagan's appointment of Kennedy and the subsequent Bush appointments, some liberal advocates had begun to concede the Court to the conservatives and look for battles where greater opportunities for success lie. However, the combination of a Democatic presidency and the emergence of a centrist group on the Court from among the Reagan and Bush appointees (most notably Souter, O'Connor, and Kennedy), has prevented the Court from becoming as conservative as the more conservative bloc of Scalia, Rehnquist, and Thomas might have preferred.

Of course, there are motivations other than affecting public policy that drive nominee opposition. Advocacy of one's cause never ceases and it is important to use whatever appropriate arena offers an opportunity for putting one's message before the public. From a leader's perspective, it is important to show the flag, to demonstrate to the membership that the leadership is active and articulate in behalf of the cause. Moreover, when the battle for one's principles can be incarnated unambiguously in a single individual in so simple an event as acceptance or rejection of a high-profile nomination, the opportunity to renew the passions of the faithful and to gain new converts—and their resources—can hardly be wasted. Conservative activist Pat McGuigan's assertion to us that the liberal lobbies used Bork as a fund-raiser and membership drive is well taken. However, as Box 4.2 illustrates, such motivations were hardly limited to the liberals.

As much as the leadership of various advocacy groups might wish to act without restraint in opposition to or support of a nominee, there are very practical constraints that prevent it. We have already noted the need to work cooperatively with allies. In addition, effectiveness requires credibility. Lest they be taken no more seriously than the boy who cried "wolf" too often, advocacy groups seek to maintain an image of reasonableness and rationality while

★ ★ ★ ★ ★   ★   ★   ★   ★

BOX 4.2
*Solicitation Letter Used to Promote
Support for Bork*

Dear Fellow American –

The time for action is NOW!

On July 1, 1987 – President Reagan nominated Judge Robert Bork to fill the vacancy on the U.S. Supreme Court left by the retirement of Justice Lewis Powell . . .

. . . And since then – nearly every liberal in America has spoken out to denounce and defame the character of Judge Bork!

They have called him a racist . . . a radical . . . an extreme ideologue . . . and a man who lacks background and experience.

But these remarks are outright lies!

VERIFICATION FORM: Moral Majority, Inc.

☐ I have mailed (or will mail) the enclosed postcards to members of the Senate Judiciary Committee immediately!

☐ Enclosed is my contribution of: ☐ $50 ☐ $25 ☐ $ _____ to help you in this campaign and the other important projects of Moral Majority.

RETURN IMMEDIATELY

Please Print:

Name:	Official Use Only:
Address:	Date:
City: State: Zip:	Code:

Reprinted with the permission of Dr. Jerry Falwell.

consistently standing by the principles that define their existence. While the conservatism of Scalia was well known—and feared—by liberal advocates, most felt that to oppose simultaneously the Rehnquist elevation to chief justice and the Scalia nomination was just too much nay-saying. They chose to put their energies into the Rehnquist nomination.

To speak of group motivations may be a collective fallacy. These groups, after all, are driven by individual effort, particularly those individuals who serve as a group's spokesperson or director, and the motivations that drive their work are diverse. On the other hand, our experiences and observations with these advocates are consistent with those of other scholars (Schlozman and Tierney 1986; Berry 1977). To a person, all to whom we have spoken are sincerely committed to their work and their partisan positions. Most are at least temporarily demoralized by their losses, concerned about the future of the country, and somewhat cynical about the motivations driving their opponents.

Group Tactics

Much of what occurs during the interim period happens behind closed doors as groups seek to establish and implement a strategy to affect the outcome of the nomination. During the Thomas nomination, for example, we sat in on a visit from six representatives of Hispanics for Thomas, an ad hoc group of former Reagan and current Bush administration people, some of whom had worked with Clarence Thomas. Hoping to catch the senator, they settled for making their points to the two staff members responsible for handling the confirmation. We crowded into the small conference room of the senator's Judiciary subcommittee and, after introducing themselves, one of them began a spiel on behalf of Judge Thomas. After their initial expression of support, they rebutted allegations of Thomas's bias against Hispanics while at the EEOC and challenged the legitimacy of the Mexican-American Legal Defense and Educational Fund (MALDEF) to speak for Hispanics in opposition to Thomas. Most made their points simply and sincerely. One was more aggressive, attacking MALDEF, maligning the Thomas opposition, and throwing in a minilecture on equal protection to boot. The staff members listened politely, asked a few questions, thanked the six for coming in, and assured them that the senator would know of their visit and their concerns. After they left, one of the staff looked over and said, "Could you believe that guy?"

Later that afternoon, we were back in the conference room, now with two representatives from MALDEF. One was a legislative staff attorney from their Washington office acquainted with the two Senate staff members; the other was from out of town. They handed over a 23-page MALDEF assessment of the Thomas nomination, summarized the basis of their concerns about Thomas, and asked if there was any information or assistance they could provide the staff. Informed of the morning session with Hispanics for Thomas, they smiled and simply asked if there were any questions stemming from that session that they could answer.

Such visits are common, especially during a controversial nomination. After all, advocacy groups deal in information. That is their primary utility, the means by which they hope to persuade others—especially senators—to their point of view. Information is the basis for the symbiotic relationship between advocacy groups and senatorial staff, staff who need information with which to prepare their senator for the confirmation hearings and for making a confirmation decision.

Advocates are especially good sources of background information regarding the issues of a nomination. They are the ones who really construct the discourse of the nomination. They raise the issues, pose the questions, and establish the language used in conjunction with the nomination. Opposition advocates are there to help the staff and senator to see how the nominee is inconsistent with certain positions or beliefs of the senator or, in other words, to increase the ideological distance between the senator and the nominee. Proponents are there to narrow that distance. What this means, of course, is that advocates most often work in conjunction with senatorial allies, are solicitous to undecided senators with offers of support and assistance in providing information, and pretty much don't work at all with the opposition. To be effective, advocates must work with the staff, establish good rapport, provide assistance to them often in the form of questions and background information suitable for use in the hearings, and maintain the utmost credibility as reliable and honest providers of useful information (Wolpe 1990, 9–15; Schlozman and Tierney 1986, 104; Smith 1988, 46–53).

Even with no vacancy anticipated, groups are still prepared for a nomination. This comes about in part because of familiarity with federal judges who already have gone through a confirmation process, albeit a process that is often pro forma. Some advocates keep files on prospective nominees and are just generally knowledgeable about the prominent names. Ruth Ginsburg and Stephen Breyer were well known in the legal community, and it would not take advocates long to prepare material on a Laurence Tribe, a Richard Arnold, or a Drew Days. On the other hand, it can be a distinct surprise to hear that a Sandra O'Connor or David Souter, both plucked from state court systems, has been nominated.

Especially in instances of relatively unknown nominees, the phone lines carry a surge of activity. Where information is the major currency, a good network is like owning a bank. Calls go out to and come in from locals who have information about the nominee. In a situation in which there was little appetite among liberal senators to fight Harrold Carswell on the heels of the Haynsworth battle, Marian Edelman, lawyer-director of a civil rights advocacy group in Washington, initiated the battle by phoning several lawyers she knew in Florida to get their views on Carswell. "The first one I got through to told me that he was a bad guy. . . . The others told me he was a *really* bad guy" (Harris 1971, 26). She heard enough to convince her and then other advocates and, ultimately, some senators that Carswell must be opposed.

The phone lines are not filled solely with interpersonal conversations on this initial day of a nomination. Binary digits (bits) stream between computers as advocates, reporters, and scholars access legal and newspaper databases in a mad scramble for every citation of a court decision, article, or other publication by or about the ·nominee. Computers, the icon of the information age, are used to gather, analyze, process, and disseminate the advocates' information, not only to Senate staff but also to representatives of the media and to the advocates' own memberships.

Groups do not gather information only about the nominee. In 1987 the anti-Bork coalition utilized social science techniques to gather information about the public as a means of plotting strategy for an effective appeal to mobilize public opinion against Bork's confirmation. An initial $40,000 was donated by the American Federation of State, County, and Municipal Employees (AFSCME) to hire a polling firm, Martilla and Kiley, to conduct a nationwide survey designed to determine effective issues around which to build opposition to Bork (Pertschuk and Schaetzel 1989, 135). Other professionals were hired to conduct focus-group sessions, particularly in the South since the votes of the southern senators were recognized as the key to the defeat of Bork. Focus groups typically assemble a dozen or so individuals selected to represent a cross section of some population. A group facilitator then moves the group through a discussion on different issues. As the name implies, this approach permits a greater focus on specific topics than does a survey poll. The information from these different sources permitted the anti-Bork coalition to disregard issues that held little concern for the public, such as Bork's role in Watergate, and focus on more fertile areas for public opposition, such as equal protection and the First Amendment (Pertschuk and Schaetzel 1989, 136–139).

While we have placed considerable emphasis on the information gathering and disseminating activities of advocacy groups, let us not lose sight that information is a means to the ends of persua-

TABLE 4.1
Advocacy-Group Tactics in the Legislative Process

1.	Testify at hearings	99%
2.	Contact government officials directly to present point of view	98
3.	Engage in informal contacts with officials	95
4.	Present research results	92
5.	Send letters to members regarding activities	92
6.	Enter into coalitions with other organizations	90
8.	Talk with people from press and media	86
9.	Consult with government officials to plan legislative strategy	85
11.	Inspire letter-writing or telegram campaigns	84
13.	Mount grassroots lobbying efforts	80
14.	Have influential constituents contact legislator's office	80
21.	Attempt to influence appointments to public office	53
23.	Engage in direct-mail fund-raising	44
24.	Advertise in media about your position on issues	31
27.	Engage in protests or demonstrations	20

Notes

The Washington Representative Survey, conducted between October 1981 and May 1982 (Schlozman and Tierney 1986, 150), asked representatives of 175 advocacy organizations operating in Washington to identify the activities performed by their organization. Of 27 different activities listed by Schlozman and Tierney, we report here the ones that are particularly relevant for influencing the Supreme Court appointment process. The activities are arranged in order of the percentage of representatives who specified that activity as one engaged in by their organization.

sion and mobilization. Advocates seek to persuade their own members, to capture the media, and to bring senators over to their point of view. By convincing others of the "rightness" of their position, they then engage in activities to mobilize those human resources to work in their behalf.

The various ways in which advocacy groups go about their business is especially well documented (Berry 1977; Schlozman and Tierney 1986; Smith 1988; Wolpe 1990; Knoke 1990; Petracca 1992). In a 1981–1982 survey of 175 different Washington advocacy-group organizations, Kay Schlozman and John Tierney itemized some 27 different activities that a majority of advocates reported using regularly (Schlozman and Tierney 1986, 150). Reported in Table 4.1 are 15 of those activities particularly relevant for the nomination and confirmation process, along with the percentage of organizations reporting that activity. Of course, some of the activities not listed (like making financial contributions to electoral campaigns) can affect those activities more directly relevant to influencing the appointment process.

Finally, for a much greater sense of the scope and intensity of advocacy efforts, we recommend the first-hand accounts published

after the Bork nomination (Pertschuk and Schaetzel 1989;
McGuigan and Weyrich 1990). Reading both permits some interesting comparisons of the liberal and conservative efforts for that nomination. More generally, fascinating accounts of the Bork and
Thomas nominations are also available (Bronner 1989; Phelps and
Winternitz 1992). All bring to life the political nature of an appointment and the considerable efforts by advocacy groups to frame the
nomination discourse in their terms as a means of winning the confirmation battle.

The American Bar Association

In Chapter 3 we traced the emergence of the ABA in the appointment process to the extent that it was involved with the executive
branch. The decline, really since President Eisenhower, of a strong
role in the initial selection process for Supreme Court nominees
has pushed the impact of the ABA back into this interim period
during which investigations of the nominee take place in preparation for Senate consideration.

In attempting to secure a role for itself, however, the ABA has
managed to alienate, at one time or another, just about everyone
involved in the appointment process. Here is an association
whose Standing Committee on Federal Judiciary concluded unanimously that Harrold Carswell was qualified to serve on the Court
while rendering a split judgment on Robert Bork, a minority of
four finding him not qualified "because of . . . concerns as to his
judicial temperament" (Tyler 1987, 6). Liberals were alienated by
the Carswell rating; conservatives were absolutely livid over the
Bork evaluation.

In a similar vein, liberals expressed some irritation that the reports from the Standing Committee regarding the assessments of
Rehnquist and Scalia in 1986 contained little detail concerning
negative views that surfaced about the nominees. However, in providing more detailed descriptions of negative views that came forward in the Bork nomination, the Standing Committee received
the ire of the conservatives on the Senate Judiciary Committee.
The record of the ABA evaluation of Supreme Court nominees is
presented in Box 4.3.

Prior to the 1980s, the committee was criticized by Senate liberals as overrepresenting the establishment to the exclusion of women
and minorities not only in its own makeup but in its solicitation of
opinions concerning judicial nominees. The legal establishment as
represented by the ABA has long been perceived by many liberals as
one dominated by conservatives. Indeed, its very creation in the late
nineteenth century was prompted by a desire to conserve a philoso-

BOX 4.3

The Standing Committee on Federal Judiciary and Its Evaluation of Supreme Court Nominees

The Standing Committee on Federal Judiciary was created in 1946 initially as a Special Committee on the Judiciary (Grossman 1965, 61–62). The first evaluation of a Supreme Court nominee came with the recommendation to confirm Earl Warren as chief justice in 1954. The committee currently consists of 15 members, one from each of the 13 judicial circuits, a chair, and a representative from the ABA board of governors.

The criteria for evaluating Supreme Court nominees have remained reasonably stable over the years: professional competence, integrity, and judicial temperament. Of course, the process of applying these criteria is not particular reliable. Committee members have exhibited differing views about how to define those criteria and how to weight them in an overall assessment.

Variation in the evaluation vocabulary of the Standing Committee over time and in the amount of detail contained in its report, conveyed in letter form, reflects the struggle to provide useful information to the administration and the Senate Judiciary Committee. During the major portion of the Eisenhower administration, letters from the ABA were rather curt and conveyed little more than the fact that the ABA had found the nominees eminently qualified to serve on the Court.

Year	Nominee	Assessment	Vote
1954	Warren	Eminently qualified	Unanimous
1955	Harlan	Eminently qualified	Unanimous
1956	Brennan	Eminently qualified	Unanimous
1957	Whittaker	Eminently qualified	Unanimous

Between the Whittaker and Stewart nominations, the ABA committee adopted a four-position scale of exceptionally well qualified, well qualified, qualified, and not qualified. Although used for only two Supreme Court nominations, the scheme was retained for evaluating judicial nominees for lower federal courts until 1990, when the highest category was dropped.

Year	Nominee	Assessment	Vote
1959	Stewart	Exceptionally well qualified	10 to 1
1962	White	Exceptionally well qualified	Unanimous

Although a 1962 letter from the ABA committee to the chair of the Judiciary Committee indicated a desire to use a system that

continued

continued

simply says a nominee is or is not acceptable and avoid "the use of any adjective which might suggest a comparative rating," the committee proceeded to describe nominees as "highly acceptable." The two evaluations of Haynsworth stemmed from revelations during the hearings that raised ethical concerns, which led to the ABA committee being asked to reevaluate his nomination.

Year	Nominee	Assessment	Vote
1963	Goldberg	Highly acceptable	Not reported
1965	Fortas	Highly acceptable	Not reported
1967	Marshall	Highly acceptable	Not reported
1968	Fortas (CJ)	Highly acceptable	Unanimous
1969	Burger	Highly acceptable	Not reported
1969	Haynsworth	Highly acceptable	Unanimous
1969	Haynsworth (reconsidered)	Highly acceptable	8 to 4

During the consideration of Haynsworth, the ABA committee decided to limit future ratings to simply qualified or not qualified. While it did so with Carswell, the language was quickly embellished after Carswell to say that the nominee "meets high standards of professional competence, judicial temperament, and integrity" and typically that the nominee "is one of the best persons available for appointment to the Supreme Court." O'Connor presented a problem in this regard, however, and the committee virtually abandoned this approach and provided a descriptive narrative indicating that "the Committee has unanimously found that Judge O'Connor has the professional qualifications required of an Associate Justice, . . . that [she] has an appropriate judicial temperament,. . . [and that] her integrity is above reproach." They said nothing about her being one of the best persons available.

Year	Nominee	Assessment	Vote
1970	Carswell	Qualified	Unanimous
1970	Blackmun	Qualified, one of the best	Unanimous
1971	Powell	Qualified, one of the best	Unanimous
1971	Rehnquist	Qualified, one of the best	9 Qualified 3 Not opposed
1975	Stevens	Qualified, one of the best	Unanimous
1981	O'Connor	Qualified	Unanimous

More recently, the ABA committee has adopted a three-position scale of well qualified, qualified, and not qualified. Letters to the Judiciary Committee are somewhat detailed, providing a classification of individuals whose assessments of the nominee were solicited, a summary of the comments that came forward, and an evaluation of an interview with the nominee.

Year	Nominee	Assessment	Vote
1986	Rehnquist (CJ)	Well qualified	Unanimous
1986	Scalia	Well qualified	Unanimous
1987	Bork	Well qualified	10 Well qualified 4 Not qualified 1 Not opposed
1987	Kennedy	Well qualified	Unanimous
1990	Souter	Well-qualified	Unanimous
1991	Thomas	Qualified	12 Qualified 2 Not qualified 1 Abstention
1993	Ginsburg	Well qualified	Unanimous
1994	Breyer	Well qualified	Unanimous

Note
CJ=Chief Justice

phy of law coming under increasingly radical challenges (Schwartz 1988, 61). The opposition to Brandeis from many of the ABA's elite on the basis of his radicalism stood as a symbol of ABA conservatism into the 1970s. From the liberal perspective, the problem with the ABA stemmed from four major factors:

•the Committee's own narrowly drawn membership;
•criteria for judicial appointments that placed a premium on lengthy experience to the detriment of the increasing number of women and minorities who were more recently admitted to the legal profession;
•assessments of judicial nominees with too little input from civil rights groups and other equal-rights advocates; and
•acquiescence to substandard nominations from conservative presidents.

On the other hand, ever since the presidency of Richard Nixon, conservatives have grown more and more alienated from what they perceive as an increasingly liberal ABA. They have been greatly disturbed by the changes in the structure of the association, which established "sections" to deal with a variety of public policy issues (Rees 1981, 288). The domination of certain sections by more reform-minded and activist lawyers has produced liberal stands on abortion, gun registration, the death penalty, and other issues. Concurrently, the Committee on Federal Judiciary responded to the liberal criticism by soliciting assessments of nominees from groups that were more likely to have liberal perspectives on equality and civil rights issues and by acting affirmatively to create greater diversity on the committee itself. Those efforts, particularly the former, provoked a severe reaction from conservatives, initiated through the Washington Legal Foundation and supported by a majority of Republicans on the Senate Judiciary Committee (Popeo and Kammenar 1989, 179–181; *Washington Legal Foundation* v. *Department of Justice* 1989; Grassley, et al. 1990, 21).

The ABA's seeming inability to satisfy both Democrats and Republicans at any one time illustrates the political sensitivity of the appointment process. The ABA purports to avoid considerations of political or ideological philosophy while examining and evaluating only a nominee's professional competence, judicial temperament, and integrity. Ultimately, such considerations are unable to command universal acceptance not just because they are subsidiary to political considerations but also because the three criteria are fundamentally political and ideological constructs themselves.

The Media

As the word suggests, the media literally are the agencies through which much of the nomination discourse is conducted. The emergence of various media mark virtual epochs in the social and political history of humankind. The printing press, the telegraph, the radio, and television have all made impressive impacts on their founding and subsequent generations. Where some see these media as a means to empower ever larger numbers of people, others see devices to manipulate and control ever larger numbers of people (Abrahamson, Arterton, and Orren 1988, 3–31). Few policy advocates and fewer politicians wish to leave to chance the images and resulting interpretations that will result from portrayals of them or their positions.

Since the first rejection of a Supreme Court nomination in 1796, the media have played a significant role in the nomination and confirmation process. Newspaper allegations of John Rutledge's insanity and their reports of his anti-Jay Treaty speech likely played a significant role in his defeat (Friedman and Israel 1969, 1:45–49). At the same time, the fact that news traveled so slowly in those days may also have contributed to his ultimate defeat. Rutledge's July 18 bashing of the Jay Treaty came after Washington's July 1 offer to him of the chief justice position but possibly prior to Rutledge's receipt of the offer (Warren 1935, 1:129–130; cf Friedman and Israel 1969, 1:45). Regardless of whether Rutledge knew of the appointment, he had actively sought it and there is little doubt that his oratory cost him confirmation as chief justice of the United States.

Today the media's contribution to the confirmation discourse is every bit as important as it was years ago, but its instantaneous and more pervasive nature makes for a more intricate and complex impact. In this age of live television coverage, the Judiciary Committee confirmation hearing has become a media event. Camera angles, the schedule time given to proponents or opponents of the nominee, the encapsulation of arguments and characterizations into sound bites—all can influence reactions to the nominee. Most analysts of the Bork and Thomas nominations gave considerable weight to the media in influencing public opinion and the ultimate outcomes of those deliberations.

In describing the role of media, we must distinguish four major functions because each plays differently upon the appointment process. One major function of the media is news reporting, in which reporters and editors determine what is newsworthy and how that news should be presented. With the advent of C-SPAN and other representatives of broadcast media, a second function of media has become, in effect, the *unmediated* transmission of events, like gavel to gavel coverage of the Judiciary Committee hearings. Certain media also become agencies for the transmission of advertising from advocates in support of or opposition to a nominee. Finally, various media, particularly the newspapers, serve up opinions from advocates and from the newspaper's own editorial board in the op-ed pages. All of these functions serve to develop the discourse that takes place throughout the appointment process.

News Reporting

On the day before the Clarence Thomas hearings began, the Sunday *Washington Post* ran the first of a two-part front-page analysis of Clarence Thomas with the headline "Thomas: Growing Up Black in a White World" (Lancaster and LaFraniere 1991, A1). It followed the next day with "Despite Achievement, Thomas Felt Isolated; Rebuffs Stung Emerging Conservative" (LaFraniere 1991, A1). Strictly speaking, analysis features are not considered "news" in the sense of events or actions, but they presumably do represent what newspapers feel they do better than the other media, namely, provide an introspective assessment of a news topic. What do these headlines and the stories that were fairly represented by them suggest about the nomination of Clarence Thomas? For one thing, they framed the nomination as one that focused on the character and the race of Clarence Thomas. The attempts by some opponents to focus on Thomas's lack of experience, intellectual capacity, and judicial temperament were largely absent from the *Washington Post* analysis. From the perspective of Thomas opponents, these analyses might as well have been written by White House staff.

News reporting is less reporting reality than it is structuring reality (Altheide 1976; Nimmo and Combs 1990). Reporters, analysts, and editors are constantly confronted with the necessity of making decisions concerning what events and actions constitute news, how to structure descriptions of that "news," and empowering individuals as credible spokespersons for these events and actions. In the news business, every decision—whether it be to commit or omit—has political consequences. Even basic journalistic ethics that seek to ensure fairness by providing balanced and reliable coverage cannot overcome the fundamental arbitrariness of journalistic decision making.

Reporters we interviewed almost universally perceive as newsworthy events that produce change and conflict. The O'Connor nomination was initially newsworthy because it constituted a historic change in the Supreme Court—the first female appointee. Coverage faded quickly in the absence of further "news," meaning controversy, about the nomination. The Bork nomination drew immediate media attention because of the instant and intense conflict it generated, conflict created in part because of the significant change it seemed to portend for the Court and the nation. Of course, the Thomas nomination moved from newsworthy to news obsessive when a charge of sexual harassment produced a turn more melodramatic than the daily soap operas.

The importance of change and conflict stems from the need for the media to find an angle, a way to frame or structure a story in order to capture the attention of the public. While change or conflict may define much that is considered newsworthy, there is also room for the human-interest and Horatio Alger rags-to-riches story. The media never tired of reminding us of Clarence Thomas's roots in Pin Point, Georgia, despite the fact that Thomas was rooted in what would be more accurately depicted as a working middle-class background. There is also no doubt that sex sells and that angle, of course, is what attracted such attention to the Thomas-Hill phase of the hearings. When reporter Dawn Ceol of the *Washington Times* crafted a balanced, though perhaps bland, headline that read "Thomas Accuser Lauded, Assailed," the editor subsequently modified it to read "Miss Hill Painted as a 'Fantasizer'" (Kurz 1991, C1, C9).

While trying to maintain their journalistic objectivity, reporters must not only battle editors from time to time, they are also besieged by advocates of one side or the other who are increasingly knowledgeable and sophisticated about what buttons to push to get reporters' attention and at providing a frame or spin to a topic that reporters can use. Ethan Bronner, a *Boston Globe* reporter, knowingly cited *New York Times* reporter Linda Greenhouse's sense of feeling like so much "raw meat" during the Bork nomination as anti-Bork advocates inundated the media with news releases and other actions that themselves were deemed as newsworthy (Bronner 1989, 147–153). A television advertisement of actor Gregory Peck denouncing the Bork nomination only ran one time as a paid political announcement but in the process became a news event that received much wider play than the ad itself.

Advocacy groups are becoming particularly adept at playing to state and local news media. Through the use of video news releases and radio actualities, the local broadcast media are seduced into giving play to the advocacy group's message, typically with little critical assessment. The video news release utilizes high-profile personalities, typically from the Washington political arena, in five-minute interview segments with local newscasters via a satellite feed, paid for by the advocacy group. For the local television station, it is a wonderful and virtually free opportunity to display the local newscaster in a one-on-one interview with a Jesse Jackson, Ralph Nader, or some other well-known political personality. The radio actuality works somewhat differently. Rather than provide an interview, a 30- to 60-second statement is recorded by the personality and a professional lead-in is then provided. The result is a self-contained presentation ready for play on the radio news. In either instance, the television or radio station may choose to do some editing, although the setup for the radio actuality is intended to be used as it is. The radio actuality is also much more likely to use prominent locals in getting the message across.

Journalism is a tough business. To a person, those top reporters that we interviewed were knowledgeable, self-aware, and competitive. All spoke of the need to get the story straight and of the desire to break it first, two goals that exist in tension with each other. Nominee supporters complain of a media that dig in the dirt searching for negative information that might raise questions about a nominee's character. When the *Capitol Times* ran an article on the movie rentals of Robert Bork, there was a widespread sense that his privacy was unduly invaded and that such information was not newsworthy in the context of a Supreme Court nomination. But as competition among the media increases, journalistic ethics are interpreted ever more narrowly. The fear that if you as a reporter don't make "it" public someone else will is behind the increasing tendency of the media to reveal all. Ethics, it seems, are defined by the least ethical.

On the other hand, there is no doubt that an active investigative effort of nominees is called for. Not all journalists agree, but most perceive the Senate Judiciary Committee investigative staff as inadequate because they tend to lack true investigative experience and are too passive in the search for information. There is a definite need for investigative journalism that will discover relevant and re-

liable information bearing directly on the character and qualifications of a Supreme Court nominee (Totenberg 1988). The media
bear a major burden and responsibility for developing the nomination discourse. Advocates for either side in a nomination can say
and do all they want, but unless the media convey the message, the
effect is largely muted.

"Unmediated" Media

The 1980s witnessed the emergence of "narrowcasting" as a major
media market force, predominantly in the form of cable television.
In particular, C-SPAN emerged as a passive observer and recorder of
political events, including gavel-to-gavel coverage of Supreme
Court confirmation hearings. Fuller coverage of the confirmation
hearings has also been taken up by CNN and, in controversial nominations, PBS, both of which accompany the coverage with reporters and commentators who attempt to provide some perspective and insight concerning the hearings.

Opening the doors of the Senate hearings to all who care to
watch is not as benign a process, however, as one might think. As if
following some principle of quantum mechanics, the mere process
of training television cameras on the hearings has certainly fixed
the physical presence of committee senators in the hearing room
more often than occurred before that intrusion. The informal proceedings that characterized even modern hearings prior to television coverage are a thing of the past. All committee members now
give opening statements. All consume their full share of time allot-
ted for questions, at least through the first round. Most, if at all possible, remain present throughout the questioning of the nominee.

Public opinion is also affected, and while the opportunity for
education about the process exists, little occurs with C-SPAN's passive coverage. To their credit, however, C-SPAN does offer program
opportunities that provide explanations and interpretations of
events by knowledgeable participants and scholars. The educational
value of coverage by CNN and PBS is largely dependent upon the
quality of the commentators they choose to get. Things are not always what they seem, and it helps to have a knowledgeable analyst
to provide perspective for viewers. In addition, the focus on the
hearings tends to overlook the significance of the interim period between the nomination and the hearings, a time that is crucial to the
development of the nomination discourse and the eventual outcome of the confirmation vote.

Advertising

The emergence of public-interest advocacy groups as major players
in the confirmation process has been accompanied by the use of the

media to advertise positions concerning the nomination. This is a major development in the overt politicization of the confirmation process. Advertising demands partisan rhetoric, not a thoughtful assessment of a nominee's strengths and weaknesses. As such, advertising contributes to the nomination discourse but in a way that generates controversy.

Advertising attempts to frame the nomination and pre-empt the discourse along the lines favored by the advertising group. This anti-Bork television ad with Gregory Peck dramatically situated in front of the Supreme Court building portrayed Robert Bork as being retrogressive on civil rights, privacy, and freedom of speech. The Bork opposition was quite successful at getting this frame to stick, placing the burden on Bork to establish otherwise. Pro-Clarence Thomas forces ran an ad in the *Washington Post* (Americans for Self Reliance 1991, A7) that pursued their strategy of focusing on his race and on the quality of character that emerged from this self-made man. Their photo of several black children in front of a ramshackle rural home was not of Clarence Thomas, but the poignant images of poverty conveyed by the picture appealed effectively to the acclaim we reserve for such people.

Editorial and Op-Ed Endorsements

The scramble for editorial endorsements from newspapers and for the publication of one's views on the op-ed page is an obsessive focus of advocacy groups. It was no surprise that the first meeting of conservative advocates for Bork articulated the following strategy: "First, we will try to alert and influence opinion makers, editorial boards, church leaders, and others with the ear of a senator" (McGuigan and Weyrich 1990, 27). While on the liberal side, Phil Sparks—an advocate for AFSCME—reported:

> We prepared, for distribution by a network that AFSCME has developed, a generic op-ed piece in Ralph's [Neas] name condemning the nomination, following exactly the lines suggested by the poll results, that we sent out to every paper in the country the week before the hearings started. Next we encouraged and helped prepare state-specific op-ed pieces for in-state authors: the dean of a law school in Florida [and] a prominent civil rights lawyer in Alabama, for example (Sparks 1991).

The preoccupation of advocates with the op-ed page seems curious at first. It is an activity that receives very little attention from scholars, even though it topped a list of 27 different activities in an early 1980s survey of Washington advocacy representatives with respect to techniques used more now than in the past (Schlozman and Tierney 1986, 155). One team of political scientists has used the editorial reactions about a nominee to measure nominee qualifications (Cameron, Cover, and Segal 1990, 529), a result that seems to work not because newspaper editors are particularly adept at assessing qualifications but because the advocacy groups are busily constructing the images of the nominee and framing the issues around which the nomination discourse will proceed.

The op-ed pages are a major turf in the confirmation battle for control of the nomination discourse. Groups recruit well-known and respected scholars and political commentators to articulate their views. They inundate editors with information designed to support their positions. They activate well-placed partisans who can influence newspaper editors and editorial boards. Then they harvest the fruits of their op-ed efforts, package them, and forward them to still other media sources, to grassroots organizations and members, and to senators' offices. The effect of the op-ed pages may not lead directly to swaying a senator's vote, but advocates view it as an essential step in controlling the discourse. To ignore the op-ed pages is to abandon the battlefield.

The Public

As we sat in the reception area of Senator DeConcini's Washington office looking over notes from a previous interview, the phone rang incessantly. "Senator DeConcini's office, please hold," was the inevitable response. "Thank you for holding. Is this call concerning the Bork nomination? And are you for or against confirmation? Thank you for calling, I'll be sure the Senator hears about your call." For days during the hearings, the calls in the Washington office started at 9:00 A.M.—6:00 A.M. in Arizona's September—and ran virtually nonstop till past 6:00 in the evening, one almost every 10 seconds. The calls, the faxes, and the mail numbered in the tens of thousands for DeConcini, Specter, and Heflin—presumably the undecided votes on the Senate Judiciary Committee. They were the special targets of advocacy groups that, as never before, were activating grassroots public opinion in an effort to influence the Senate confirmation vote.

In the meantime, the *Atlanta Constitution* had commissioned the Roper Organization to conduct a poll throughout the southern states for a series on the state of the South. Planned before the Bork nomination, they nonetheless were able to develop questions concerning the nomination. Bork proponents didn't need to consult an astrologer to see that there was an ill-fated convergence regarding their nominee. No fewer than seven new Democratic senators had just been elected from the South, most through coalitions of blacks and moderate to liberal whites, and they were about to cast the highest profile vote of their very new careers. The polls showed a slight preference overall to reject Bork, but the demographics revealed that the Bork opposition centered precisely among those constituents who elected these senators.

The polls further suggested that Bork's nomination was a more intense and salient issue for opponents than proponents. In one NBC poll, 19 percent of the respondents indicated that a senator's vote to confirm would make them less likely to vote for that senator in the future. Only 11 percent indicated a favorable confirmation vote would induce a greater likelihood to support the senator (NBC and *Wall Street Journal* 1987). The sense that opponents cared more about the outcome than did supporters made it easier for senators, should they so choose, to vote against confirmation. For a senator, constituency opinion offers a wonderful rationale for explaining one's vote, so much so that it is difficult to know when it really matters. In the Bork vote, our best guess is that it was quite significant for these southern senators (Gitenstein 1992, 287–288).

The Clarence Thomas nomination produced an even greater outpouring of public interest and public action. For a Senate phone exchange that normally handles a busy 375,000 calls a day, there were over 600,000 calls handled on the first day of the Thomas-Hill hearings. On the day before the Senate vote, the number climbed to 1,011,600, with even more (1,021,508) calls on the day of the vote. Pollsters ran daily surveys, trying to document shifts in opinion should they occur. The fact that all polls indicated a public preference for Thomas's confirmation and a willingness to credit his testimony over Anita Hill's led most commentators to declare Thomas the "winner" in this Hill versus Thomas hearing. That declaration was misleading.

The fact is that a preference for Thomas was already quite clear prior to the public allegations of Hill. Cognitive dissonance theory has long since explained to us that individuals will engage in selective and biased perception as two means of rendering potentially conflicting information compatible with preexisting beliefs. In other words, most of the public was already predisposed to believe Thomas rather than Hill, so we should expect that most will in fact believe Thomas rather than Hill. Over 90 percent of those who supported Thomas held fast in their support through the Hill phase of the hearings (ABC and *Washington Post* 1991b). Only about 15 percent of the sample in this ABC/*Washington Post* survey reported that the Thomas-Hill hearing had brought about a change in opinion, and for 61 percent of those, that change involved a decision to oppose Thomas' confirmation. Only 21 percent were persuaded to support Thomas. In effect, the Thomas-

Hill confrontation was not held on a level playing field. People do not suspend beliefs or opinions just because a new accusation comes forward. Supporters will tend to dismiss the negative information; opponents will tend to embrace it as further evidence justifying their opposition. Thomas's support going into the Hill phase of the hearings gave him a distinct advantage, and while Anita Hill's testimony persuaded some to change their minds and to form an opinion against confirmation, her testimony was not enough to change the outcome.

Public opinion seems destined now to play a significant role in Supreme Court confirmations, at least in controversial nominations. In large part this is due to the fact that the advocacy groups constituting the major players in confirmation politics have made grassroots appeals a basic tactic in the confirmation battle. The greater media exposure given particularly to controversial confirmation hearings also promotes public interest. Public opinion remains something that must be mobilized, however. In general, the public is largely uninformed about Court nominees. It is not at all

---

BOX 4.4
How the Public Views the Roles of the President and the Senate in Evaluating Nominees to the Supreme Court

	President (1987)	Senate (1987)	Senate (1991)
Consider qualifications and background only	38.4%	38.9%	35.6%
Consider also how nominee might vote	52.7%	53.8%	59.1%
Don't know/no answer	8.9%	7.4%	5.3%
Number of respondents	839	839	1,233

The public seems quite willing to let the president and Senate consider a nominee's political views in reaching a judgment about the suitability for a Court appointment. The 1987 data are from a CBS/*New York Times* poll taken just prior to the Bork hearings on September 9 and 10. Two questions asked whether the Senate and president, respectively, should " only consider that person's legal qualifications and background or . . . also consider how that nominee might vote on major issues the Supreme Court decides" (CBS and *New York Times* 1987a, 2). The 1991 data for the Senate came from

unusual for 60 percent or more of the citizenry to report not hearing or knowing about a nominee preceding the Judiciary Committee hearing (e.g., CBS and *New York Times* 1987a). While a hearing will increase the visibility of a nomination, even then 57 percent of the respondents in one ABC/*Washington Post* poll report not paying very close attention to the initial Thomas hearing (ABC and *Washington Post* 1991a). It remains true that the people must be persuaded that any particular vacancy or any particular nomination deserves their attention.

On the other hand, people do possess some fundamental opinions about the appointment process. For example, people are willing to permit political issues and considerations for both the president and Senate in their assessment of nominees (see Box 4.4). They also see a vigorous role for the Senate. Yet the public and even lawyers and political scientists have difficulty reconciling their acknowledgment that the appointment process is political with a desire for the process to somehow rise above politics, ostensibly to focus only on the nominee's qualifications of competence, tempera-

---

an ABC/*Washington Post* poll conducted during the initial Thomas hearing prior to the publication of Anita Hill's allegations (ABC and *Washington Post* 1991a). Specifically, the question asked whether the Senate should "consider only the nominee's background and qualifications or whether it should also consider the nominee's political views."

The public also seems to accept the role of the Senate in making an independent assessment of the president's nominee. While the data below come from a poll conducted by Marttila and Kiley from August 13 to 17, 1987 (Kiley 1987) on behalf of the anti-Bork opposition, the results are consistent with other polls finding support for a Senate role apart from the president. However, the Marttila and Kiley poll put the question more directly than others, asking respondents to agree either that the president "has a right to appoint whomever he wants to the Supreme Court, . . . so the Senate should approve [the nominee] as long as he meets acceptable standards of competence and personal honesty," or "the Senate should carefully examine [the nominee's] background, his beliefs about the Constitution, and his past decisions as a judge, and should approve him only if they conclude that his addition to the Court would be for the good of the country" (Kiley 1987, 3).

President's right to appoint whomever	15%
Senate should examine carefully	82%
Not sure	3%
Number of respondents	1008

ment, and integrity. Thus, the Clarence Thomas hearings in 1991, galvanized by the public and graphic testimony of Anita Hill alleging sexual harassment, simultaneously fascinated and shocked the American public.

Developing the Discourse

While the president has the first opportunity to frame the nomination and the nominee, the determination of whether the nomination will become controversial hinges on the actions of those who represent the president's political opposition. Moreover, it is this interim period between the initial introduction of the nominee and the opening of the Senate Judiciary Committee hearing that likely will determine the level of opposition. If the nomination is to be challenged, then opposition must surface relatively quickly before the public and the Senate acquiesce in the notion that the nominee must be suitable. To a nominee, no news is typically good news. The absence of negative discourse in the interim period will do much to ensure a smooth confirmation.

Modeling the Development
of Nomination Discourse

We previously have identified two underlying dimensions of the nomination process, one of which is the setting at the time of the vacancy, which establishes the presumption in favor of the president's nomination and thereby the potential for controversy. Nomination settings can be arrayed from those that are least supportive of a president to those that are most supportive. The other dimension concerns the qualifications of the nominee. Although nominee qualifications can similarly be arrayed from low to high, the same degree of specificity obtained for nomination setting is not possible with regard to a particular nominee's qualifications. Qualifications are established through an iterative process engaged in by presidents and their supporters on the one hand and opposition political actors on the other.

Figure 4.1 presents the relationship between these two dimensions of the nomination process, illustrated through four particular nominations. Data for the nomination settings and nominee qualifications were presented previously in Figure 3.1. As we have noted, the setting and qualifications dimensions are not independent of each other. As the situation becomes less favorable to the president, opposition groups are likely to challenge the president's depiction of the nominee as one of the best people available and perceptions of a nominee are likely to vary much more widely, as indicated by the increasing length of the boxes in Figure 4.1. In addition, as the situation becomes less favorable to the president, an increasing number of groups and other political actors are willing to engage in the nomination discourse, as depicted by the increasing density of dots within the boxes.

Figure 4.1 does overstate the case. While the depiction of the nominee is not independent of the nomination setting, neither is it totally dependent on the setting. Ultimately, what one can say about a nominee does depend upon the background, experiences, and character of the nominee. There are nominees so universally accepted as qualified that the effect of the nomination setting is constrained. Hoover's appointment of Cardozo, Nixon's of Powell, and Ford's of

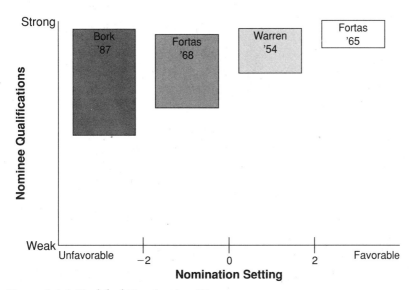

Figure 4.1 A Model of Nomination Discourse
This diagram reflects the impact of nomination setting upon the characterization of nominee qualifications. Four nominations of the modern era illustrate the model: Fortas in 1965, Warren in 1954, Fortas in 1968, and Bork in 1987. The length of the boxes reflects how opinions about a nominee's qualifications can be quite diverse. The density of dots within the boxes represents the intensity of the debate and, to some extent, the number of groups and individuals that become involved in that debate. The model suggests that characterizations of the nominees' qualifications are a function of the nomination setting. In a very favorable setting, nominees are generally perceived as qualified and there is little debate otherwise. As the setting becomes less favorable, opposition surfaces and portrays the nominee's qualifications in less favorable light than the nominee's supporters. Controversy develops, engages more people, and produces competing perceptions about the qualifications of the nominee.

Stevens all rank as particularly nonpartisan, nonideological appoint-ments in settings less than favorable to the president.

Indeed, the absence of an ideological agenda appears to be the key. Nominees with strong credentials are more readily accepted if it is perceived that they bring no strong ideological or partisan bag-gage with them. Ruth Ginsburg is a good case in point. Her record as an activist in the cause of women carried the potential of tainting her as a liberal ideologue of sorts. However, her 14-year service on the federal bench preceding her nomination permitted her to estab-lish a judicial reputation that was much more centrist than liberal and much more restrained than activist, a fact that Republican con-servatives found very comforting in the first nomination of Bill Clin-ton. On the other hand, Robert Bork carried considerable ideological and partisan baggage in his trip to the Senate. In this unfavorable set-ting, opposition to Bork was certain, swift, and vituperative.

While granting some level of independence between nominee and setting, the connection that does exist between the two sug-gests some interesting consequences. For example, a nominee who might otherwise be perceived as very well qualified during a period favorable to the appointing president may be perceived as less qual-ified during a period that is not so favorable to the president. We have suggested already that the change in perception of Fortas's qualifications between 1965 and 1968 may be more a function of the nomination setting than any real change in his qualifications.

The logic of this model suggests a strategy for understanding nomination controversy. The first step is to establish how favorable the setting is for the president at the time of the nomination. In set-tings favorable to the president, controversy is less likely to emerge because there is less opposition out there to fight the nomination. The strength of the president's position discourages the emergence of opposition. In settings that are less favorable, more opposition to the president, his programs, and his nominations is likely to sur-face. Nomination opponents will attempt to push the perception of the nominee's qualifications downward as supporters attempt to push that perception upward.

The perception of the nominee's qualifications can then be traced through the four stages of discourse—from the president's characterization to the ultimate definition offered by the Senate. In stage 1, the president makes the nomination and proclaims the nominee to be highly qualified. During stage 2, the interim period between the nomination and the Judiciary Committee hearings, op-ponents will attempt to develop a negative discourse that portrays the nominee as lacking in qualifications. As Figure 4.1 illustrates, there may ultimately be very different perceptions about the nomi-nee's qualifications, especially in nomination settings unfavorable to the president. Ultimately, the Judiciary Committee (stage 3) and the full Senate (stage 4) will enter the field, sometimes focusing and refining the discourse, but often just reflecting the views developed through the interim period.

Discourse Development in Three Cases

Let us round out our discussion by performing a simple analysis on the development of negative discourse for the Bork, Souter, and Thomas nominations—three relatively recent nominations in which the discourse and the outcomes were quite different from each other. The opposition discourse involving Bork started immediately and eventually overwhelmed his ability to rebut it. For Thomas, opposition built more slowly, and he was given time to construct a positive image that helped him weather more severe opposition later. For Souter, no substantial negative discourse ever developed, and his nomination was confirmed with relative ease.

As noted earlier, advocacy groups are involved in varied types of communications to a number of different political actors. Some communications are publicized in the media and others are not. For simplicity's sake, our analysis of the interim discourse in these three nominations is restricted to the public discourse, as evident through publication in the *Washington Post*. Our focus is also on the emergence of opposition that attempts to stimulate controversy regarding the nominee. If public opposition does not arise, controversy does not arise, and the nominee is insured smooth sailing, at least into the Judiciary Committee hearing.

Initial Reactions to the Nominee

Opponents to a nomination face a bit of a dilemma in deciding when and how to assert their opposition. To speak out in opposition too quickly conceivably risks an appearance of prejudging the nominee and politicizing the process. On the other hand, to fail to respond quickly abandons the initial phase of the discourse to the president. This permits the president to frame the nomination and construct an image of the nominee in ways most favorable for confirmation. The resulting positive image of the nominee can have a lasting effect on the public and the Senate.

Liberal opponents did not accept for a moment Ronald Reagan's invitation to evaluate Robert Bork in terms of his legal experience and competency. Even before the nomination was announced, Kate Michelman of NARAL had threatened that "We're going to wage an all-out frontal assault like you've never seen before on this nominee, assuming it's Bork" (Cannon and Kurtz 1987). Within hours of the Bork nomination, Senator Edward Kennedy had entered the nomination discourse, providing an alternative frame to the debate by characterizing Bork as an "extremist" and out of the mainstream of contemporary political thought—someone who was unqualified because he lacked judicial temperament (see the quote that opens Chapter 1).

The day after the nomination 80 organization leaders and lobbyists held a planning meeting in Washington for the Block Bork Coalition. In the next two weeks, at least one powerful civil rights group and a key member of the Senate Judiciary Committee had announced their intention to oppose the nominee. Benjamin Hooks, Executive Director of the NAACP, vowed "an all-out battle" against the Bork nomination (UPI 1987). Joseph Biden, chair of the Judiciary Committee, also indicated his intention to oppose the nominee (*Washington Post* 1987). All of these groups and individuals took on the task of defining Bork as biased and lacking in judicial temperament. Bork's extensive public record of actions and writings helped mute any claim by supporters that opponents were prejudging the nominee. Opponents were able to claim that Bork was all too well known.

While the immediate response to the Thomas nomination was not uniformly positive, opposition was not nearly as rapid nor as vehement as it was with Bork. For example, there were no speeches about Thomas's America. No members of the Judiciary Committee quickly opposed the nominee. Civil rights groups that had almost immediately opposed Bork were now described as having "mixed feelings, uncertainty about the nominee" (Duke 1991). The strongest early negative characterization of Thomas was by an African-American Harvard Law School professor, Derrick Bell, who said of the nominee, "To place a person who looks black and who, in conservative terms, thinks white, is an insult" (McCarthy 1991).

Most important to the early discourse was the NAACP's decision to defer a decision whether to support or oppose Thomas (Duke 1991). While the civil rights group did eventually oppose the nominee it was not until a month later (Marcus 1991a). Liberal opposition was frozen in place during this month because it was very difficult for any such organization to actively oppose an African-American nominee to the Court without similar opposition by the venerated civil rights organization. Thus, the strategy of appointing an African American to control negative liberal discourse worked, at least in the early stages of the discourse.

The initial response to Souter was even more reserved. In fact, it was reserved to the point of being nonexistent. While liberal groups expressed immediate concern, there was no serious initial opposition. There was a distinct wait-and-see attitude (Rusakoff 1990). President Bush's attempt to structure the nomination discourse appeared successful. By appointing someone with no paper trail, liberal opposition was forced into a holding pattern, hoping that some negative information on the nominee's qualifications could be dug up. As the *Washington Post* put it, the opposition was "Hunting for Souter's Smoking Gun" (Rusakoff 1990).

Moving into the Interim Period

During the period between the initial response to the nominee and the beginning of the formal Senate consideration of the nominee, advocacy groups and the media carry the weight of the nomination discourse. In recent times this has been particularly true because vacancies on the Court typically have been announced at the end of a Court term in June and the Senate consideration has not begun until September after the summer recess. This "down time" for the Senate gives advocacy groups and the media a clear field to offer their view of the nominees' qualifications.

Figure 4.2 traces the negative discourses about Bork, Souter, and Thomas through this interim period as reflected in *Washington Post* articles. Circles in the figure represent expressions of concern about a nominee as expressed by a spokesperson for some group, while squares represent explicit statements of opposition. For Robert Bork, opposition mounted rapidly. Within two weeks of his nomination, a half-dozen major advocacy groups had announced their opposition. They continued to press their claim that the nominee lacked judicial temperament—that his positions were out of the mainstream of American legal thought.

Particularly significant was the entry of a new actor on the nomination scene, People for the American Way, which would orchestrate much of the anti-Bork discourse leading up to the Judiciary Committee hearings. Also very important to the late summer discourse was the split decision approval by the ABA of Bork as well qualified for the Court (Marcus and Kamen 1987). While eleven members of the ABA Committee on Federal Judiciary judged Bork to be well qualified, one member voted not opposed and four voted not qualified. The four not qualified votes came from members who defined Bork as being unqualified because of his extreme stands and lack of judicial temperament. Response to this characterization was immediate and condemning from the conservatives (Orrin Hatch, for example), but these votes from the ABA committee provided much-needed support for the discourse theme that liberals had been pushing, namely, that Bork was unqualified to be on the Court because he lacked judicial temperament (Marcus 1987).

For Thomas, opposition grew during the interim period but it did not do so at nearly the rate or intensity of the Bork nomination. For example, while People for the American Way spent over $1 mil-

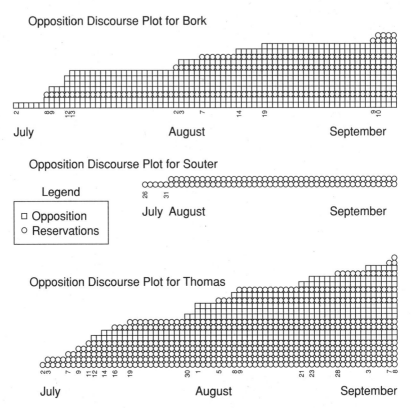

Figure 4.2
Development of Negative Discourse for Bork, Souter, and Thomas

lion on their campaign against Bork, they spent less than $100,000 in opposition to Thomas. Nevertheless, as Figure 4.2 shows, there was an inextricable increase in opposition during the summer.

One difference between the Bork and Thomas discourses was the level of positive discourse. Many conservative activists blamed the Reagan White House for the defeat of Bork, arguing that Reagan should have entered the nomination discourse earlier and more aggressively. In the Thomas nomination, not only did the president speak often in favor of his nominee, but conservative advocacy groups almost immediately went on the offensive to support Thomas. For example, as the hearings approached there was a series of TV ads run in Washington, D.C., and in key states attacking the character of three liberal members of the Senate—Biden, Kennedy, and Cranston (Marcus 1991b)—in an effort to undermine the legitimacy of the opposition discourse.

The ABA also helped frame the debate on Thomas. Unlike Bork, Thomas did not receive any well qualified votes. Twelve members of the committee did characterize him as qualified. However, there were two dissenters who called Thomas not qualified and one abstainer. The liberal Alliance for Justice immediately tried to place a spin on the ABA's rating as the lowest of any nominee since the ratings had begun. The absence of well qualified votes and the two negative votes were used by the opposition to fuel concern about the nominee's lack of judicial experience and to question his judicial temperament (Torry 1991).

The interim period was a nonevent in the Souter nomination. Figure 4.2 reveals almost no negative discourse during that summer of 1990. Indeed, there was little discourse about the nominee at all. The strategy of a stealth nominee seemed to be vindicated. Also helpful to the pro-Souter forces was the unanimous well qualified rating by the ABA.

As these three nominations headed to the Senate Judiciary Committee, there were three distinctly different patterns of discourse: Souter had sailed through the interim period with little or no attacks upon his qualifications. Bork had been immediately and persistently attacked as unqualified for the Court by an ever increasing number of individuals and groups. Thomas's qualifications had been questioned by several groups, but their opposition lacked the intensity and persistence present during the Bork nomination.

The closing of the interim period does not signal an end to the activities of the political actors prominent during this period. It does, however, signal the beginning of the most public part of the confirmation process, a phase in which the public and, more importantly, the senators themselves, begin to focus more attention on any issues that have been raised during this interim period.

CHAPTER FIVE

The Senate Judiciary Committee

> Senator, may I tell you, I have listened here and I saw these senators come and say, "If something developed, it might change our mind." I am talking only to you, Senator. I want to say I object. . . . We come down to the end of the road, sir, I think this thing has been stacked. . . . I sat here and listened at every senator here on the bench, I listened to them, and a majority have already said they are going to vote for her, so how in the world could we even change their minds at the present time with a five-minute speech.
>
> *Dr. Carl McIntire*

No aspect of the nomination and confirmation process is less well understood, both by the general public and academics, than the role of the Senate Judiciary Committee. The lament of the Reverend McIntire concerning his testimony in the presence of only a single senator at the O'Connor hearings illustrates a common public misperception, namely, that the Judiciary Committee consists of senators open-mindedly awaiting testimony on the pros and cons of a nominee in order that they might reach a judgment about the nomination (Senate 1981, 344–345). Given all that has come before the actual hearing, the senator who enters the hearing without some predisposition one way or another is much less common than one who is very much predisposed toward, if not already decided on, a particular vote.

The opposite mistake is to assume that all senators have, in fact, made up their minds in advance of the hearings. For situations in which the interim period prior to the hearings has generated little controversy or opposition, there is a tendency for senators to assume confirmation, as happened with Lewis Powell or Sandra O'Connor. However, for nominations that stir advocacy-group activity, only those senators who systematically support the president on such matters—typically members of the president's own party and ideological views—are sure bets to vote a particular way, that is, in support of the nominee. Advance opposition to a nominee by Judiciary Committee members is less common, although the Bork nomination certainly showed it can surface. President Clinton's style of publicly identifying potential nominees, however, has encouraged senators to speak publicly as well. Whether this portends a permanent change in the informal process must await future presidents and senators.

A third misunderstanding about the nature of committee confirmation hearings is to assume that they make no difference in the outcome of the confirmation vote of the full Senate. A string of easy confirmations from the early 1930s to the middle of the 1960s made the hearings stage of the process seem pro forma (Grossman and Wasby 1972, 558). But there is a difference between assuming that hearings are pro forma and understanding that the factors determining controversy may have simply played out in a noncontroversial manner. In reality, the committee hearings play a very significant role in continuing to develop and refine the nomination discourse and in serving to guide the full Senate to its conclusion.

This chapter begins with an overview of how the structure and operation of the Judiciary Committee affects the confirmation process. We then address the committee's role in furthering the nomination discourse leading up to the hearings. The hearings are covered in considerable detail, including factors that influence the vote of the committee senators. Finally, we provide an assessment of the impact of the hearings on the nomination discourse.

Overview of the Judiciary Committee's Role

Like all Senate committees, the Judiciary Committee gathers information on behalf of and makes recommendations to the full Senate. Once a nominee's name has been forwarded to the Senate for its advice and consent, the first step is to refer that name to the Judiciary Committee for its evaluation. While the most visible portion of this task in recent years has been public hearings where the nominee and other witnesses are questioned by the committee members, a number of significant steps occur before the hearings, away from the public's view.

As soon as the nomination is announced by the president, staff members of the Judiciary Committee begin to gather information about the nominee. This first step is duplicated within each committee member's office as each senator becomes an independent collector of considerable printed material concerning the nominee and the nomination. In addition, letters and calls come into the Senator's office. At the same time, staff members make phone calls to friends and associates of the Senator in the nominee's home state and elsewhere in an effort to secure information on and evaluations of the nominee. Almost without exception, special attention is paid to any known liabilities or problems concerning the nominee, such as past memberships in exclusive clubs or suspect financial dealings.

The second step in preparation for the hearings is the collection of information from official sources. The FBI report will be received by the committee and held in relatively tight confidence for senators to peruse. A request will be sent to the ABA for its Committee on Federal Judiciary to report back with an assessment of the nominee's qualifications. More recently, the committee has also solicited a report from the Congressional Research Service that delves into the legal background and writings of a nominee. In addition, the chief counsel for the committee, in cooperation with the minority counsel, will send the nominee a questionnaire from the committee designed to provide extensive information, not only with respect to the nominee's experience but also regarding financial holdings, potential conflicts of interest, and other personal matters. The questionnaire also asks a couple of open-ended questions, one submitted by the majority counsel and one from the minority, which often deal with matters of judicial philosophy. For example, a common question for recent nominees from the Republican side of the committee has asked the nominee to respond to a critique of "judicial activism." A Democratic question of recent times has asked nominees to specify actions in their professional and personal lives that demonstrated concern for "equal justice under the law."

A third step in the prehearings agenda involves a private meeting by the nominee with each of the senators on the committee, as well as the Senate leadership, and—in the case of Thomas—with just about every other member of the Senate. This is an important part of the process for both the nominee and the senator. From the nominee and administration's perspective, it provides insights into the concerns of the committee members and permits a preview of the kinds of questions that are likely to be put to the nominee during the formal hearings. It also personalizes the process and gives the nominee an opportunity to alleviate concerns that a senator may have about the nomination. All of the senators, in turn, are able to evaluate various aspects of the nominee and check out any reservations that they may have.

The hearings provide the public with its first real look at the nominee and at how the members of the committee view the nominee. By that time, considerable information has already been gathered to assist the senators in their evaluation. In a noncontroversial nomination the hearings may be little more than a coronation of the new justice. However, in a controversial nomination the hearings continue the nomination discourse as supporters and opponents vie for control of the issues and images that will characterize the nomination and the nominee. Senators will have opportunities to clarify their positions. Various political actors and advocacy groups will have a chance to offer their assessments of the nominee. The public will have its opportunity to evaluate the claims and counterclaims and to see and hear the nominee first-hand.

At the completion of the hearings, typically within a week, the committee will vote to support or oppose confirmation. A majority vote in support of confirmation automatically sends the nomination to the full Senate with a recommendation to confirm. However, a negative vote (as with Bork) or a split vote (as with Thomas) may require another vote in committee regarding whether to forward the nomination to the full Senate. Often in the legislative process, a negative vote in committee simply kills the matter under consideration right there. It is difficult, however, in this era to think that the committee might not forward the nomination. The potential for adverse public reaction is simply too great. Once forwarded to the Senate, all that remains is for the Senate to debate and vote.

Committee Structure

"By what right does Ted Kennedy get to sit in judgment of Clarence Thomas?" the irate caller queried. That person wasn't the only one during this particular call-in show to challenge the makeup of the Committee. On talk shows and letters-to-the-editor across the country, various Thomas supporters expressed their irritation with a Democratically dominated committee that had all too many liberals on it. The answer to the caller's question, of course, is that the Judiciary Committee is a standing committee, meaning that members appointed to the committee serve continuously from one session of Congress to the next. By the time of the Thomas nomination, Senator Kennedy was in his thirtieth year of service on the committee. The median length of service among the 14 Committee members was at 13 years, a time during which six other confirmation hearings had been held. For better or for worse, Clarence Thomas was simply another judicial nominee to come before this particular panel of senators.

Standing Committees

The creation of standing committees to handle the work of the Senate dates back to 1816, when eleven such committees, Judiciary among them, were created by a Senate resolution (Congress 1854, 30). As with all Senate committees, Judiciary has fluctuated over the years with respect to its size, its procedures, and its subcommittee structure, but from the beginning it has handled appointments to the federal judiciary, including the Supreme Court. Generally, then, only committee members participate in confirmation hearings by directing questions to the nominee. A notable exception was the grilling in 1957 of nominee William Brennan by the infamous Senator Joseph McCarthy (Senate 1957).

Another important structural feature of Senate standing committees is their organization along partisan lines. The majority party in the Senate controls a majority of the committee seats, typically in rough proportion to the split in the full Senate. Thus, in 1980 when the Republicans captured the Senate and turned a 41 to 58 deficit into a 53 to 46 advantage (there being one Independent in the Senate), the distribution in the Judiciary Committee swung from a 10 to 7 Democratic majority to a 10 to 8 Republican advantage. Since two of the Judiciary Committee Democrats lost their Senate seats (Bayh and Culver), the committee was restructured by simply adding new Republicans while permitting sitting Democrats to maintain their seats. After regaining control of the Senate as a result of the 1986 election, the Democrats reasserted their majority status in the committee.

The ways in which adjustments are made to committee control and size may seem innocuous but they are not without consequences. Suppose, for example, that the Democrats in 1987 handled the switch back to Democratic control by increasing the number of Democrats rather than just reducing the number of Republicans. More than one liberal advocate complained to us that the Democrats missed an opportunity to establish a stronger liberal presence that would deal critically with Reagan conservative appointees to the courts. As one lamented, "Can you imagine how the presence of a Barbara Mikulski [a Democrat from Maryland] could have altered the handling of Anita Hill in the Thomas hearings?" The consequence of retaining an all-male committee was this kind of criticism in the wake of the Thomas hearings. In an effort to bring some diversity to the Judiciary Committee, the Senate Democratic leadership decided to increase the size of the committee in 1993 to permit the addition of two newly elected women, one of whom was an African American, on the Democratic side. Because the party split in the Senate had not changed, it was also necessary to add two new Republicans, changing the committee size from 14 to 18.

The Committee Chair

The complaints of the liberal advocates regarding committee composition were actually directed at the new committee chair in 1987,

Joseph Biden, because it is the chair who controls so much of the committee structure and procedures. Many observers of the committee suggested that Biden valued harmony with the minority party and its ranking member at the time, Strom Thurmond, more than battling the nominations of a conservative Republican president. Their perception of Biden's handling of the committee changeover from Republican to Democratic control was almost surely correct. The liberal Biden and conservative Thurmond constitute one of the Senate's more prominent "odd couples" (Smith 1988, 106–107).

Change comes slowly to Senate committees, in part, because the membership remains largely unchanged from one session to the next, but more importantly, because the chair retains that position over lengthy periods of time. When change does come, however, it can be sudden and dramatic. Ted Kennedy's ascension to the chair in 1979 marked the end of a 22-year reign by James Eastland, a conservative Democrat from Mississippi. Kennedy became chair because his 16 years represented the longest consecutive tenure among Democratic members of the Committee. Eastland's departure more generally signaled the end of southern conservative Democratic dominance of standing committees in the Senate. Kennedy immediately set about to strengthen the committee's ability to investigate nominees and gather more information on them. In part, this was accomplished by adding significantly to the staff of the committee under Kennedy's control. Among the new staff was the chief counsel, Stephen Breyer, whose 2 year service would help pave the way for his subsequent Supreme Court nomination.

Kennedy's tenure was short lived, however, because the Republicans came to power in 1981 and the chairship went to Strom Thurmond from South Carolina, a committee member for 16 years although he had been a member of the Senate since 1954. When the Democrats regained control of the Senate in 1986, Kennedy, of course, still had the longest continuous service on the committee. However, he had already relinquished his status as ranking Democrat to Biden in 1981 and subsequently as chair in order to chair the Labor and Human Resources Committee—Senate rules permit a senator to chair only one major standing committee. So it was in 1987 that the Judiciary Committee chairship went to Joseph Biden, a 10-year veteran of the committee.

For liberal advocacy groups, the Kennedy decision was not necessarily a welcome one, at least in terms of Supreme Court nominations. Kennedy was perceived as being tougher and more willing and capable of establishing a hard line against conservative forces. Nonetheless, Biden's style has seemed to serve the committee well through some turbulent nominations between 1987 and 1992.

Moreover, he has presided over and, to a great extent, initiated changes that continue to move the committee in the direction of a more critical assessment of Court nominees.

The chair's control of the committee is more limited today than it was in the days of James Eastland and before. The 1970s witnessed structural changes in the Senate that dispersed power more widely among individual senators. The control of the Senate by senior members was diminished by reducing the number of committees they could serve on, limiting everyone to no more than a single chairship on a major committee, and most importantly increasing the number of staff to serve senators (Smith and Deering 1984, 35–57).

Subcommittees

Particularly relevant for the confirmation process have been changes in the subcommittee structure. From 1946 to 1974, the number of subcommittees in the Senate ballooned from 44 to 140. The Judiciary Committee typically had 15 or so during this period of time, all appointed by the chair of the committee and two or three of which he chaired personally. With a major reduction in subcommittees in 1977 (Kravitz 1990, 394), a system evolved in which each member of the majority party chairs a subcommittee and each minority member serves as the ranking minority member on a subcommittee, except for the committee chair and ranking minority member, whose leadership status is directed to the service of the whole committee. Such a system has helped to provide staff and space for each member of the committee, majority and minority alike. However, the 1993 expansion of four additional committee members did not bring new subcommittees into being, and those new committee members must, for the moment, make do with what they otherwise have.

Until 1993 the significance of this arrangement had been that all of the senators had their own subcommittee staff to assist them, not only with their subcommittee work but also with their committee work more generally. Each subcommittee has office space and staff existing separately for the majority and minority ranking members. For most senators on the Judiciary Committee, it is the staff in the subcommittee who are responsible for handling that senator's effort in the confirmation process. Of course, the chair of the committee and the ranking minority member direct majority and minority staff on the Judiciary Committee itself. As this book goes to print, the Republicans are preparing to assume control of the committee, and it remains to be seen whether the subcommittees will be restructured to provide each Republican member with a subcommittee and staff to assist committee business.

Staff

The term *staff* actually covers a variety of personnel, ranging from attorneys to student interns. Typically, the Judiciary Committee and each of the subcommittees have a chief counsel, who serves at the pleasure of and as chief advisor in committee matters to the respective majority party members. Similarly, each minority senator is served by a minority counsel. Additional professional staff serve each senator under the direction of the counsel, typically four or five more for majority party senators and two or three more for minority party senators. Senators' offices also abound with eager and bright students who serve as interns. In a controversial nomination, it is not unusual for as many as a half-dozen staff members, from counsel to intern, to work on the nomination for any given senator.

The committee chair and the ranking minority member have somewhat more resources at their disposal, including investigators who help gather and evaluate information on a nominee. In addition, the staff director for the Judiciary Committee carries a heavy burden in organizing and directing the actual mechanics of the confirmation hearings. The close working relationship between Strom Thurmond and Joe Biden, as leaders of their respective parties from the nominations of O'Connor through Thomas, helped ensure good working relationships in the development of protocols for the hearings. Their good will was insufficient to prevent acrimonious exchanges between Biden and Orrin Hatch as well as other committee members during the Anita Hill phase of the Thomas hearings.

Generally, staff see their role as preparing their senators for the confirmation hearings. The hearings have become the focal point of the Senate's role in the process. It is certainly the most visible aspect, one that provides Judiciary Committee senators with media time and thus requires a degree of preparation to help them look good or, at least, not look bad. To this end, each senator's staff acquires a veritable library on the nominee, relevant constitutional issues, and the confirmation process itself. Senator Kennedy's staff amassed over a half-dozen file drawers full of information regarding the Bork nomination, a process nearly duplicated in each of the other committee member's office. Typically, such information consists of any publications by nominees, including court opinions they may have authored, publications about them, relevant newspaper articles, analyses of nominees submitted by any number of advocacy groups, the background package on the nominee from the Congressional Research Service, and other information relevant to the nomination. For example, some play was given during the Thomas nomination to the philo-

---

★ ★ ★ ★ ★   ★   ★   ★   ★

BOX 5.1
Table of Contents from a Senator's Briefing Book

Each senator on the Judiciary Committee enters the hearings on a nominee with a reasonably thorough briefing book prepared by the senator's staff. Below is the table of contents of the briefing book used by Senator Dennis DeConcini for the Souter nomination.

Briefing Book for the Hearings of Judge David Souter to be Associate Justice of the Supreme Court

Table of Contents

A. Opening Statement
B. Questions to ask Judge Souter
C. Summary of Supreme Court 5-4 Decisions
D. Academic Perspective of the "Advice and Consent" of the Senate
E. Equal Protection and Gender Discrimination
F. Judicial Discipline
G. Right of Privacy and Abortion
H. Statutory Construction
I. ABA Approval Letter
J. Listing of Interest Groups and Their Positions Toward Souter
K. The Senator's Past Questions of Supreme Court Nominees

---

sophical concept of "natural law," a notion of a higher law that transcends and supersedes mere statutory or "man-made" law. Thomas's use of the concept in support of his own jurisprudential musings would gain considerable attention in the confirmation hearings (Phelps and Winternitz 1992, 110–112, 176–178) The month prior to the September hearings found staff members in more than a few senators' offices reading up on natural law and its implications for constitutional law.

Usually the end result of all of this preparation is a briefing book for the senator (see Box 5.1.) Briefing books develop out of the particular needs of the senator, either as directed by the senator or as anticipated by the staff or a combination of the two. Such reference sources will provide background information on the nominee, on significant political and constitutional issues likely to catch the senator's attention, and other relevant matters. They seek to provide sufficient background to keep the senator informed while avoiding so much information that the senator cannot find it and process it easily.

Staff also prepare a senator's opening statement and the questions to ask the nominee. For every one question asked, there may be a half-dozen prepared, especially for the lower-ranking senators on the committee whose question time follows their more senior colleagues. There is a certain amount of collaboration among staff from different offices and between staff and representatives of different advocacy groups, but it varies considerably, depending on the senator and on the nomination. In the Bork nomination, there was fairly close cooperation between certain staff members of liberal committee senators and certain advocacy representatives. Similar communication occurred between conservative groups and Senate staff, joined to some extent by the White House and Justice Department. There were many complaints from conservative senators and staff, however, that support from the Reagan administration was too little and of questionable utility.

Partly as a result of knowing each other as well as they do, there is less collaboration among staff of different senators and among the senators themselves than we had expected. We are certainly not alone in this observation of the modern Senate's operation (Smith and Deering 1984; Malbin 1980). Nor are we alone in observing how the increase in staff size has not reduced a senator's workload but rather increased the amount of paper and documentation that is brought to the senator. The belief that larger staffs have made senators more distant from the subject of their work seems to hold in Court nominations as well as other areas.

On the other hand, Judiciary Committee senators are usually on that committee because of their interest in the subject matter, although neither of the two Democratic women appointed to the Committee in 1993 apparently preferred that assignment. It is not a constituency-oriented committee. In fact, Judiciary is not considered a particularly good committee from the perspective of gaining positive publicity. Thus, while all the Senate committee members rely heavily on staff to prepare them for confirmation hearings, some do a considerable amount of the background research themselves. We were told by one of Senator Specter's aides that

> He didn't rely on us [his staff] at all. He very much likes to pursue these things himself. And he doesn't like secondary sources either. When I sent him material on flag burning that relied fairly heavily on a standard text, I got a quick note back to provide him with the original sources relied on by the text. He is very much his own counsel.

Despite the significance of their work, there is little to suggest that staff play a determinative role in the confirmation decisions of their senators. Staff members often have very strong views on issues and on nominees, but those views are usually compatible with the senator. Where they are not, staff will raise the issues but not press personal views. Many staff on the Judiciary subcommittees have legal training and they are able to draft questions and statements in either direction on an issue. One staff member conveyed to us how he had been directed by his senator to draft two statements justifying his Bork vote, one favoring confirmation and the other rejecting the nomination. How the senator would ultimately vote, he did not know.

In addition to their staff, most Judiciary Committee senators appear to have confidants, advisors, or trusted sources to whom they turn to gain insight concerning a nominee. Often these people are judges, well-connected lawyers, or law school professors who are familiar with the nominee either personally or by reputation. Such contacts are likely to carry considerable weight with senators. They help to structure the manner in which a senator frames the nomination and the nominee, and they help the senator to interpret the massive amount of information that inevitably accompanies a nomination.

Staff members work hard. Their hours are long. During a controversial nomination, the intensity and the pressure are quite high. So much work goes into preparing each senator, yet so much is duplicated in office after office. In some corollary to Parkinson's Law, which states that work expands to fill the time available, staff produce enough paper to fill the binders that will document the constitutional issues, nomination history, and the nominee's record and background, all the time knowing that most of this material will never be utilized by the Senator. There is no doubt that the preparation for a nomination is more thorough now than before the increases in staff sizes. It can be doubted, however, whether all of that preparation—all of that material—leads to better judgments about the nominees.

The Structure of Confirmation Hearings

Time and again we have drawn examples of previous appointments and earlier controversies in a "history repeats itself" theme to disclaim that controversial nominations are unique to the modern era. Yet by the very process of identifying a "modern era," we draw a distinction between now and scarcely two generations ago. Most of the major changes in the process involve the role of the Senate Judiciary Committee, especially, though not exclusively, in the manner confirmation hearings have evolved.

The Development of the Modern Hearings

Confirmation hearings, as we have come to know them since the 1980s, are a distinctly recent phenomenon. The major characteristics of the modern process are these: hearings; publicly conducted; by the entire Judiciary Committee; with direct questioning of the nominee; and broadcast live on television. In addition to these features of the hearings themselves, other aspects surrounding the hearings are distinctly modern, such as more thorough and formalized investigations of a nominee and visitations to the committee senators by the nominee. Let us examine the development of each of these changes.

Until 1868, there was no rule to refer nominations to the Judiciary Committee. Even then, referral to the committee did not mean that there would be hearings. More often than not, the committee felt no need to hold hearings as a device for gathering information and making decisions. Rather, the committee would simply evaluate the nomination in executive session and submit a recommendation to the Senate. On a few occasions, the committee would not report the nomination out of committee, letting it languish. Hearings for Supreme Court nominations tended to be reserved for the controversial choices. What purpose would be served by going through the motions if there was little or no opposition?

Until the mid–twentieth century, confirmation hearings were rare indeed, reserved for sensitive nominations in which hearings were deemed politically useful. Democrats used hearings in the Brandeis nomination as a device to gain time and credibility for a nominee who initially seemed destined for defeat (Harris 1953, 102). In general, hearings were used as a means of clarifying the nomination discourse, identifying and articulating those issues on which the nomination would be decided. The incidence of hearings increased after the Brandeis nomination, in part because of the precedent set by the Brandeis hearings and prompted by substantial liberal opposition to Republican nominations in the 1920s.

It was the nomination of Hugo Black in 1937 that ultimately precipitated the Senate rule mandating hearings on a Court nominee. Black was one of the Senate's own, a New Deal Democrat from Alabama, and Henry Ashurst, chair of the Judiciary Committee, saw no need to have the nomination referred to his committee, let alone have hearings. Ashurst's motion to bypass the committee was defeated, but he rushed the nomination through the committee without hearings. The vote was 13 to 4 in Black's favor. The Senate confirmed the nomination, but shortly thereafter a series of articles in the *Pittsburgh Post Dispatch* renewed previously aired charges about Black's connection with the Ku Klux Klan and alleged his continuing ties to the Klan. The uproar soon subsided, in part from

Black's firm response and more significantly from his record on the bench. The Senate, however, felt that its reputation had been damaged by its failure to hold hearings that would adequately air the charges against Black. A Senate rule was adopted that established hearings as the norm for nominations to the Supreme Court.

Even when hearings were conducted in these earlier times, however, they were different from what we know today. First of all, they tended to be held in executive session—closed to the public. From its inception, the Senate had engaged in secrecy with respect to its deliberations and its votes. In part, this followed the logic of the framing of the Constitution. Secrecy presumably promoted honest and frank discussions while protecting the reputations of all involved. That argument persists through contemporary times and is still compelling enough in light of the Thomas hearings of 1991 to result in the Judiciary Committee's return to nonpublic executive sessions concerning sensitive areas of concern regarding Court nominees.

Challenges to the norm of secrecy involving nominations came as early as 1841, and over the years many famous senators including Salmon Chase, Stephen Douglas, Orville Platt, William Borah, and Robert LaFollette supported motions to open committee deliberations. In conjunction with the controversial nomination of Harlan Fiske Stone to the Court in 1925, Senator Clarence Dill, a Stone supporter, attempted to force an open discussion of the nomination by asserting that "public business . . . ought to be discussed in public" (Harris 1953, 252), a statement that gained more attention when uttered by George Norris in 1929 (Harris 1953, 253). The open-session forces finally gained their victory in 1929 with a resolution that made open rather than closed sessions the norm when considering nominations.

Another way in which early hearings differed from those of today involved the use of subcommittees. A subcommittee of five members handled the Brandeis nomination. Similar subcommittees were used for Stone (1925), Parker (1930), Frankfurter (1939), and others. Subcommittees were generally regarded as the appropriate means by which investigations and information gathering were most efficiently conducted. The subcommittee held hearings and then reported back to the full committee, which in turn made its own recommendation concerning the nomination.

The move to conduct hearings by the full committee rather than a subcommittee coincided in part with significant changes in the structure and staffing of the Senate in 1946. The Legislative Reorganization Act of 1946 established a professional and clerical staff for Senate standing committees (Davidson 1990). The Senate also permitted individual senators to add an administrative assistant to their personal staffs. Possessing a staff to investigate and gather information paved the way for hearings conducted by the full committee. Full committee hearings were held for Clark and Minton in 1949, but a subcommittee was used for Earl Warren's nomination to be chief justice in 1954. Beginning with John Harlan in 1955, the full committee has conducted the hearings without the use of a subcommittee.

The next major development in the evolution of modern hearings was the appearance of the nominee at the hearings. For most of our history, it has been considered inappropriate for a nominee to make such an appearance. The first to appear was Stone in 1925. Stone had alienated a handful of senators in part from his law firm's representation of J. P. Morgan, one of the wealthiest businessmen in the country, and from his refusal as attorney general to dismiss a land fraud case against Montana Senator Burton K. Wheeler. Stone offered to be interrogated by the Judiciary Committee, which included Montana's other senator and counsel to Wheeler, Thomas Walsh, in order to defuse the issue, a strategy which worked rather nicely. There were only six negatives in the subsequent Senate vote (Mason 1956, 188–199).

Stone's appearance did not immediately set a precedent. In fact, the Judiciary Committee rejected the initiative of John Parker in 1930 to testify in support of his troubled nomination, a result which likely sealed his rejection. Slowly, the Judiciary Committee came to prefer an appearance by the nominee. Frankfurter first balked at his invitation in 1939, but the appearance at his hearings of fringe anti-Jewish and anticommunist advocates persuaded him to uphold his good name. Frankfurter's appearance was so compelling that all opposition faded and he was confirmed unanimously (Harris 1953, 309–311).

Once again, however, this appearance of a nominee did not establish the precedent. There was no dramatic event that changed the norm. The committee or subcommittee did not always invite the nominee to appear as with Tom Clark in 1949. William O. Douglas literally stood ready to testify in his 1939 nomination, but the subcommittee felt it unnecessary to call him in. On the other hand, Sherman Minton in 1949 turned down a request to appear as inappropriate. The committee, which had issued the invitation by a narrow vote, subsequently reversed itself and withdrew the request. From that point on, however, the committee has requested each nominee to appear and, in turn, each nominee has assented to the request. The only exception has been Abe Fortas' refusal in 1969 concerning his elevation to chief justice, but this refusal came only after he already had testified, and it involved a request to return to the committee to answer allegations of impropriety in certain financial transactions while on the Court.

By the time John Harlan's nomination came before the Senate in 1955, these most fundamental aspects of the modern confirmation process were established, namely, public hearings before the full Judiciary Committee with testimony by the nominee. Still, there was less ceremony and a greater casualness about nominations in this early modern period than we see today. We are not likely to see again hearings of a single day as we did with Whittaker (1957), Stewart (1959), White (1962), Fortas (1965), and Blackmun (1970). Nor are we likely to see the chair of the Judiciary Committee open a hearings with the invitation, "Is there anyone here who desires to testify either in favor or in opposition to this nominee?" as Senator Eastland did in Potter Stewart's hearings (Senate 1959, 11).

Additional refining characteristics that mark the process today are the prodigious amount of information gathered on the nominee, individual visitations by the nominee to committee senators and Senate leaders, formal opening statements and more extensive questioning of the nominee by each of the committee senators, and more careful screening of witnesses to testify in support of and opposition to the nominee. Of course, the greater involvement of advocacy groups and the media, discussed in the previous chapter, are also distinct characteristics of nominations since 1981.

Most of these refinements can be considered to have escalated the stakes in the confirmation process. They have come about as a response to the expanded role of the Court; the explosion of advocacy groups attending to Court nominations; the increased sensitivity of everyone to the financial, social, and personal lives of nominees; and the presence of divided government in the latter part of the Reagan and all of the Bush administrations. Moreover, televising the hearings provides a visibility to this whole process that increases the stakes for the participants in the game. Reporters compete for stories; advocates compete for attention; senators seek to ensure that their questioning time in the hearings reveals them to be well prepared and seriously involved in the process. In reality, however, the quality and value of the confirmation discourse is rarely promoted through competition among journalists and among advocacy groups, and some senators still manage to look ill prepared and ill equipped for the hearings, despite the best efforts of their staffs.

The Basic Format of Confirmation Hearings

With the introduction of television for the O'Connor nomination, the current more formal procedures for the hearings emerged. Hearings now begin with opening statements from each of the members of the Judiciary Committee. Typically, each one notes the magnitude of this responsibility. Some supporters may use the time to praise the nominee while others will be more circumspect, but it is a good opportunity to sense where senators stand at this opening stage of the formal confirmation process.

The senators' opening statements are followed by endorsements of the nominee by prominent supporters, typically home-state senators, as was done with David Souter. Clarence Thomas was preceded by senators from his home state of Georgia, his residential state of Virginia, and from Missouri, where he had worked for Senator John Danforth. For Robert Bork, even former Chief Justice Warren Burger and former President Gerald Ford were brought in to introduce and endorse the nominee.

These initial introductions are courtesies extended to the nominee and not to be taken particularly seriously. That's why it was so surprising when Dennis DeConcini, a moderately conservative Democratic senator, interrupted the supportive introduction of Judge Bork by Ford, asking point-blank whether Ford had actually read any of Bork's judicial opinions or articles (Senate 1989, 11). Ford, of course, was relying on what support staff had prepared for him to say. For DeConcini to embarrass a former president on his lack of preparation perhaps bordered on rudeness. Yet in today's public broadcasting of such hearings, DeConcini scored a significant point, namely, that the Bork hearings involved complex issues about a complex nominee. The hearings were no place for someone who hadn't done his homework. More importantly, DeConcini signaled that the Bork hearings were not going to be a slow-pitch game. It was hardball from the beginning.

Once the introductions are given and any of the nominee's family in attendance are introduced, the nominee is invited to give an opening statement. This opening statement provides an opportunity for nominees to frame their own nomination and to short-circuit opposition efforts. One of the more effective uses of an opening statement was by David Souter. Advocacy groups had tried to characterize him as having no understanding or compassion for the poor and disadvantaged, who become victims of the establishment bias of the legal system. Souter, who had indicated to the committee and the media that he would have no opening statement, had in fact crafted an eloquent statement alluding to his pro bono work for poor clients and his trial judge experience that suggested a sensitivity to the human condition heretofore not ascribed to him.

> Two lessons [from those experiences] . . . remain with me today.
> The first lesson, simple as it is, is that whatever court we are in,
> whatever we are doing, whether we are on a trial court or an ap-
> pellate court, at the end of our task some human being is going to

be affected. Some human life is going to be changed in some way by what we do. . . . The second lesson that I learned in that time is that if, indeed, we are going to be trial judges, whose rulings will affect the lives of other people and who are going to change their lives by what we do, we had better use every power of our minds and our hearts and our beings to get those rulings right. (Senate 1991a, 51–52)

The effort to portray Souter as lacking the sensitivity needed to support equal protection and other civil rights and liberties was dead in the water.

The next stage of the hearings process involves the questioning of the nominee by the senators. It is customary to proceed in order of ranking, with the chair of the committee leading off for the majority party, and then alternating back and forth between the parties and following rank within each party, meaning that the ranking member of the minority party is next. Agreements will have been reached about the length of time permitted for questioning by each senator—15 minutes in the O'Connor hearings but 30 minutes for the first round with Thomas and somewhat less for subsequent rounds.

With this structure, the more senior senators get first crack at the more interesting and controversial issues. This permits them to stake out territory to be covered during their questioning of the nominee. With respect to Thomas, it was clear that Biden would pursue questions concerning natural law and what role that played in Thomas' judicial philosophy. Kennedy, on the other hand, would pursue Thomas' record at the EEOC. Like a basketball team whose players have learned each others' moves, senators develop styles and topics that define their interests. One did not have to consult Senator Thurmond's staff to know he would use his lead-off position for the Republicans to step Republican-appointed nominees through a series of questions that offered the nominee an opportunity to address in open-ended fashion the major issues that had been raised during the interim period since the nomination.

Questioning for the less-senior senators is more challenging. The good questions may have been taken by the time the last three or four questioners are reached. The challenge for the staff of these senators is to find an interesting, if not critical, line of questioning that will still permit their bosses to look good. Of course, junior senators do have an opportunity to pursue questions based on the earlier responses of the nominee. Another strategy is to pursue questions that address matters other than constitutional or judicial issues. In the first phase of the Thomas hearings, the most junior Democratic senator, Herbert Kohl, probed the role that the executive branch played in preparing and advising Thomas concerning the hearings, a ploy that gained widespread press attention, which was a considerable accomplishment for someone who was last in the questioning.

One standard question that a late questioner often gets to ask is "Why do you want to be an associate justice of the Supreme Court" (Senate 1989, 854)? Such a simple question seems harmless enough, and it was intended to be so when a Bork supporter, Senator Alan Simpson, tossed it up as a final question to Judge Bork. Yet Bork's answer that "it would be an intellectual feast just to be there" was seized upon by opponents as further evidence that Bork was essentially an unfeeling, uncompassionate conservative who saw the Court as an intellectual playground (Bronner 1989, 275–276).

After the testimony of the nominee, other witnesses follow and lend their support or opposition to the nomination. Before the recent emergence of so many advocacy groups, the committee would accept testimony from just about any individual who wished to testify. That is no longer done. While the committee continues to accept written communications for the record, potential witnesses are now screened for the relevance and value of their testimony. Individuals are often grouped together, as we saw during the Thomas hearings, where groups of four in support and then in opposition appeared.

Such testimony rarely adds significantly to the discourse because it rarely brings anything new. Advocacy-group claims have already entered the public discourse through the media. We began this chapter with a frustrated witness who found himself testifying about Sandra O'Connor before only the committee chair. As the television camera panned the hearings chamber, empty seat after empty seat was revealed where senators had sat only the day before listening to the nominee. Only Strom Thurmond sat listening to the testimony, while other senators would hear from staff whether anything significant had transpired.

The Thomas hearings were different. Never before had the testimony of a single witness played such a role in Supreme Court confirmation hearings. Anita Hill presented testimony, not previously aired, that could deny Thomas confirmation. Many more witnesses followed, but they played only supportive roles as witnesses customarily do. And with that the hearings closed.

Senator Role-Playing in the Hearings

The formalization of the hearings encouraged by the intrusion of television has required committee senators to give more thought to the kinds of roles they must play to achieve their goals for the hearings. For some, the goal may be to help the nominee achieve confirmation. For others, it may be to prevent confirmation. Still others want to use the hearings to determine how they will vote on the nominee. Others may have alternative goals in mind. Regardless, virtually no senator today will enter the hearings room casually. All have some direction, some goal that will direct their personal behavior (Stookey and Watson 1988).

Senators begin the committee hearings with a considerable amount of information about the nominee. Briefing materials prepared by the staff have put the senator in touch with where the discourse stands as the hearings begin. Reports from the FBI and the ABA, the nominee's own questionnaire responses, and an indeterminate number of discussions with colleagues and others have had their impact. More significantly, each senator has had private time with the nominee, providing an opportunity to size up the nominee. Moreover, all of this information is processed within a situational context—those factors that establish the level of presumption in favor of a president's nominee as well as situational factors facing each senator within the context of a particular political constituency.

As the hearings begin, committee senators are in one of three states of mind. They may already be certain, barring some extraordinary new piece of information, that they will support or oppose the nominee. Alternatively, they may be quite uncertain and genuinely undecided in which direction they will vote. Finally, there is a middle ground of being somewhat certain and possessing a predisposition to vote in a particular direction but with sufficient mental reservations to preclude the near certainty that they may have felt with other nominees. It is the level of certainty, in combination with the level of controversy that surrounds the nomination and the perceived ideological distance of the nominee, that determines a senator's role-playing behavior in the confirmation hearings.

Types of Roles

In the confirmation hearings since that of Justice O'Connor, we can identify at least four different role motivations among committee members. We label them the evaluator, the validator, the partisan, and the advocate roles.

The Evaluator

> Your answers at this hearing, not your previous record, will determine my estimate of your position on this and other issues. . . . It is my earnest hope that your responses will be neither broad nor

bland, because I will base my single vote on those responses. (Senate 1981, 29)

Senator Jeremiah Denton's opening statement in the O'Connor hearings typifies the evaluator role, namely, that of senators who use the hearings to make up their minds concerning how they will vote on the nominee. The archetypal evaluator might be described as one who listens to all the evidence and poses carefully framed questions designed to determine the fitness of the nominee. In reality, evaluators are more likely to be uncertain or unsettled about the nominee on some particular issue that involves the senator's core requirements for a Supreme Court justice. For evaluators, then, the line of questioning is clear. They must ask questions that address their concerns, questions that will permit them to decide how to vote.

Jeremiah Denton's critical issue was abortion, and he questioned O'Connor intensively on this issue. Taking extra time permitted by committee chair Strom Thurmond, Denton put 23 questions to the nominee, 17 of which dealt directly with abortion as well as two others that dealt with parental rights concerning a daughter's abortion decision. Denton was not happy with the responses he heard, and he seemed prepared to oppose O'Connor. Ultimately, he bowed to collegial pressure, abstaining on the committee vote and voting affirmatively in the full Senate.

The Validator

Judge Scalia is an accomplished scholar. . . . There can be little question about the fact that he is qualified for the position of associate justice. To my knowledge there are no allegations of impropriety or misconduct. . . . My only area of concern relates to some of the views Judge Scalia has stated in a number of critically important areas such as the proper approach to constitutional interpretation, separation of powers, and the circumstances under which citizens may seek relief in federal court for government action.

I have an open mind on this nomination. . . . we have an obligation to conduct thorough and complete hearings. . . . (Senate 1987, 13–14)

Senator Metzenbaum's "open mind" regarding nominee Antonin Scalia in 1986 may sound like an evaluator. The difference is in the level of certainty. The validator role is played by senators who are, in fact, reasonably certain about voting to confirm the nominee. Yet, they also remain reasonably open to counterevidence and will use the hearings to pursue a line of questioning designed to probe the validity of this initial favorable predisposition. Elsewhere, we have drawn an analogy with a doctoral dissertation defense (Watson and Stookey 1988, 191). Validators tend to ask questions that probe the mental capacities of the nominee and give insight to what kind of justice this person will be. Conceivably, the responses may reveal unanticipated weaknesses or flaws that lead to a change of mind. More often, just as with doctoral exams, the validating senators find no reason to change their predisposition to vote for confirmation.

The Scalia nomination found many of the Democratic liberals playing the validator role. They didn't like Scalia's conservatism, but the political realities presented by the situation suggested that opposition to Scalia would be counterproductive. First of all, they could not defeat Scalia given Republican control of the Senate. Second, given that the Scalia and Rehnquist nominations occurred simultaneously due to the latter's elevation to chief justice, prudence dictated that the Democratic liberals limit their opposition to only one of the nominees. Rehnquist had more of a record on which to build opposition. Third, Scalia provided little fodder for opposition on the traditional grounds of competence, integrity, or temperament. There were other reasons too, but they all boiled down to most of the liberal Democrats assuming they would confirm unless something arose at the hearings that would permit them to exploit some negative aspect of Scalia's record or character.

When Senator Biden queried Scalia concerning the scope of First Amendment free speech, Biden expressed "relief" at Scalia's acceptance that certain physical actions could constitute speech (Senate 1987, 52). Biden's reaction was genuine and the possibility that Scalia would (and ultimately did) support action as speech helped validate, in Biden's mind, his vote to confirm Scalia. Had Scalia given a much narrower interpretation of the First Amendment, Biden might have been placed in a position of reevaluating his intended support. Such a reevaluation likely would have involved an assessment by liberal Democrats concerning whether there was some basis for framing Scalia as outside the mainstream of judicial-legal thought and attempting to generate widespread discontent with the nomination.

The Partisan

> Mister Chairman, I feel honored to welcome to the committee one of the most qualified individuals ever nominated to serve on the United States Supreme Court. His résumé—outstanding law student, successful trial practitioner, leading law professor, esteemed author and lecturer, excellent solicitor general, and respected judge on the District of Columbia Circuit—speaks for itself.
>
> Senator Orrin Hatch

> Above all, . . . a Supreme Court nominee must possess the special
> quality that enables a justice to render justice. This is the at-
> tribute whose presence we describe by the words such as fairness,
> impartiality, open mindedness, and judicial temperament, and
> whose absence we call prejudice or bias. These are the standards
> by which the Senate must evaluate any judicial nominee. And by
> these standards, Robert Bork falls short of what Americans de-
> mand of a man or woman as a justice on the Supreme Court.
>
> Senator Edward Kennedy

Certainly these opening statements from Senators Hatch and
Kennedy dispelled any doubt that might have existed that they intended to pursue aggressive partisan roles in the confirmation hearings of Robert Bork. Partisans come to the hearings having already
decided how they will vote on the nomination, but what distinguishes partisans from others who may already be certain is their
active efforts in the hearings to secure or defeat the nomination.

Positive partisans, those in support of confirmation, will use
the hearings to assist the nominee. It often begins with an opening
statement that extols the qualifications of the nominee and, on occasion, puts down the opposition, as Senator Hatch proceeded to do
after the segment quoted above. In the questioning round, the positive partisan may ask questions that permit the nominee to show-
case a strength or rebut a criticism. Strom Thurmond often used his
lead-off position on Reagan nominees for this purpose. For example,
he attempted to let O'Connor defuse the abortion issue with the
following question: "Would you discuss your philosophy on abortion, both personal and judicial, and explain your actions as a state
senator in Arizona on certain specific matters?" (Senate 1981, 60).

Other positive partisans may use their question time more to
deliver a monologue in support of the nominee than to ask questions. Senator Hatch probably best exemplifies that particular role
performance throughout the nominations of Presidents Reagan
and Bush.

> Judge [Bork], you're doing very fine in your concise and cohesive
> answers. As a matter of fact, I don't see how anybody watching
> this could doubt that you're an eminent scholar, with a brilliant
> mind, who is in the mainstream of judicial life, who in sitting in
> more than 400 cases on the Circuit Court of Appeals for the Dis-
> trict of Columbia have never been reversed, who has been
> within the mainstream with his liberal colleagues on the courts,
> if that's an appropriate term, as you have with your conservative
> colleagues, having agreed 90 percent of the time with Judge
> Ruth Bader Ginsburg, 83 percent of the time with Judge Mikva,
> right on down to Judge Skelly Wright around 75 percent of the
> time.

. . . Now in recent years we have heard a great deal of commentary about the problems of judicial activism. How would you define judicial activism, because this seems to be really one of the central core matters here? (Senate 1989, 180)

Negative partisans, those who oppose the nomination, have a somewhat narrower range of behaviors open to them. Their efforts are constrained by the relatively narrow grounds that are currently accepted as legitimate for rejection. Basically, they want to make nominees look bad, perhaps by framing them as nonresponsive, incompetent, politically extreme, lacking integrity, or lacking judicial temperament.

In one round of his questioning, Democratic Senator Patrick Leahy pursued a line of questioning with Judge Bork concerning the lack of pro bono work during Bork's lengthy legal career. Pro bono activity refers to donating one's time on behalf of a client who could not otherwise afford legal assistance. Such work is widely regarded as a responsibility by those in the legal profession. Leahy sought to portray Bork as uninterested in the plight of the common people to take away supporters' efforts to make Bork a sympathetic figure. Leading Bork through his career, Leahy secured a succession of "No" responses from Bork about whether he had engaged in pro bono work during various stages in his legal career, finally concluding with

Judge Bork, you are acknowledged by everyone of us here as a brilliant lawyer. You don't think that those talents could have been brought to bear somewhere in pro bono work? (Senate 1989, 418)

Leahy's questioning of Bork, however, pales as an example of badgering in comparison to Strom Thurmond's treatment of Justice Fortas. When Fortas came before the committee in the hearings for his appointment as chief justice, Thurmond pursued a line of questioning that Fortas felt inappropriate to answer and refused to do so. Thurmond persisted in asking, however, punctuating each Fortas demurral with "So you refuse to answer that question?" (Senate 1968, 180–190). In opposing Thurgood Marshall, Thurmond coyly referred to Marshall's expertise on the Thirteenth and Fourteenth amendments and then launched into a complex series of questions on the legislative history of those amendments in an effort to portray Marshall as uninformed and perhaps unqualified for the Court. "Now on the Fourteenth Amendment, what committee reported out the Fourteenth Amendment and who were its members?" Thurmond deadpanned at one point (Senate 1967, 164).

The Advocate

> You are a tremendous asset. You are a woman and the first one on
> the Court; don't let these folks, me included, run you out of being
> that. You are a woman; you do stand for something that this
> country needs very badly. We need spokespersons in positions of
> high authority. Don't lock yourself in, in this hearing or any other
> hearing, to do things that you are not proscribed from doing in the
> canons of ethics.
>
> It is your right, if it were your desire, to go out and campaign
> like the devil for the ERA. It is your right to go out and make
> speeches across the country about inequality for women, if you
> believed it. Don't wall yourself out. Your male brethren have not
> done it. Don't you do it. (Senate 1981, 140)

Joseph Biden's plea to Sandra O'Connor illustrates a very different role performance than any of the others we have seen because it has nothing to do with the confirmation decision. The senator already indicated he would vote for confirmation, so his
decision, like that of the partisan, is certain, but this is not partisan behavior. Rather it is behavior driven by an advocacy motivation, a desire to use the hearings as an opportunity to inform and
perhaps influence another's behavior in ways unrelated to the confirmation decision.

That "other" may be the nominee, as it was here with Biden.
Senator Kennedy explicitly acknowledged this role with his statement to Antonin Scalia of a hope that "as a result of these hearings,.
. . [you] will look with greater sensitivity on [the] critical issues" of
race discrimination and women's rights (Senate 1987, 25). Such a
hope may seem naive, but as Senator Metzenbaum told us during
O'Connor's hearings,

> I guess I always have the hope that by calling these matters to her
> attention, maybe, just maybe, at a time of reflection, when the is-
> sue is before her, that she will think about it and do the right
> thing. (Metzenbaum 1981; see also his questioning of Anthony
> Kennedy in Senate 1988, 162–163)

Other targets of the advocacy role may be fellow senators.
Senator DeConcini used some of his time in the O'Connor hearings to talk about gun regulation he had introduced into the Senate and, in effect, lobbied for its passage. Senator Kennedy frequently uses time in less-controversial nominations to enlist the
nominee's support in talking about problems confronting women
and minorities. One motivation here is to help educate the American public about these problems. Another may well be for sena-

tors to associate themselves with a concern about these problems. Advocacy tends to combine these educational and advertising functions.

The advocacy role is almost exclusively the domain of senators who have made their decision. In the days before television coverage of the hearings, senators were generally content to cease asking questions at that point. To relinquish the exposure that television brings does not come naturally to a senator, however. Without the motivations for partisan, validator, or evaluator behavior, what remains is to make some use of the time available, and the advocacy role provides some purpose to otherwise purposeless behavior.

Frequency of Roles

Let us reemphasize that senators may play multiple roles in any given hearings. Having said that, there is also a tendency for senators to enter their first round of questioning driven by some specific motivation. In a noncontroversial nomination in which confirmation is certain, senators search for a line of questioning that will permit them to pursue issues of interest to them. This often gives rise to playing the advocacy role. Controversial nominations, on the other hand, are controversial because there may be a significant number of undecided senators, which casts doubt on the outcome, or because there is a significant and heated difference of opinion regarding the nominee. When committee senators are undecided, there is only one role to play: the evaluator. Even being somewhat certain typically requires taking care of business first by validating one's predisposition and eliminating any doubts about the decision. Finally, in a controversial nomination, those who are decided will almost surely play partisan roles initially. After all, the outcome is at stake. Committee members are likely to feel some sense of responsibility to have the courage of their convictions and to establish a record in the hearings that will justify their votes and those of their Senate colleagues.

Continuing the Discourse

First, we have a duty to the Senate to develop a complete and detailed record on all issues pertaining to the fitness of Judge Kennedy to serve on the Supreme Court, and to recommend to the Senate, based on that record, whether it should give its consent to this nomination. (Senate 1988, 58)

Senator Patrick Leahy's opening statement in the Anthony Kennedy confirmation hearings portrays the significance of the committee's investigation and public hearings for the development of the nomination discourse as ultimately evaluated by the Senate. The Judiciary Committee is the recipient of a nomination and a nominee whose background and record have been dug through, framed, and spun into a mosaic of competing claims. It is largely up to the Judiciary Committee to form those pieces into a discernible portrait that defines the issues and the nominee.

Senators influence and shape the discourse through their public statements, their questions to the nominee and others who testify at the hearings, and the committee report and individual statements that summarize the hearings. We have already witnessed how Senator Kennedy's immediate public response to the Bork nomination helped to establish a line of negative discourse, portraying the nominee as an extremist outside the mainstream of American legal thought. It was an effective framing of the nomination, one which placed Bork in an untenable position and set him up for the fatal blow in the hearings.

Senators' questions in the hearings further develop the discourse. In the case of Bork, the success of the initial frame required him to explain and to appear to alter previously published perspectives regarding constitutional interpretations. To the extent that he tried to do so, he was tagged with the label of "confirmation conversion," a spin put on his testimony by Senator Heflin and others. From out of the hearings, then, came additional vocabulary for the nomination discourse, vocabulary that carried over into the public consciousness and into the Senate as well.

In other instances, the scope of the discourse is diminished. Judge Scalia's acceptance of the First Amendment as permitting certain action as speech, in response to Senator Biden's question quoted earlier, prevented that potentially explosive issue from emerging into the discourse. Similarly, Judge David Souter's skillful opening statement at his hearings, along with several of his responses to senators' questions, blunted a nascent opposition from portraying the reclusive judge as having no heart or compassion for those caught up in the judicial system.

On occasion, the hearings provide a forum for a witness that profoundly affects the discourse. The most notable occurrence of such an event was the appearance of Anita Hill, a University of Oklahoma law professor, in the confirmation hearings of Clarence Thomas. Her assertion of sexual harassment by Thomas, her former boss, became *the* issue on which the fate of the confirmation seemed to hang. The facts that the committee had already split seven to seven on confirmation and that most of the other senators had already decided how they would vote were overshadowed by the media and the public's love of sexual politics. Nonetheless, the senators now had to incorporate this aspect of the hearings into the explanation of their personal vote decisions.

The committee places its final stamp on the nomination discourse with its report in which supporters and opponents make their respective cases for confirmation or rejection. It is also common for a few senators to make individual statements that articulate their particular points of view, to the extent that they differ from the group's consensual perspective. For the Thomas nomination, the committee report, which followed the initial hearings and was prior to the Anita Hill testimony in the second set of hearings, spanned six pages and concluded

> A motion to report with a favorable recommendation the nomination of Judge Clarence Thomas to be an Associate Justice of the U.S. Supreme Court failed by an evenly divided vote of 7 to 7. A motion to report the nomination to the Senate without recommendation passed by a vote of 13 to 1. (Senate 1991c)

However, the additional and supplemental views of the individual committee members took another 164 pages. It is this report, along with the transcript and media reports of the hearings, that usually finalizes the vocabulary and issues of the nomination discourse.

Appropriate Questions

Considerable debate has raged over the years among scholars and senators about the kinds of questions that are appropriate for senators to ask and for nominees to answer (Melone 1991; Biden 1987; Hatch 1987; Ross 1987a; Reske 1987; Rees 1983; Powe 1976). At one level, few senators would disagree with the ruling of Senator Eastland in Potter Stewart's hearings in 1959.

> The chair does not think that any senator should be precluded from asking whatever questions he desires. If the nominee thinks that the question is improper, then, of course, it is his duty to try to answer thusly. Each member of the committee has the duty to his country, to his office, to ask whatever questions he thinks are meritorious in order to enable him to make up his mind and to so advise the Senate when the matter gets to the floor of the Senate. (Senate 1959, 44)

The issue is not what questions are permissible. As Senator Hatch has articulated, "Senators are free to ask a nominee any question they wish, no matter how misleading, abusive, unfair, or foolish" (Senate 1991b, 19). The issue is what questions carry reasonable expectations of an answer from the nominee? More importantly, what should be the consequence to the nominee for failing to respond to questions that possess a reasonable expectation of a response?

For the most part, debates between senators have difficulty escaping the partisan positions in which they find themselves. Generally, senators who support the nominee argue for a narrower range of reasonableness than do the opponents. Conservative Strom Thurmond's badgering of the liberal Abe Fortas for refusing to answer certain questions in 1967 contrasts sharply with his great deference to Reagan and Bush nominees, with Thurmond advising them to feel free not to answer any question they thought inappropriate—a decision to be respected by the Senate, at least as argued by Thurmond.

The most widely accepted limitation regarding questions for which responses should not be expected is any request for the nominee to assess some issue pending before the Court. The source most often cited for excluding questions of this type is the Code of Judicial Conduct, which mandates that "A judge should abstain from public comment about a pending or impending procedure in any court" (ABA 1972, 12). The rationale for that limitation was articulated by Justice Souter in his confirmation hearings.

> If the judicial process is nothing else, it is a process in which in every court and on every issue that may come before a judge the people who come before him can have a fair hearing. . . . A fair hearing requires a willingness of the court not only to listen, but genuinely to examine the position which the court is inclined at that point to take.
>   Anything which substantially could inhibit the court's capacity to listen truly and to listen with as open a mind as it is humanly possible to have should be off-limits to a judge. . . . can you imagine the pressure that would be on a judge who had stated an opinion, or seemed to have given a commitment in these circumstances to the Senate of the United States, and for all practical purposes, to the American people? (Senate 1991a, 194)

The central issue involving senators' questions is to what extent the senators can ask and expect responses that reveal the nominee's views on constitutional issues and judicial philosophy. The desire by evaluators, validators, and negative partisans to explore a nominee's judicial philosophy and for supporters (the positive partisans) and the nominee to limit such exploration has prompted considerable debate over the years. Senator George Norris in the 1929

Parker hearings, Senator John McClellan in the 1959 Stewart hearings, Senators McClellan and Sam Ervin in the Marshall hearings, and many others since then have argued, in Ervin's words, that "the Constitution . . . requires [a senator] to ascertain as far as he humanly can the constitutional philosophy of any nominee to the Supreme Court" (Senate 1967).

The argument in favor of addressing judicial philosophy is the right of the people to understand what kind of justice the president proposes to place on the Court and for senators to be able to make an informed judgment based on that information (Biden 1987). The case against is the avoidance of any appearance that the nominee has prejudged important constitutional questions that may come before the Court and the avoidance of any "ideological inquisition," in the words of Senator Orrin Hatch (Hatch 1987, 16), that would stir up political partisanship concerning the nomination.

Given the significance of the appointment to the Court, it is difficult to justify a position that nominees can withhold their views regarding the meaning of the Constitution and their assessment of the foundations and reasoning used in reaching the decisions that interpret the Constitution. The people and their senators have a right to know what kind of justice this nominee will be. Nominees should exhibit the personal integrity to discuss freely their views on judicial decision making and constitutional interpretation (Rees 1983). They should be willing to accept rejection as the Senate's view, political though it may be, that a nominee with that particular judicial philosophy is not in line with the Senate's view of what the Court needs.

As Senator Biden invited nominee David Souter to join in a dialogue on the Constitution, the senator also pointed out quite correctly that

> No one is entitled to be a Supreme Court Justice. . . . Put
> bluntly, the burden of proof is on you—Judge Souter, the nominee. . . . A Supreme Court justice can assume his post only if the Senate is persuaded that the nominee is the right person for that position at that particular juncture of American history. (Senate 1991a, 4)

The Senate has reached a point of reasonable acceptance regarding the suitability of questions pertaining to a nominee's constitutional and judicial philosophy. It has not reached a point at which the burden of proof has been laid on the nominee and the nominee's supporters. That likely will not happen until some senator, some day, stands up to vote "no" on a nominee because of the nominee's refusal to be forthcoming in response to questions from the Judiciary Committee.

Nominee Responses

Senators constitute only part of the discourse equation to emerge from the hearings. The nominee obviously plays a critical role in all of this as well. A slip, a misstatement, or a departure from the game plan crafted to frame oneself in a particular way can lead to real trouble. On the other hand, the nominee has the distinct advantage in controlling the image projected. The goal is to appear competent and exhibit the appropriate amount of integrity, thoughtfulness, sensitivity, and temperament.

To that end, the nominee is flooded with advice on how to respond to questions at the hearings. Nominees are subjected to mock hearings at which members of the president's team from the Justice Department and/or the White House ask questions and evaluate the responses. Senate supporters advise the nominee to remain circumspect in responding to questions, while potential opponents will stress the importance of responding fully and openly to questions.

In fact, the most helpful advice is simply to recognize how the opposition seeks to frame the nomination and avoid responses that will permit a spin in support of that frame. Felix Frankfurter did not wish to testify before a Judiciary subcommittee in 1939 but his nomination had hit a snag, in part because of "crank" advocates (one opponent cited Frankfurter's foreign birth as disqualifying) and in more serious part because of the opposition of Senator Pat McCarran and other "patriots" who distrusted Frankfurter's association with the American Civil Liberties Union. The opposition frame, then, was to mark Frankfurter as a radical with communist sympathies. McCarran, however, was no match for Frankfurter. In the following exchange, Frankfurter takes control and then one-ups McCarran's effort to frame Frankfurter as supportive of Harold Laski's sympathetic treatise on *Communism* (Laski 1927).

M.: Have you ever read any of his publications?

F.: Oh, certainly.

M.: Do you agree with his doctrine?

F.: I trust you will not deem me boastful, if I should say I have many friends who have written many books, and I shouldn't want to be charged with all the views in books by all my friends.

M.: You can answer that question simply.

F.: No, I cannot answer it simply. If you have a recent book of his, you will find the list of books he has written, some 12 or 15 or 20. He is an extraordinarily prolific writer. How can I say I agree with his doctrine? That implies he has a doctrine.

M.: Do you know whether or not he has a doctrine?

F.: I assume he has more than one. All people have.

M.: I refer now to a publication entitled *Communism*, and ask you whether you have read that?

F.: I have read it.

M.: Do you subscribe to his doctrine as expressed in that volume?

F.: Senator McCarran, how can I answer that question without making a speech about my views on government and the relations of the various branches of government to one another?

M.: You say you have read it and know the author, and you know the sentiment prevailing in this country now in regard to socialism and communism. If you have read this small volume, you can surely answer whether you subscribe to the doctrine?

F.: Have you read the book?

M.: I have just casually glanced at it.

F.: What would you say is its doctrine?

M.: The doctrine is the advocacy of communism.

F.: You see, we could debate all day on whether that is in fact the doctrine of the book.

M.: Do you believe in the doctrine set forth in this book?

F.: I cannot answer because I do not know what you regard as the doctrine. You have never read it. I understand that it is a study of certain beliefs, of a theory called communism. So far as I know, it would be impossible for me to say whether I agree with the doctrine in that book or not, because I think it is impossible to define what the doctrine is.

M.: If it advocates the doctrine of Marxism, would you agree with it?

F.: Senator, I do not believe that you have ever taken an oath to support the Constitution of the United States with fewer reservations than I have or would have now, nor do I believe that you are more attached to the theories and practices of Americanism than I am. (Senate 1939, 125–126)

Frankfurter was unanimously recommended for confirmation by the Judiciary Committee.

On other occasions, there is reason to suspect that a response from a nominee is simply disingenuous. In his confirmation hearings in 1957, Justice William Brennan faced a hostile Senator Joseph McCarthy, who was permitted by the Judiciary Committee to question the nominee even though not a member of the committee. Mc-Carthy thought Brennan too liberal, particularly concerning upcoming Supreme Court cases involving efforts to criminalize association with the Community party. When McCarthy asked, "Do you approve of congressional investigations and exposure of the communist conspiracy setup?" Brennan responded,

> Not only do I approve, Senator, but personally I cannot think of a more vital function of the Congress than the investigatory function of its committees, and I can't think of a more important or vital objective of any committee investigation than that of rooting out subversives in government. (Senate 1957, 17)

While Brennan might claim fidelity to such an utterance, in the context of the Smith Act and Subversive Activities Control Act, Brennan's statement seems to belie his stance on the Court in protecting individuals' First Amendment right to free speech (*Scales* v. *U.S.* 1961) and Fifth Amendment protection against self-incrimination. (*Communist Party* v. *SAC Board* 1961)

We may never know whether Justice Thomas's responses to the harassment accusations of Anita Hill were true or false. We certainly do know that Thomas adopted an uncompromising stance that attempted, with some success, to paint the hearings as a "high-tech lynching" by his political opponents rather than an effort by the committee to find some truth in the competing claims. To a certain extent, he was correct. The media attention certainly made it high tech, and the hearings had less the appearance of seeking truth rather than opponents and supporters locked in a battle to establish credibility. On the other hand, while it surely didn't seem like it to Thomas, the Democratic senators were really quite constrained. The Democrat most capable of mounting a vigorous assault, Senator Kennedy, was hamstrung by his own vulnerability to allegations of misconduct with sexual overtones. And with the "lynching" spin, Thomas also played the race card effectively enough to dampen the will of the other Democratic (and white) senators to pursue the allegations more aggressively.

A different approach to overcoming a potential opposition frame that could damage one's nomination is to admit past inadequacies or mistakes and assert a new, more politically "correct" position. In response to questioning by Senator Kennedy concerning membership in an athletic club that apparently maintained a white male membership specifically excluding blacks and women, nominee Anthony Kennedy basically repudiated his earlier club membership and cited a growing sensitivity to such matters, culminating in his resignation from the club.

Over the years, I have tried to become more sensitive to the existence of subtle barriers to the advancement of women and minorities in society. This was an issue on which I was continuing to educate myself. (Senate 1989, 105)

Such a strategy does not always work. Harrold Carswell had a long row to hoe in recanting his statement 20 years previous when he uttered,

I yield to no man as a fellow-candidate or as a fellow-citizen, in the firm, vigorous belief in the principles of white supremacy, and I shall always be so governed. (Harris 1971, 15–16)

Opponents ultimately succeeded in diminishing the effect of Carswell's categorical retraction of that statement by providing testimony alleging racial prejudice in his more recent judicial demeanor.

We have referred more than once to Robert Bork's inability to satisfy concern over his previous writings and opinions by asserting, in part, that he no longer felt that way. Opponents to his confirmation were successful in getting the "confirmation conversion" label to stick in the minds of a significant part of the public and the Senate. Despite Clarence Thomas's more successful outcome, he was not particularly adept at overcoming opponents' portrait of him as unqualified and as having turned his back on the very political principles that helped him attain his own status.

These numerous examples of nominees in action testify to the integral part that they play in the development of the nomination discourse. In a noncontroversial nomination, the nominee is doubly blessed. The absence of a determined opposition means that the discourse is already free from efforts to frame the nomination in especially negative terms. It further means that the nominee is freer to respond because efforts to place some negative spin on those answers are largely absent. The nominee can afford to be generous and communicative.

If a nominee can blow such a positive situation, Antonin Scalia may have flirted with the possibility. His lack of responsiveness to questions provoked resentment from senators already predisposed to support his nomination. One could argue that Scalia was simply exhibiting how open minded he was rather than evasive, for example, when he equivocated regarding the acceptance of *Marbury* v. *Madison* (1803) as definitively giving the Court the power to declare acts of Congress unconstitutional (Senate 1987, 83–85). Senators Specter and DeConcini, two who would play pivotal roles in the defeat of Bork, were sufficiently irritated to draft a resolution designed to coerce nominees into more forthcoming behavior in

confirmation hearings. Scalia may not have suffered any consequences from his behavior, but there is little question that he
helped to move some senators in the direction of requiring more responsiveness from nominees.

The situation is much different whenever the nomination has already been framed as controversial. Here the nominee's responses are
very critical in determining the final disposition of the nomination
discourse. As we have observed, an adept performance by a nominee
can effectively neutralize opposition attempts to frame the nominee
in particular terms. Some nominees have even successfully established their own frame of the nomination. Finally, nominees can use
their testimony to place their own spin on events and behaviors, successfully orienting the discourse in the direction they desire. Thus,
while public testimony by the nominee is historically a recent phenomenon, it has become the true defining moment of the confirmation process. In a controversial nomination, the nominee's testimony
will figure quite prominently in the outcome of that nomination.

The Committee Report

After the hearings conclude it remains for the committee to generate its report, which serves to wrap up the discourse and put forward the final arguments prior to the Senate's confirmation decision. From this point on, little new language will inform the
nomination discourse. Of course, the Thomas nomination represented a spectacular exception in which the sexual harassment
charges became public after the initial vote of the committee.

The most significant aspect of the committee report is the actual committee vote on whether to recommend confirmation or rejection of the nominee. This vote is a strong indicator of the ultimate outcome in the full Senate. A unanimous vote in the
committee is inevitably a signal that there will be little or no opposition in the Senate. On the other hand, if there is some degree of
opposition on the committee, then the committee vote will provide
a cue as to the level and likely sources of the opposition. This statement implies that any discussion of committee voting should focus
on the two related questions of (1) what factors cause opposition to
emerge, and (2) when there is opposition, what determines the size
and basis of the conflict?

The Emergence of Opposition

We have suggested already in Chapter 3 that the source of nomination controversy lies in the political setting at the time of the

nomination. That connection between the setting and the emergence of controversy, as reflected by opposition to the nomination in the Judiciary Committee, is depicted in Figure 5.1 When the political setting substantially favors the president, as indicated by the shaded "favorable" setting in Part A of Figure 5.1, committee opposition is unlikely to emerge. Eight nominations between Warren's in 1954 and Breyer's in 1994 occurred in settings that were quite favorable for the president, with favorableness defined as a score of 2.0 or higher on our composite index of nomination setting (see Figure 2.5). Of those eight nominations, seven generated unanimous votes for confirmation in the committee. Only Thurgood Marshall's nomination proved the exception. In these very favorable settings, the president has a natural reservoir of support that precludes both the opportunity and motive for opposition. Similarly, such a strong political position reduces the likelihood that a negative frame or spin regarding the nominee's qualifications will be attempted.

In settings less favorable for the president (less than 2.0) attention focuses more on the nominee, and political opponents of the president are more likely to raise questions regarding the nominee. This is particularly true if the nominee is perceived as having any partisan or ideological biases that the president is trying to bring to

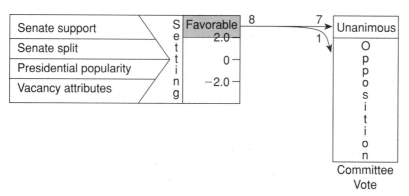

Figure 5.1 A. Modeling the Development of Opposition
Very favorable settings usually produce unanimous committee votes. One key to whether opposition to a nomination will surface in the Judiciary Committee is the setting in which the nomination takes place. The box on the left above captures the four variables we identified in Chapter 2 as central to defining the nomination setting. In Figure 2.5, we displayed a graph of a nomination setting scale. A score of +2.0 or higher was defined as being a particularly favorable setting for the president and nominee. The graph above shows that eight nominations in the modern era (since 1954) have occurred in these favorable circumstances. Seven of those eight nominations resulted in unanimous recommendations for confirmation by the Judiciary Committee.

the Court. The need to base opposition in terms of the nominee's qualifications will generate efforts to dispute and question the nominee's qualifications. Applying the qualifications measure used in Chapter 3, we can identify 11 nominations of this modern era in which the nominee's qualifications were disputed (Figure 5.1B). Of those 11 nominees, only Anthony Kennedy escaped any opposition in committee. Opposition to the other 10 ranged from a single opponent for Souter (Senator Kennedy) to a majority (9 out of 14) for Robert Bork. Nonetheless, even a single opposing vote in committee is likely to signal some greater opposition in the full Senate.

The presence of a less-positive setting does not necessarily mean that controversy will arise. We have noted previously the ability of a president to mitigate a less-positive setting, even one that is quite negative, by appointing a nominee who is particularly well respected and qualified. Effectively, this may also mean appointing a person whose partisanship and ideology seem to play a relatively minor role in the nominee's recent political history. Seven nominees emerged in this modern era who were perceived as particularly well qualified in spite of the less-than-optimal setting for the president—Stewart, Burger, Blackmun, Powell, Stevens, and Ruth Ginsburg (Segal, Cameron, and Cover 1992, 107). Six of the seven (Figure 5.1C) proceeded to attain the unanimous support of the Judiciary Committee. Only Potter Stewart re-

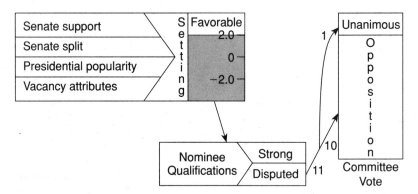

Figure 5.1 B. Modeling the Development of Opposition
Opposition emerges in less-than-favorable settings when the nominee's qualifications are disputed. When the nomination setting is less than very favorable to the president and nominee (<2.0), more attention focuses on the nominee and the nominee's "qualifications." As Part B of the figure shows, 11 nominations in the modern era occurring in less than the most favorable setting for the president produced disputes over the nominee's qualifications. All but one of those 11 nominations produced at least some opposition in the committee.

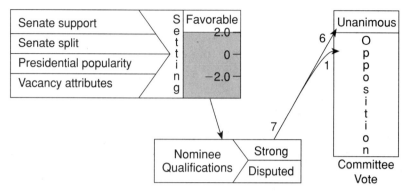

Figure 5.1 C. Modeling the Development of Opposition
Opposition is avoided in less-than-favorable settings by appointing a nominee
with strong qualifications. Of the six people nominated in settings less than
strongly favorable to the president (<2.0) and who were widely perceived as
possessing strong qualifications for the Court, five sailed through the Judiciary
Committee with unanimous support. Only one—Potter Stewart—sustained
opposition.

ceived general acclaim in the media for his qualifications and still
was confronted with committee opposition. Even then, the opposing southern senators acknowledged his qualifications and based
their opposition more as a matter of principle on the direction
that the Court had taken with respect to desegregation than on
Stewart's credentials.

The Scope of Opposition

The significance of committee opposition rests not so much in
the absolute magnitude of the opposition as it does in the makeup
of the opposition. The five votes cast against Thurgood Marshall
represented almost one-third of the committee, but the full Senate
vote found only 11 senators (15 if paired votes are counted) voting
in opposition. A paired vote occurs when two members who in-
tend to vote on opposite sides of a question agree to link their
votes, in effect canceling each other's vote, permitting them to go
on record as favoring or opposing the question but not actually requiring their presence at the vote. Paired votes are not actually
counted in the vote tally, hence the Marshall vote was reported as
69 to 11 rather than 73 to 15. Clearly this is a courtesy that senators are more likely to indulge when a vote is not expected to be
close. In the Marshall nomination all negative votes in the committee and in the Senate, like Stewart before him, were from
southerners. This southern opposition to Marshall signaled both
the scope and the limits of the opposition.

As we have suggested throughout, nomination controversy is inevitably politically driven. From the single vote of Senator Kennedy against David Souter to the nine votes in opposition to Robert Bork, opposition in the committee seems most easily accountable in terms of political ideology and partisanship (see Table 5.1.) In the case of Robert Bork, the nine opponents (all eight Democrats and one Republican) were all more liberal than the five conservative Republicans who supported the nomination. The Thomas vote split almost along the same lines, except that this time the Republicans stayed together while one Democrat (DeConcini) came to his support. Straight liberal Democrat opposition highlighted the nominations of both Rehnquist and Carswell. On the other hand, the Fortas vote for chief justice cut across party lines, reflecting a fairly straight split by ideology. Thus, Republican and Democratic conservatives opposed the nomination while Republican and Democratic liberals favored it.

While opposition from southerners in the 1950s and 1960s had a regional focus, its basis was also ideological, stemming from the shifting role of the Court as represented by the monumental *Brown* v. *Board* case in 1954, which began the Court's dismantling of segregated public schools. On this issue, however, the southern conservatives, who were all Democrats until Strom Thurmond switched parties and joined the Committee as a Republican, could not generally attract the nonsouthern Republican conservatives. This essentially southern opposition surfaced in the nominations of Stewart and Marshall and to a lesser extent in those of Warren and Harlan.

Two nominations brought some mix across ideological lines. While Haynsworth was generally opposed by liberals of both parties and favored by conservatives, the defection of the moderately conservative Republican Robert Griffin was a blow to Haynsworth supporters. Griffin was brought into opposition, in part, by the way his opposition to Fortas had been framed just the year before. By focusing on Fortas's ethical problems, Griffin led a group of similarly situated Republicans who were persuaded that Haynsworth had problems very similar to Fortas. Substantially different was the 1955 nomination of John Harlan. Opposition from South Dakota's William Langer was expressed as a protest to appointments going to individuals from large states. From a different perspective, Idaho's Herman Welker expressed concern that Harlan would fail to uphold American sovereignty, alluding to Harlan's association with an international organization called Atlantic Union. Harlan also caught the opposition of a couple of southern Democrats. All in all, his four negative committee votes produced only 11 negatives in the Senate vote.

A yes vote in committee does not always signify support for the nominee. Democrat Quentin Burdick and Republican Charles Mathias made it quite clear in the Carswell vote that they did not favor confirmation and that their yes votes should be interpreted as moving the nomination forward to the full Senate. Republican Hugh Scott had done the same in the Haynsworth nomination. Their explicit reservations about the nominees would prove to be important in the Senate vote to come. Mathias's statement in the committee report spoke more significantly than his vote and reinforced the negative discourse surrounding Carswell.

> I would not have chosen him. . . . the issue of personal competency or qualification becomes . . . one for the judgment of the Senate. In this instance that means submission of the nomination to the full Senate for debate and decision. On this basis and for this purpose I have voted in the Judiciary Committee to report the nomination to the Senate. (Senate 1970, 11–12)

TABLE 5.1
Committee Votes on Nonunanimous Nominees Since Earl Warren
In Order by Number of Negative Votes

Nominee	President	Year	Committee Vote	Composition of Opposition
Bork	Reagan	1987	5 to 9	liberals and Democrats
Thomas	Bush	1991	7 to 7	most Democrats
Haynsworth	Nixon	1969	10 to 7	liberals and mix
Fortas	Johnson	1967	11 to 6	conservatives
Rehnquist (CJ)	Reagan	1986	13 to 5	liberal Democrats
Marshall	Johnson	1967	11 to 5	southerners
Carswell	Nixon	1970	13 to 4	liberal Democrats
Harlan	Eisenhower	1955	10 to 4	mix
Rehnquist	Nixon	1971	12 to 4	liberal Democrats
Stewart	Eisenhower	1959	12 to 3	southerners
Warren	Eisenhower	1954	12 to 3	some southerners
Souter	Bush	1990	13 to 1	Kennedy

Notes

CJ=Chief Justice

The Haynsworth committee vote is somewhat misleading. Senator Hugh Scott, the Republican whip, made clear that he did not support the recommendation of the majority to confirm and that his yes vote was intended to support moving the nomination forward to the floor of the Senate. Scott voted against Haynsworth on the floor.

Similarly, in the Carswell vote two senators—Burdick, a Democrat, and Mathias, a Republican—voted with the majority as a means of moving the nomination to the full Senate, but their statements indicated severe reservations about the nominee. Both subsequently voted against confirmation.

To the extent that the committee is representative of the full Senate, the actual committee vote count can serve as a reasonably good predictor of what will happen in the Senate. The more sophisticated analyst will observe the statements of the senators to see if their words are consistent with their votes. Then the careful observer will pay attention to the partisan and ideological split in the vote, anticipating that the Senate will pretty much follow suit. After all, that is what the senators themselves will do as they prepare to receive the report of the committee.

CHAPTER SIX

The Senate

I cannot find a single distinguishing aspect of Mr. Thomas's legal career that would warrant his consideration for the Court.

Senator Donald Riegle, Democrat from Michigan

I based my decision on a careful review of the nominee's intellectual capacity, his background and training, and his integrity and reputation.

Senator Alan Dixon, Democrat from Illinois

There . . . are doubts about the nominee's legal experience, his legal maturity, his legal theory, and now, sadly, his character.

Senator Jim Sasser, Democrat from Tennessee

I have heard from a number of Alaskans and visited with them last week during our recess. . . . they are telling me by a substantial majority, that they favor the confirmation of Judge Thomas by this body.

Senator Stan Murkowski, Republican from Alaska

The last thing I did before I decided was to call my wife. I believe Anita Hill was telling the truth.

Senator Harry Reid, Democrat from Nevada

[Senator Danforth] convinced me some time ago that Thomas is an outstanding man. . . . I saw no reason not to support him again.

Senator Ted Stevens, Republican from Alaska

This is a confirmation process, not a judicial process. No individual has a particular right to a Supreme Court seat. Why give him the benefit of the doubt? I shall vote against Judge Thomas [because] he not only effectively stonewalled the committee,. . . [but because] I frankly was offended by his injection of racism into the hearings.

Senator Robert Byrd, Democrat from West Virginia

> In my mind, if there is substantial doubt, you resolve that doubt in favor of the accused.
>
> *Senator David Boren, Democrat from Oklahoma*

> In a case of this vast magnitude, where so much is riding on our decision, the Senate should give the benefit of the doubt to the Supreme Court and to the American people, not to Judge Clarence Thomas.
>
> *Senator Edward Kennedy, Democrat from Massachusetts*

> I thought I should err on the side of caution.
>
> *Senator Joseph Lieberman, Democrat from Connecticut*

What motivates senators to vote for or against confirmation? The statements above reveal an interesting array of basic philosophies—from very different evaluations about the nominee to reliance upon constituency opinion to reliance upon a spouse to reliance on a colleague to voting yes when in doubt to voting no when in doubt. To the political scientist, however, the explanations seem little more than rationalizations that support underlying political philosophies. As we have emphasized throughout this book, nominations are part of the political process, and political considerations are preeminent in determining the final outcome of a confirmation vote. This is not to say that individual senators do not agonize about their votes—it is to say that there is some predictability about the ultimate outcome of that agony.

For first-term Senator Joseph Lieberman, a Democrat from Connecticut, it was the most difficult vote of his heretofore brief political career in the Senate. Having initially decided to support Clarence Thomas, he found himself swayed into opposition by the riveting testimony of Anita Hill, only to be brought back by the compelling rebuttal of Judge Thomas. As witnesses supported the character of each of these two antagonists, Lieberman found himself swinging from one side to the other. He was lobbied by President Bush in behalf of Thomas and by his own daughter against. He listened to other supporters and opponents and considered the calls from his constituents, which were running three to two against the nomination. Ultimately, and only minutes before the vote, he decided to oppose confirmation with the explanation cited above.

This chapter brings us to the culmination of the appointment process. We shall first pay attention to how the political discourse that has framed the nomination is continued within the full Senate. That discourse both shapes and is shaped by the vote decisions reached by the senators. We shall then analyze the votes of the more controversial nominations with a particular focus on the importance of political ideology and partisanship along with an assessment of a number of sources that serve as cues to senators about their confirmation votes. In particular, these cues involve the role of a senator's own constituency and the influence of other senators.

Concluding the Discourse

By the time the nomination emerges from the Judiciary Committee, the discourse is largely established. The committee majority and minority have articulated the bases on which the confirmation will be argued in the Senate. Advocacy groups have refined their claims. The media have distilled their analysis into a focus on one or two "critical" issues. Any debate in the Senate and among senators is largely a reiteration of that which has come before. After all, these are the sources that have primarily informed the vast majority of the senators regarding any confirmation issues.

With a controversial nomination, certain issues may have been so well defined that they must be incorporated into any explanation that a senator gives for a vote. The most obvious example of such a nomination is how each senator had to explain support for or opposition to Thomas in light of Anita Hill's testimony. Supporters had a somewhat more difficult road. One could not accept Hill's testimony as true and still publicly support Thomas since to do so would be to confirm a perjurer to the Supreme Court. Opponents of Thomas, however, didn't have to believe Hill to feel that Thomas was not qualified to sit on the Supreme Court.

Moreover, to reject Professor Hill's testimony as false was difficult for Thomas supporters. One could do so only at the risk of trivializing sexual harassment or alienating those impressed with her testimony. For Thomas supporters, then, it was generally important to acknowledge that sexual harassment is a serious issue but not the issue before the Senate. While some felt comfortable enough trying to discredit Hill's testimony, many felt compelled to add a new wrinkle to the confirmation discourse, applying the criminal law principle of "innocent until proven guilty" to the nomination process. In other words, a nominee against whom allegations are made should be given the benefit of any doubt. To do otherwise, they argued, would place any nominee at the mercy of opponents willing to make any unsubstantiated charge. Efforts by Thomas opponents, notably Senators Kennedy, Heflin, and Byrd, placed a different spin on the principle, to the effect that any doubt should be resolved in favor of protecting the Court by rejecting the nominee. Their argument simply could not win the day.

Generally, the purpose of posthearings debate is not to introduce new issues or to give some new spin to existing arguments. Senators simply want to get on the record, to explain their vote in ways that will minimize repercussions. The fact that they are repeating comments that have come before does not matter. Once Thomas supporters pronounced their sensitivity to and abhorrence of sexual harassment, they could proceed to adopt any of the basic lines already established in the discourse as reasons for supporting Thomas. For Thomas opponents, it was important to deny political or racial motivations in part by shifting responsibility for any injection of race into the discourse to the president and to Thomas himself. From then on, they could stress the credibility of Anita Hill, argue against any presumption of innocence standard in a confirmation hearing, and otherwise adopt any of the various lines already established in the discourse as reasons for opposing Thomas. In many respects, statements on the floor of the Senate are a "CYA" operation designed to gain the plaudits of those back home who agree with the senator's decision and placate those who disagree with that decision by showing sensitivity to their particular point of view. This effort is perhaps best epitomized by Senator Larry Pressler's press release: "Senator Supports Thomas, Praises Hill's Testimony."

The Vote

> The question is, will the Senate advise and consent to the nomination of Clarence Thomas, of Georgia, to be an associate justice of the U.S. Supreme Court? The yeas and nays have been ordered.

Once the speeches are over, there is nothing left to do but vote. In times previous, many of these votes were simply voice votes, particularly in relatively noncontroversial nominations. So it was with Earl Warren in 1954, William Brennan and Charles Whittaker in 1957, Byron White and Arthur Goldberg in 1962, and Abe Fortas in 1965—but not since. The opposition to these nominees, and there was some opposition, was overwhelmed by the voices in support. As the process has become increasingly formalized, voice votes have given way to votes of record, which have provided social scientists with an opportunity to analyze voting behavior in these appointment decisions.

Predicting Senate voting in some nominations is not a difficult task. If the Judiciary Committee has been unanimous in its support of a nominee, there is little doubt that the Senate will be nearly unanimous as well. In the 14 instances of nominations in the modern era (since 1954) that drew no announced opposition in committee, the most negative votes occurring in the full Senate appears to have been the nine cast against Stephen Breyer in 1994, an unusually high number of negatives given the absence of committee opposition. "No" votes in the face of general unanimity are often

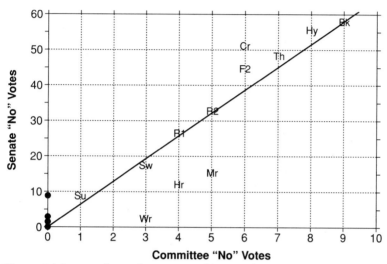

Figure 6.1 Scatterplot and Linear Prediction of Senate "No" Votes as a Function of Judiciary Committee "No" Votes for Supreme Court Nominations between 1955 and 1994

Committee no votes are adjusted to reflect the realities of interpreting committee member votes. Specifically, the Haynsworth "no" votes were adjusted from seven to eight to reflect Senator Hugh Scott's "yes" as being merely a transmittal vote to send the issue on to the full Senate. Similarly, the Carswell vote was adjusted from four to six "no" votes to reflect the transmittal votes of Senators Burdick and Mathias. All three senators indicated that their "yes" votes should not be interpreted as an endorsement for confirmation. Their explicit separation from nominee supporters left the unmistakable impression that they did not support the nomination and, indeed, all did vote against confirmation in those respective Senate votes.

Senate "No" votes reflect announced pairs. The largest impact in so doing was to increase the Marshall negatives from 11 to 15. Single votes were added to Harlan, Fortas (chief justice), and the first Rehnquist nomination. The Fortas vote for chief justice was not on confirmation but on whether to close debate on the confirmation. The failure to close debate doomed the nomination. Finally, Warren's voice vote was announced as unanimous, but we recorded the three committee "no" votes as remaining against him in the full Senate.

The regression results that underlie these straight-line predictions are: $b = 6.5$; $a = -0.5$; adjusted $R^2 = 0.90$; $P < 0.0001$

Abbreviations for the nominees receiving one or more "no" votes in committee are:

Bk Bork	Hr Harlan	R1 Rehnquist 1st	Sw Stewart
Cr Carswell	Hy Haynsworth	R2 Rehnquist 2nd	Th Thomas
F2 Fortas 2nd	Mr Marshall	Su Souter	Wr Warren

rather idiosyncratic. For example, the lone "no" vote against Lewis Powell came from Oklahoma's Fred Harris, who objected to Powell as a representative of the nation's political elite. William Langer of North Dakota claimed to have opposed Harlan's nomination in 1955 as a protest against the failure by the president to appoint nominees from any of the small states. Strom Thurmond stated for the record his opposition in the voice vote for Goldberg in 1962, but he did not state the basis for his opposition.

Division in the Judiciary Committee portends division in the Senate. In the nominations of the modern era, the committee vote has been an excellent predictor of the vote count in the full Senate. The scatterplot in Figure 6.1 utilizes a statistical procedure that summarizes the data points of the two variables—committee vote and the Senate vote—with a straight line. That line serves to predict the number of "No" votes in the Senate confirmation vote based on the number of "No" votes cast in the Judiciary Committee. It reveals that each committee "No" vote projects an average of 6.5 "No" votes in the full Senate. This rough estimate would have predicted 58 negatives in the Senate against Bork based on the nine committee "No" votes, which was exactly correct. For Thomas, the prediction was off by only two votes. Only the Warren, Harlan, and Marshall votes exhibit much deviation from the committee predictions and, quite frankly, we're not sure about Warren, whose casual voice vote obscured how much opposition actually existed.

The relationship between the committee vote and the full Senate vote stems from the committee being representative of the full Senate, which it is designed to be. To have it otherwise would mean that output from the committee might often be rejected by the whole Senate, a poor use of time for committee members and the Senate as a whole. In part, representation is built in by structuring a partisan division in the committee that mirrors that in the Senate. If the Senate were 60 percent Democratic, the committee would be approximately 60 percent Democratic. In addition to reflecting the partisan division in the Senate, the committee more often than not also provides a reasonable approximation of the ideological makeup within each party.[1] In this way, the

---

[1] We conducted a number of statistical tests of the representativeness of the committee over time including the years of 1969, 1972, 1987, and 1991, in which nominations had sigificant opposition. We tested for differences in ideology by using the ADA voting scores and checking for central tendency (means and medians) differences, as well as goodness-of-fit tests (Chi Square and Kolmogorov-Smirnoff). There were no statistically significant differences between committee member scores and scores of all Senate members.

range and distribution of political views on the committee are generally representative of the range and distribution of political views in the full Senate.

Assuming then that the committee is politically representative of the Senate, the strong correlation between committee votes and the Senate votes can come about for two reasons. One explanation assumes a relatively passive role for the committee and simply assumes that members of the full Senate are likely to arrive at similar views of a nominee's qualifications independently of their colleagues on the committee. The committee, in other words, is simply a representative sample of the whole Senate. A second explanation perceives a more active role for the committee and posits that members of the full Senate, who are not as intimately familiar with a nominee's record as are members of the committee, will look at how committee members voted and use the voting of politically like-minded members of the committee as a cue on how to view the nominee and how to vote.

Regardless of whether the explanation is passive and like-minded agreement or more active cue-giving, it is important to understand the underlying factors that shape how most senators, whether on or off the Judiciary Committee, perceive the nominee and the nomination and how they will vote on that nominee. A constant theme that has appeared throughout this book from the initial setting in which the vacancy occurs through the presidential appointment through the committee process is the importance of politics, defined both in terms of partisanship and political ideology. That these factors should play a significant role in the Senate vote on confirmation is hardly surprising. Both have figured prominently in the history of congressional voting (Poole and Rosenthal 1991, 228–230).

Partisanship and Ideology

Ideology implies a way of structuring the political universe that permits a coherent evaluation of political phenomena according to some logically interrelated system of values. Despite the oversimplification and misuse of the liberal and conservative labels, it is significant that they remain commonly accepted terms to describe ideology and to describe Supreme Court nominees. Thus, Abe Fortas was framed as an activist ultraliberal justice and Robert Bork was painted as so conservative that he fell outside the judicial mainstream. Assuming a political motivation for senators, we ought to expect that their ideology will serve as a guide to their voting. The more senators perceive a nominee's ideology as consistent with their own, the more likely they are to support that nominee. Conversely, a nominee who is perceived as in opposition to one's own ideological position is more likely to be perceived as unacceptable.

Partisanship may be viewed as more than just which political party a senator affiliates with. Realistically, it denotes how often one affiliates with positions taken by a majority of one's own political party, especially in votes that pit the majority in one party against the majority in the other party. Given the structure of the appointment process, it is difficult not to think of a nominee as representing the president's party. This assertion is particularly true given the fact that 90 percent of all Supreme Court nominations have involved the president nominating someone from his own party. Partisanship is more likely to play a role where the nomination or the nominee is viewed as having a partisan basis. Among more recent nominees, Rehnquist, Bork, and Thomas had fairly strong partisan records, which prompted relatively quick acceptance by most members of the president's party and considerably more skepticism by the stronger partisans within the Democratic party. On the other hand, considerable leeway is granted by most senators in tolerating previous partisan activities by nominees. It is not too surprising that Senator Kennedy's effort to pin partisan Watergate activity on Robert Bork as a way of generating opposition simply fizzled. Senators are quite willing to accept that an individual can shed the coat of partisanship when donning the robe of justice.

Combining ideology and partisanship suggests a rather straightforward set of expectations about Senate voting in controversial nominations. The senators most likely to vote yes on a nominee will be those who are both strongly supportive of the president's party and ideologically close to the president and the nominee. Conversely, the surest no votes will be from senators who strongly oppose the president's party and are ideologically distant from the president and the nominee. Logically, therefore, assuming some reasonably even split between opposing sides, the ultimate outcome in a controversial nomination depends upon those senators who form both the ideological and partisan middle grounds.

Given these general expectations, the actual relationships among ideology, partisanship, and voting will vary across nominations and time periods. For example, some nominations may be framed as primarily partisan battles while others will be fought largely on ideological grounds. Additionally, the relationship between ideology and partisanship may change across eras. During some periods, party differences may closely mirror ideological cleavages; at other times partisans of a particular party may exhibit great diversity in their ideological beliefs. The only true way to examine the predictive power of partisanship and ideology is to observe how these factors have actually played out in controversial nominations over time.

In the last half of the twentieth century, ideology and partisanship have become increasingly aligned and the Senate has polarized along these partisan-ideological dimensions. Box 6.1 illustrates the Senate alignment along these two dimensions in 1968, the year of the Fortas nomination, and 1991, the year of the Thomas nomination. In 1968 there was much less distance between the centers of the two parties and considerably more variation within each party with respect to both party support and ideology scores. In 1991 ideology and party support were nearly synonymous—to be liberal was to be Democratic, to be conservative was to be Republican. Prior to the 1980s, conservative southern Democrats often abandoned the Democratic party and joined with conservative Republicans in Senate votes. On the Republican side, gone are liberals like Jacob Javits and Kenneth Keating, who led New York's delegation through much of the 1960s. Republicans Clifford Case of New Jersey and Edward Brooke of Massachusetts had voting records that rivaled many liberal Democrats.

BOX 6.1
A Portrait of Ideological and Partisan Alignment from 1968 to 1991

The makeup of the Senate has changed over time. Although the Democratic party held a comfortable 63 to 37 advantage over the Republicans in 1968, there existed a bloc of 10 to 15 Democratic senators, primarily from the South, who voted regularly with Republicans to form conservative majorities on certain issues, the Fortas nomination being one of them. In the charts on the following pages, the Rs are the positions of Republican senators and the Ds indicate the Democratic senators. The vertical axis reflects political ideology as measured by a senator's Americans for Democratic Action (ADA) voting score, a 100 meaning that a senator voted in favor of positions supported by the liberal ADA 100 percent of the time. A 0 defines the most conservative senators—senators who never voted in accordance with the position of the ADA (see Appendix D for details concerning ADA scores). The horizontal axis provides partisanship scores, or essentially how often senators voted with their party when a majority of one party opposed a ma-

continued

continued

jority in the other party. On this scale, the 50 in the middle indicates voting half the time with the Democrats and half the time with the Republicans. Moving toward the right end of the scale indicates how often senators voted with the Democratic majority. Moving to the left signifies how frequently senators voted with the Republicans. Thus, a score of 80 to the right of 50 indicates voting with the Democrats 80 percent of the time while a score of 80 to the left of the 50 specifies having voted with the Republicans in 80 percent of these partisan votes.

The charts reveal some similarities. For instance, the charts are more alike than different on the partisanship dimension. Republicans are still more likely to vote with other Republicans than they are with Democrats and vice versa. So for any given level of ADA score, Rs will almost always appear to the left of the Ds. In addition, the alignment of ideology and partisanship casts a distinctive lower-left to upper-right tilt to the data. As Republicans become more liberal, placing them higher on the chart, they also move from left to right and away from supporting their own party in the direction of the Democrats. Similarly, as we move down from the top among the Democrats, they simultaneously move to the left in the chart, voting less often with the majority of their fellow Democrats.

More apparent than the similarities are the differences. The two charts *look* different. The senators in 1968 are more widely dispersed, especially vertically. Democrats and Republicans appear across the full range of ideological scores. In 1991 conservative Democrats are simply gone, and many fewer Republicans are seen above a score of 25. If ideology and partisanship were perfectly aligned, all senators would fall along the straight line drawn diagonally through the data. While this is certainly not the case, you can observe that there is much less variation from the line in 1991 than in 1968.

The statistical calculations bear out this increased alignment. One measure of the amount points deviate from the line is their standard deviation. A 0 would indicate all points are on the line—perfect alignment. For 1968, the standard deviation is 25.2; for 1991, it drops drastically to 9.4. Similarly, the tables immediately below the charts report the medians and interdecile ranges of the data for both the ideological and partisanship measures. The median may be interpreted as the party's center point; half of the senators are above that point and half are below. The interdecile range drops off 10 percent of the senators from both extremes, much like certain performance sports drop the highest and lowest judges' scores for a competitor's evaluation. What remains is the range of scores—the difference between the highest and the lowest scores—for the middle 80 percent of the senators. This measures how much diversity exists with respect to senatorial voting behavior.

In 1968 the ideological centers of the two parties were separated by 36 points on the scale (57 to 21). By 1991 that separation had grown to

70 points, with the Republican center becoming more conservative, exhibiting a median of 10, while the Democratic median had increased to 80. At the same time, both parties exhibit much less diversity in their ideological makeup as revealed by the considerable reductions in their interdecile ranges—79 to 45 for the Republicans and 86 to 45 for the Democrats. There are simply fewer moderates and liberals within the Republican party and fewer moderates and conservatives within the Democratic party. Less dramatic but in the same direction are changes in the partisanship measure. All of this suggests that ideology and partisanship are increasingly aligned. Being conservative and being Republican go together as do being liberal and being Democratic.

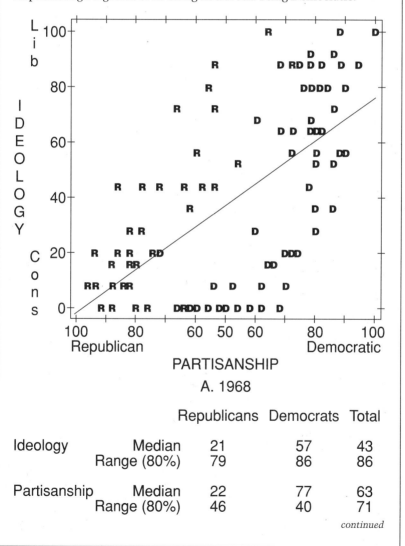

A. 1968

		Republicans	Democrats	Total
Ideology	Median	21	57	43
	Range (80%)	79	86	86
Partisanship	Median	22	77	63
	Range (80%)	46	40	71

continued

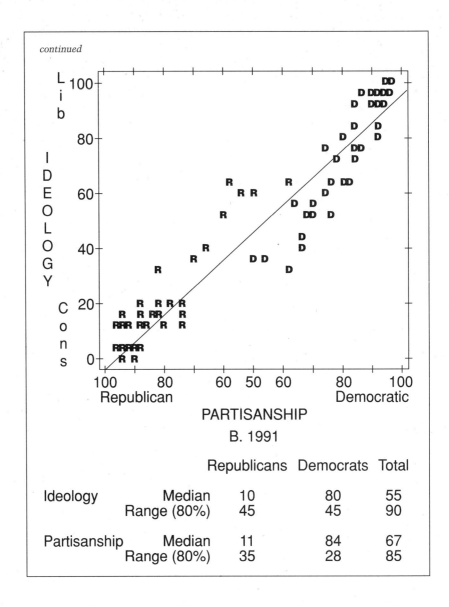

continued

PARTISANSHIP

B. 1991

		Republicans	Democrats	Total
Ideology	Median	10	80	55
	Range (80%)	45	45	90
Partisanship	Median	11	84	67
	Range (80%)	35	28	85

Much of this change came about as successive Republican presidential candidates, beginning with Barry Goldwater in 1964, touted the Republican party as the ideological home for conservatives. To a certain extent with Richard Nixon and more completely with Ronald Reagan, the Republicans succeeded in establishing themselves as the conservative party. Other political leaders like Senator Strom Thurmond, who switched from the Democratic to the Republican party in 1964, hastened this merging of ideology and party. As the Republicans pulled in conservative voters and politicians, they also abandoned the liberal wing of the party to the Democrats. This worked fine for the Republican party in 1980, when they gained control of the Senate and made considerable inroads in the traditionally Democratic South. However, in 1986 the Democrats regrouped and wiped out the freshman Republicans from the South, replacing them not with the conservative southern Democrats of old but with a new generation, distinctly more liberal and more supportive of the Democratic party than any of those who came before them.

When partisanship is compounded with an ideological bias, opposition becomes increasingly likely in any nomination that occurs in a less-than-optimal setting for the president unless the president short-circuits such opposition with a nomination viewed as free from partisan or ideological overtones. Opposition first appears at the most extreme point of ideological and partisan opposition. More often than not, opposition at one extreme will then activate support from those at the opposite extreme of partisanship and ideology. In this manner, controversy begins at the extremes and moves toward the middle. The intensity increases as both sides move simultaneously in the space toward those senators who demonstrate weaker levels of partisanship and more moderate positions along the conservative/liberal ideological dimension.

This pattern is illustrated quite clearly as we examine the controversial nominations of the modern era. Up until the rejection of Abe Fortas as chief justice, no nominee in the modern era had met serious opposition. When opposition did appear, it was usually limited to senators from no more than six to nine southern states because it focused so exclusively on the Court's *Brown* v. *Board* school desegregation decision. Virtually no serious effort was made to frame the nominee in a way that would question his qualifications. Indeed, many of Potter Stewart's opponents in 1959 made a point of finding no fault with his qualifications, basing their opposition on his support of the Court's desegregation decisions. Few senators outside the South were willing to oppose on that basis.

By 1968, however, the political setting had begun to take on a look that the country had not witnessed since the time of Herbert Hoover. The popularity of President Lyndon Johnson had declined from record highs to record lows as the nation soured on the Vietnam War abroad and increasing strife at home. Senate support for the president had waned, and opposition to a liberal Court's insistence on the rights of the accused during a period of increasing crime in the streets presaged a difficult time for a president to elevate one of the more liberal justices and a close personal friend, Abe Fortas, to be chief justice. During this same period, Court opinions along with the social agendas of the Kennedy and Johnson administrations had generated substantial opposition from a coalition of southern conservative Democrats and a considerable portion of conservative Republicans. The expectation in 1968 that Johnson would be replaced by the more conservative and Republican Richard Nixon fueled an effort by these combined forces to stall, if not defeat, the Fortas nomination.

What transpired over the next three and a half years was truly extraordinary for twentieth-century American politics: Eight men would be named by two different presidents to fill only four different vacancies. Johnson's attempt to fill Chief Justice Earl Warren's vacancy with Abe Fortas would be effectively stalled, negating the nomination of another Johnson friend, Homer Thornberry, to fill a Fortas vacancy that never occurred in Johnson's term. Warren's vacancy would be filled by Richard Nixon's first appointee, Warren Burger. However, Nixon would then fail in two consecutive efforts to replace Abe Fortas with southern conservative nominees before succeeding with the highly regarded Minnesotan, Harry Blackmun. Two other nominations would give Nixon the most appointment opportunities for a first-term president since Warren Harding. While both nominations were successful, with Lewis Powell replacing Hugo Black and William Rehnquist replacing John Harlan, Powell would sail through the Senate while Rehnquist encountered substantial opposition (26 negatives).

Despite the varied arguments surrounding each of these Court nominations, all four exhibit very similar patterns with respect to which senators voted to confirm and which voted to reject. Figure 6.2 graphs the yeas and nays along the two dimensions of partisanship and ideology for these four controversial nominations. For each nomination we have demarcated this space into zones of opposition (the shaded area) and support for the nominee. This demarcation is based on a statistical procedure designed to estimate the probability of voting either "yes" or "no" on the basis of partisanship and ideology. These zones serve two purposes. First, they allow easy visualization of how ideological and partisan characteristics appear to have influenced the confirmation vote. Second, they also help us to identify senators who seem to be voting in a way that is inconsistent with what would be expected for one in some particular ideological and partisan position. For example, noting a senator who falls into the opposition zone but nonetheless votes "yes" on a nominee suggests that we might look for explanations other than ideology or partisanship for that senator's vote. Moreover, the greater the number of such inconsistent votes—or "errors," as it were—the more likely we are to conclude that voting in that particular nomination was not motivated by ideological and partisan considerations.

It is very apparent that the upper-right and lower-left quadrants are the consistent strongholds of supporters and opponents. The up-

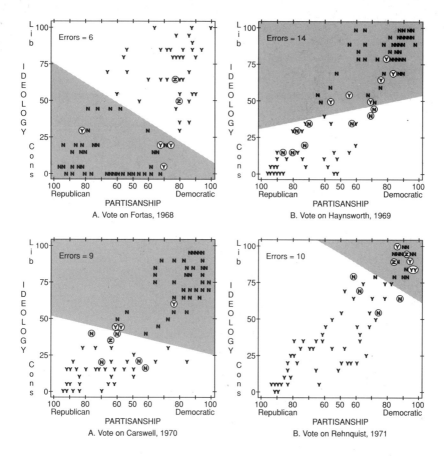

Figure 6.2 Confirmation Votes by Ideology and Partisanship, 1968–1971
The Ys and Ns in the charts represents the senators' yeas and nays regarding
whether the nominee should be confirmed. In the case of Fortas, the actual issue was not to confirm but to stop debate in order to vote on the confirmation.
The letter Z represents two or more senators with identical scores on the ideology and partisan variables but who voted differently regarding confirmation.
The shaded area represents a zone of opposition as specified by a probit statistical analysis using ideology and partisanship as predictors of the vote. Circled
letters indicate errors in the statistical prediction of senators' votes based on
their position on the ideology and partisanship variables.

Ideology is measured by the ADA voting score as provided by the Americans
for Democratic Action. Corrections are made according to the procedures indicated in Appendix D. A 100 represents having voted 100 percent of the time in
accordance with the position of the ADA, which defines the liberal position. A
0 indicates never voting in accordance with the position of the ADA, which defines the conservative position.

Partisanship is measured by the party support scores reported in the annual
editions of the *CQ Almanac*, published by Congressional Quarterly. *CQ* defines party support as voting with one's party on issues in which a majority of
voting Democrats opposed a majority of voting Republicans. We eliminated
nonvoting from affecting the scores. We also transformed the scale such that
the 50 in the middle indicates voting half the time with the Democrats and
half the time with the Republicans. Moving toward the right end of the scale
indicates how often one voted with the Democratic majority. Moving toward
the left indicates how often one voted with the Republican majority.

per-right quadrant consists of liberal partisan Democrats, who voted overwhelmingly for Fortas (Figure 6.2A) and overwhelmingly against Haynsworth and Carswell (Figures 6.2B and 6.2C). The lower-left quadrant, composed of conservative partisan Republicans, voted exactly the opposite. Thus, for the votes on Fortas, Haynsworth, and Carswell, the "no" votes begin broadly in one corner and move toward the middle. Only then, for the most part, do the votes begin to interweave as some in the middle area vote "yes" and others vote "no." Only in the Haynsworth vote (Figure 6.2B) do the opposition votes reach deeply into the more conservative and Republican corner of the ideological-partisanship graph.

The Rehnquist vote exhibits a different pattern. Some mixed voting is apparent even among liberal Democrats (the upper-right corner). In his case, the opposition simply could not muster the kind of case against Rehnquist necessary to attract all of those who typically voted in a liberal Democratic direction, let alone secure the numbers among the middle part of the ideological-partisanship space that would have been necessary to seriously contest the confirmation. It is interesting to observe that Rehnquist was the only one of these four nominations in which the opposition discourse relied almost totally upon an ideological appeal, namely the nominee's conservatism, yet this is the nomination that was least successful in mustering the solid support of the liberals in that cause. In fact, the nomination failed to gain even a single vote from the senators in the middle ground.

While the data are compelling in connecting ideology and partisanship with voting, it remains true that reasons other than ideology alone must be provided as justification for one's opposition—especially if the opposition has any hope of gaining the votes of those senators in the middle. There is a certain irony to the fact that the confirmation battles most sharply divided along partisan and ideological lines will ultimately be decided by those senators who are least influenced by ideological and partisan claims. By definition, those in the middle on party support are less drawn to partisan arguments and are more willing to vote against their own party majority. Moreover, these same individuals often fall in the middle on the ideology scale, indicating that their votes across a number of issues tend to cross ideological positions as well. In short, appeals to the liberalism or conservatism of the nominee or to partisan loyalties don't work very well with this middle group of senators who will ultimately tip the confirmation vote one way or another.

The Carswell nomination was predominantly an ideological battle in which the opposition took advantage of concerns over his competence and alleged racial bias—framed as a judicial temperament issue—to make inroads among the so-called moderates. The interleaving of both "yes" and "no" votes in this middle space illustrates how this argument was successful with some but not with others. Statistical analysis of the data reveals only nine errors in trying to say how senators would vote based only on their position on the ideological and partisanship factors, and five of those are right along the demarcation line where predicting or explaining senators' votes on the basis of ideology or partisanship is much more problematic.

The discourses in the Fortas and Haynsworth nominations, to the extent that they dealt with judicial ethics and conflicts of interest, were quite similar to each other. But make no mistake: The ethics charges against both of them had less to do with ethics and more to do with politics. As Robert Byrd pointed out in the Haynsworth hearings, the ethics charges were largely a smokescreen: "The real opposition is based on judicial philosophy, nothing more, nothing less; judicial philosophy, pure and simple" (Congress 1969, 34376). He was mostly correct, but what he failed to observe was that Haynsworth's support was also based on judicial philosophy or, more accurately, on political philosophy. Conservatives, largely Republican but with a number of southern Democrats, supported the Nixon nominees and opposed Abe Fortas, the Johnson nominee. Liberals, mostly Democrats but with some Republicans, typically supported Fortas while opposing the Nixon nominees.

Despite the similarities, the Haynsworth vote stands in curious contrast to that of Fortas. The respective demarcation of the zones of support and opposition for the two have very different looks. The Fortas nomination has the traditional demarcation line that cuts perpendicular through the lower-left to upper-right diagonal that characterizes the relationship between ideology and partisanship. Such a demarcation establishes the upper-right part of the graph as one zone and the lower left as the other. This pattern is consistent with an explanation that gives preeminence to ideology and partisanship as explanations of the vote. The fact that there are only six mistakes in the statistical effort to assign likely vote outcomes for Fortas supports the significance of those two factors

On the other hand, the most errors of any of the nominations (14) occur in the Haynsworth nomination. The demarcation line for the zones also takes a different angle than in the other three charts, somewhat more parallel with rather than perpendicular to the ideological-partisan diagonal of the senators. This different direction of demarcation is brought about by the failure of the partisanship variable to operate as it does in the other nominations. There were significant defections deep within the Republican party, which otherwise supported Haynsworth. There were also a few Democratic partisans who supported Haynsworth amid the more general opposition. These defections occurred in addition to the expected inter-leaving of support and opposition that occurs along the demarcation line of support and opposition.

These data suggest that ideology and partisanship actually had more to do with the Fortas outcome than with Haynsworth, making Senator Byrd's comment above actually more appropriate to the former than the latter. This also conforms with our earlier description of how Robert Griffin and certain other Republicans felt compelled to oppose Haynsworth after having publicly proclaimed their opposition to Fortas on ethical grounds just the previous year. Their votes, then, were not based on ideological or partisan criteria but either on conviction regarding the conflict of interest or out of a felt need to remain consistent in their public response to such charges.

After the Rehnquist appointment in 1971, there would be only one other Court vacancy for the remainder of the decade, and the potential for controversy had rarely been greater. However, with an appointment that illustrates how easily a president can diffuse a potentially controversial situation, Republican President Ford selected John Paul Stevens, who had immediate bipartisan support from liberal Democrats and conservative Republicans, diffusing any opposition that might have arisen in such a situation. With the election of Ronald Reagan and a Republican Senate in 1980, the political setting entered a period distinctly more favorable to the president. The O'Connor and Scalia appointments, in 1981 and 1986 respectively, occurred in those most favorable settings in which we expected and got unanimous confirmations.

At the same time as the Scalia nomination, however, Justice William Rehnquist was nominated by Reagan to be chief justice. In our measure of the nomination setting, the supposedly higher stakes of the chief justice position were sufficient to reduce the favorableness of the setting for the president from one of an almost certain unanimous confirmation to one that is open to some controversy. Just as with Fortas not quite 20 years earlier, Rehnquist became a sitting target for dissatisfaction with the direction of the Court. This time, of course, it was the liberals' turn to generate the opposition, but the basis for their opposition had really not changed since Rehnquist's initial appointment in 1971. Efforts to resurrect ethical charges of blatantly partisan behavior in working to disqualify minority Democratic voters in his early political days did not take hold any better in 1986 than in 1971. With no straightforward way to challenge Rehnquist's qualifications, the result was pretty much the same—substantial opposition (33 negatives) but with virtually no support from those senators in the middle of the ideological and partisanship continuums (see Figure 6.3A).

If the liberals managed to rally a third of the Senate into opposition in a political environment that was distinctly positive for the president, it was clear that the situation would become more combative after 1986, a year in which the Democrats reclaimed control of the Senate. In regaining that control, party and ideology became more synonymous than ever before, setting the stage for two of the most monumental battles over a Court nomination in our history—Robert Bork's nomination to replace Lewis Powell in 1987 and Clarence Thomas's succession to the legendary Thurgood Marshall. Both nominations were essentially a face-off between liberal Democrats and conservative Republicans, both of whom felt the other sought to politicize the Court. As the charts in Figure 6.3 show, whoever controlled the middle ground would win the confirmation battle.

The ability to assign likely vote outcomes of the senators based on ideology and partisanship is generally better in these three confirmation votes than the earlier ones from 1968 to 1971. This is almost surely a result of the more clear-cut alignment of ideology with partisanship. In addition, the discourse surrounding these nominations was more patently ideological in nature. There is a slow but perceptible increase in the willingness on the part of some senators to cast their opposition vote more openly in terms of philosophical differences with the nominee. Errors in the statistical assignment of likely vote outcomes based on senators' ideological and partisan positions produced five mistakes for Rehnquist, six for Thomas, and seven for Bork.

Minding One's Cues

Senators give a wonderfully diverse set of explanations to help account for their voting behaviors in Court confirmations, but rarely do these explanations allude to ideology or partisanship. The more sophisticated social science predictive models also include variables other than ideology and partisanship. Among the more prominent factors included in such predictions are constituency influence and advocacy-group activity (Segal, Cameron, and Cover 1992, 107–108). In addition, the explanations for voting in the Thomas confirmation that opened this chapter revealed other influences, including family members and fellow senators. Regardless of the various sources of influence, a common process is involved—that of taking cues from others to help inform the voting decision.

Ideology and partisanship are characteristics of the individual senators' psychological and behavioral state of mind. Cueing factors involve entities like other senators, advisors, constituents, advocacy groups, and the media. Senators do not collect information re-

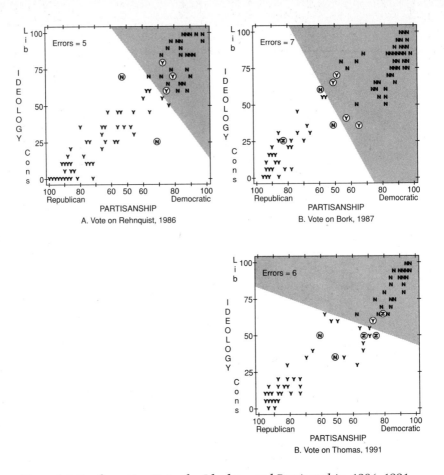

Figure 6.3 Confirmation Votes by Ideology and Partisanship, 1986–1991
The Ys and Ns in the charts represents the senators' yeas and nays regarding whether the nominee should be confirmed. The letter Z represents two or more senators with identical scores on the ideology and partisan variables but who voted differently regarding confirmation.

The shaded area represents a zone of opposition as specified by a probit statistical analysis using ideology and partisanship as predictors of the vote. Circled letters indicate errors in the statistical prediction of senators' vote based on their position on the ideology and partisanship variables.

Ideology is measured by the ADA voting score as provided by the Americans for Democratic Action. Corrections are made according to the procedures indicated in Appendix D. A 100 represents having voted 100 percent of the time in accordance with the position of the ADA, which defines the liberal position. A 0 indicates never voting in accordance with the position of the ADA, which defines the conservative position.

Partisanship is measured by the party support scores reported in the annual editions of the *CQ Almanac,* published by Congressional Quarterly. *CQ* defines party support as voting with one's party on issues in which a majority of voting Democrats opposed a majority of voting Republicans. We eliminated nonvoting from affecting the scores. We also transformed the scale such that the 50 in the middle indicates voting half the time with the Democrats and half the time with the Republicans. Moving toward the right end of the scale indicates how often one voted with the Democratic majority. Moving toward the left indicates how often one voted with the Republican majority.

garding a nominee in a vacuum and then process this information through their ideological and partisan filters to reach an independent, isolated judgment. Rather, they look to others to help them acquire, process, and evaluate information that will help them formulate a judgment about what to do.

While this appears to introduce a number of new variables into any prediction equation, it is also clear that ideology and partisanship are intimately involved in the selection and evaluation of cues. Various sources serve as cues in the first place because of their relevancy to ideological and partisan matters. Senators look to like-minded individuals for assistance, whether those individuals be advisors, constituent groups, advocacy groups, fellow senators, or others. Similarly, those who seek out senators to give their advice generally seek out senators they perceive will be receptive to the message, namely, those with similar ideological and partisan views.

Senators as Cues

> I am convinced after . . . talking to people I respect, who are strongly in support of this nomination, that Judge Thomas brings no personal agenda to the Court. I am referring specifically to Senator Danforth of Missouri. I do not know of any other individual in this chamber that I have more personal regard for in terms of the high standards that he demands not only of himself but of the people who work with him. In large measure I have turned to Jack Danforth to tell me about the character of Judge Thomas.
>
> William Cohen

This frank admission of reliance upon another senator as the basis for interpreting the debate surrounding a Supreme Court nominee (Congress 1991, S14683) points up the importance of one's fellow senators as sources of information and influence.[2] The Bush administration, more than any other before it, made strong use of a Senate sponsor for the nominee. For David Souter, Senator Warren Rudman took the initiative to such an extent that the two never seemed to be apart. Missouri Senator John Danforth, for whom Clarence Thomas had worked at one time, labored tirelessly as Thomas's campaign manager, press secretary, and cheerleader all rolled into one. In the absence of such support, Souter may have taken more heat and Thomas may well have lost. Both senators

---

[2] It is probably worth noting that William Cohen had not yet been appointed to the Senate Judiciary Committee by the time of the Thomas appointment. Committee members are more likely to speak of their own assessment of the nominee rather than of their reliance on others.

were well respected by their colleagues, and their careful and successful handling of the nominations surely recommends this strategy to future presidents who fear Senate opposition to a nominee.

There is simply no doubt that peer influence is an important factor in legislative voting behavior (Kingdon 1989). Controversial Supreme Court nominations are decided only through the considerable efforts of a relatively few senators to persuade their colleagues.[3] In this respect the Judiciary Committee vote is especially critical. Most senators are not that familiar with the pros and cons of a nominee's record and qualifications. There is considerable dependence on the Judiciary Committee to establish the basis of support for or opposition to the nominee. Indeed, *the* major function of the confirmation hearings is to create a record that can serve as a handle for senators to grasp in support of their vote.

It is not necessarily the committee vote outcome that is the most significant factor, however. The Judiciary Committee reported favorable votes for Clement Haynsworth (10 to 7) and for Harrold Carswell (13 to 4), two Nixon nominees who lost support at the full Senate level with 45 to 55 and 44 to 52, respectively. Senators look instead to the votes of particular committee senators as cues. In those two nominations, opposition surfaced from liberals on the committee, who represented only a minority on the committee but who networked with the controlling liberal majority in the Senate as a whole. Moreover, even though the committee vote in the Carswell nomination was formally 13 to 4 to forward the nomination to the full Senate, 2 of the 13 refused to endorse the majority report in support of the nomination by noting that the purpose of their votes was to forward the nomination to the full Senate.

One of those two was Republican Charles Mathias, who submitted an individual report that became part of the committee record (see page 169). The clear signal from Mathias was that he had considerable doubt about this nomination and likely would vote to reject Carswell. One does not raise questions about a nominee's competency and qualifications if he has resolved such issues in favor of the nominee. Indeed, Mathias was one of two moderate Re-

---

[3] The flavor of senators' efforts to win confirmation battles is best captured in writings about specific nominations. For Fortas, read Bruce Allen Murphy's *Fortas: The Rise and Ruin of a Supreme Court Justice* (1988). For Carswell, see Richard Harris's *Decision* (1971). For Bork, read Ethan Bronner's *Battle for Justice: How the Bork Nomination Shook America* (1989); Patrick McGuigan and Dawn Weyrich's *Ninth Justice: The Fight for Bork* (1990); and Mark Gitenstein's *Matters of Principle: An Insider's Account of America's Rejection of Robert Bork's Nomination to the Supreme Court* (1992). For Thomas, read *Capitol Games: Clarence Thomas, Anita Hill, and the Story of a Supreme Court Nomination* (1992) by Timothy M. Phelps and Helen Winternitz.

publicans from the committee who ultimately were joined by 11 other Republicans in opposition to Carswell.

More recently, in the 1980s and early 1990s Senators DeConcini and Heflin may have served as cues to the relatively conservative Democrats both in the South and elsewhere. A "no" vote from these two committee members alerted certain senators that a nominee might have some disturbing traits that deserved their attention and consideration. Similarly, Republican Senator Arlen Specter surely served as a cue to moderate and liberal Republicans. During the Reagan and Bush administrations, a "no" vote from Specter signaled trouble; a "yes" vote was more reassuring for those whose natural inclination was to support the president.

There's no reliable way to determine which Judiciary Committee senators may serve as cues to which other members of the Senate short of asking each of them. We can, however, effectively analyze the frequency with which senators vote together.[4] Figure 6.4 illustrates such an analysis in 1969 during the year of the Haynsworth vote. Particularly noteworthy in this analysis is cluster group 5, a relatively small grouping of five Republican moderates, four of whom voted against Haynsworth. A key figure of that group was Judiciary Committee member and Republican Minority Whip Robert Griffin, who was one of two Republicans (Mathias was the other) to oppose Haynsworth in the committee vote. In a grouping that otherwise could have been expected to support their Republican president's nominee, Senator Griffin almost surely took some Republicans with him in deciding to oppose the nomination. In the subsequent Carswell nomination, a different four out of those five, including Griffin, cast their votes in favor of Carswell.

Recall that our earlier analysis of the Haynsworth vote produced the least satisfactory estimate of voting outcomes based on ideology and partisanship with 14 errors in assigning votes based on those two factors. The table in Figure 6.4 reveals only seven senators departing from the majority in their respective clusters, a number that drops to six when ideology and partisanship are joined with the voting clusters. For the Haynsworth nomination, then, cue voting may have played a very significant role in the outcome. Later in the Bork nomination, which had seven errors when using only ideology and

---

[4] We apply to the ADA vote record for the Senate in 1969 Ward's cluster analysis technique utilizing SPSS-X 3.0 on an IBM 3090. We ultimately chose to work with a six-cluster solution, which was the maximum number in most nomination years that had at least one Judiciary Committee member in each cluster. Moreover, beginning with the 1980s, the six clusters produced groups that could clearly be designated as representing conservative, moderate, and liberal groups of each of the two parties.

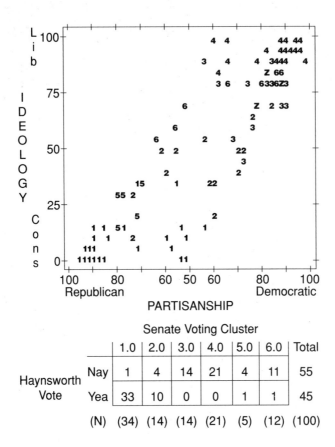

	1.0	2.0	3.0	4.0	5.0	6.0	Total
Nay	1	4	14	21	4	11	55
Yea	33	10	0	0	1	1	45
(N)	(34)	(14)	(14)	(21)	(5)	(12)	(100)

Figure 6.4 Senate Voting Clusters in the Haynsworth Nomination
In the chart, ideology is measured as the percentage of time that a senator
voted in accordance with the position advocated by the liberal Americans for
Democratic Action. See Appendix D for details on the ADA measure. Partisanship is measured as the percentage of time one supports either the Democrats
or Republicans on issues in which a majority of voting Democrats opposed a
majority of voting Republicans. The 50 in the middle indicates voting half the
time with the Democrats and half the time with the Republicans. Moving toward the right end of the scale indicates how often one voted with the Democratic majority for those who most often voted with the Democrats. Moving toward the left indicates how often one voted with the Republican majority for
those who most often voted with the Republicans.
The numbers 1 through 6 in the body of the chart represent the six voting clusters defined by a statistical procedure known as *cluster analysis*. It was performed on the votes identified by the ADA as key votes for the purpose of creating its scale. Senators could have nearly identical scores on ideology and
partisanship yet still be in different clusters. For example, two senators could
have scores of 50 on the ADA scale without having voted the same way on any
of the issues. Cluster analysis attempts to group together individuals who have
very similar voting behaviors. See note 6 in this chapter. The letter Z in the
chart identifies where two or more senators with identical ideology and partisanship scores belong to different clusters.

partisanship as the predictors, the addition of the six-cluster cueing factor reduced the number of prediction errors to only three.

Cueing on other senators, even when it moves the explanation beyond the sole effects of ideology and partisanship, nonetheless reinforces the importance of those two factors to the decision-making process because senators take cues from colleagues who are essentially like minded. These voting clusters are based largely on the similarities of ideological and partisan views. Senator Terry Sanford spoke to us of having consulted with Judiciary Committee member Patrick Leahy regarding the Bork and Thomas nominations. Both were situated in 1991 in a liberal Democratic cluster of 35 Democrats, all of whom opposed the Thomas nomination.

The significance of William Cohen's use of Danforth as a major cueing source, as quoted above, is that Cohen is one of a handful of rather liberal Republicans—only five in the 1991 cluster analysis. Thomas opponents needed to make inroads with this group to offset the "yes" votes to be cast by southern Democrats. Danforth, on the other hand, fell in a cluster of distinctly more conservative Republicans, though perhaps still moderate by Republican standards. Nonetheless, three of those five liberal Republican votes went to Thomas. While it would be easy and perhaps correct to credit the cueing power of Danforth and perhaps Arlen Specter, the moderate to liberal Republican member of the Judiciary Committee at that time, it remains true that Cohen and his liberal Republican colleague, Mark Hatfield, also supported Robert Bork in a nomination where other liberal Republicans voted against him.

In the final analysis, then, what determined Cohen's vote? As a relatively liberal Republican with a relatively low record of voting support for the Republican party, Cohen may have been swung in the direction of opposing Thomas. Cohen reported that sentiment in his state seemed to be running against Thomas. However, Cohen is also one who seems to look for reasons to support the nominations of Republican presidents, as he did with Bork. In the end, only two Republicans opposed their president's nomination of Clarence Thomas. The pressure was on and it came to Cohen through the person of Jack Danforth, but it came because Cohen was in a partisan and ideological position that made him simultaneously susceptible to the pleas of Thomas supporters while not really requiring all that much persuasion in the first place.

Constituency Cues

Public opinion has never been considered particularly influential in Supreme Court nominations. To the extent that this is true, it is because nominations do not often command the attention of the public. As observed in Chapter 4, nominees are usually unknown to the public, and unless advocacy groups generate opposition, the salience of a nomination will remain low among most senators' constituencies. Voters remain largely ignorant about the qualifications of any particular nominee, and opinions are often split and not intensely held. Such situations presumably give senators some slack in toeing the constituency line, permitting them to vote their own rather than the constituency's preference, a situation sometimes referred to as *shirking* (Kalt and Zupan 1990).

Contributing to any tendency of senators to shirk from constituency opinion is the six-year term of office. The late Senator Hubert Humphrey is quoted as saying, "The first four years are for God and country; the last two are for the folks back home" (Elling 1982, 75). Indeed, there is evidence that representatives with two year terms more nearly reflect constituency opinion than do those with longer terms (Kuklinski 1978). Other evidence suggests that senators are more likely to moderate their voting behavior as election time nears (Elling 1982). A somewhat more refined assessment reveals that senators seem to reflect views of their own party constituents during periods when reelection is not imminent, while an upcoming election leads senators to move away from the party position in states where the party is not dominant while remaining with the party view in those states where the party is dominant (Shapiro et al. 1990).

It is hardly a new thought that there is more than one constituency for an elected representative (Huntington 1950). For a senator, the state electorate represents the geographical constituency. Senators attend to the needs of this constituency when they engage in activities designed to benefit the general welfare of the state or engage in specific work in behalf of a single constituent. There is sufficient diversity of opinion in most states, however, that this geographical constituency of voters cannot be considered to hold a single view on an issue. By definition, of course, the term *issue* denotes some division of opinion. When opinion is divided, senators are most likely to take positions that are consistent with their electoral constituency, those voters who support the senator at election time (Clausen 1973; Markus 1974). A considerable portion of that constituency is inevitably found within the senator's own political party (Shapiro et al. 1990). Consequently, analyses of senatorial voting behavior will show high correlations between those votes and partisan measures of the constituency (Carson and Oppenheimer 1984; Kalt and Zupan 1990).

Constituency is even more complex than this two-level model. Senators can face threats to reelection from within their own party as well as from opposition-party candidates. In 1992, Senator Arlen

Specter had to fend off conservative opposition from within his own party in Pennsylvania's primary election. Liberal advocates who attempt to explain how Senator Arlen Specter could change from a firm antagonist in the Bork nomination to the outspoken protagonist in behalf of Clarence Thomas and inquisitor of Anita Hill inevitably focus on his 1992 reelection needs. Expecting tough conservative Republican opposition in the primary, Specter's ADA score dropped from an 80 to a 40 between the Bork and Thomas nominations, and his party support score in voting with fellow Republicans increased from 44 to 63 percent. There is little doubt in the minds of these observers that Specter was positioning himself for his primary reelection campaign. At the same time, he had to be mindful that moving to the right to help ensure a victory in the Republican primary could work against him in the general election against a more liberal Democrat. Specter ultimately did win reelection but only by a very narrow margin against a female Democratic candidate who did in fact make an issue of Specter's role in the Anita Hill phase of the Thomas hearings.

The linkage between senators and their constituencies is a complex one from the standpoint of knowing in which instances and in what ways constituency may influence the senators' decisions. Generally, we can say that there is a reasonably close match between a particular electoral constituency and the senator they elect. People try to elect like-minded legislators. Legislators, in turn, have a vested interest in establishing a reputation that permits their electoral constituencies to identify them as representatives of the people. For outspoken liberals and conservatives, voting decisions in the face of controversy can be fairly clear-cut. Liberals may safely oppose a conservative nominee; conservatives may safely oppose a liberal nominee. They want to and their electoral constituency expects them to. So has the constituency been influential in such a vote? Probably not, but the statistical correlation will support the assumption of constituency influence for those who wish to assert it.

A senator in the middle, with no consistent ideological bias, cannot base a decision explicitly on ideological grounds. It is inconsistent with that self-constructed image of being nonideological. More often than not, such a senator is trying to build an electoral constituency that crosses partisan and ideological lines. Such a senator must therefore establish a viable position of virtual nonpartisanship regarding nominations. This can be done, in part, by asserting the president's prerogative, which carries the subliminal message not to expect opposition to a nomination. Another part of a moderate's strategy is to defer judgment on a nomination until all of the evidence is in and a careful assessment of the nominee's credentials and qualifications can be made. In these ways, the moderate senator hopes to avoid alienating potential supporters while promoting an image of fairness and nonpartisan thoughtfulness.

It is these senators in the middle who must pay closer attention to constituency opinion while recognizing at the same time that they themselves influence constituency opinion. The Bork and Thomas nominations began more or less typically, with more than two-thirds of the electorate expressing no opinion on or awareness of the nominee even a couple of months after the announcement of the nomination. However, by the time the Judiciary Committee voted, polls estimated that more than three-fourths of the electorate were now prepared to express an opinion (ABC and *Washington Post* 1991b; Hugick 1991a; Gallup 1987, 221, 241; NBC and *Wall Street Journal* 1987). The outpouring of constituency concern was reflected in a flood of phone calls and mail that inundated the offices of a number of senators and, in the case of Bork, particularly those of the presumably "undecided" senators on the Judiciary Committee. That level of attention, even if driven by advocacy groups, does get the attention of the senator.

There is little doubt that the newly elected southern Democratic senators were influenced by polls that indicated a preference for rejecting Bork, especially among those segments of voters who constituted the electoral constituency of these Democratic senators, namely, blacks and urban whites. On the other hand, polls concerning Thomas reflected an ambivalence among blacks as well as whites regarding his confirmation. These southern senators who defeated Bork ultimately voted to confirm Thomas (Overby et al. 1992).

The question of constituency influence has a normative side as well as an empirical one. Those who argue against "undue" pressure by constituents work from the presumption that public opinion can be manipulated by special-interest and political appeals. The end result is politicization of the judiciary through the tyranny of public opinion. Conversely, to argue that constituency opinion should not be considered has a distinctly antidemocratic ring. As Felix Frankfurter noted in writing about the nomination of Charles Evans Hughes to be chief justice, "In theory, judges wield the people's power. Through the effective exertion of public opinion, the people should determine to whom that power is entrusted" (Frankfurter and Landis 1928, 185–186).

Other Cues

Senators and the electoral constituency are not the only sources of cues for senators. We have alluded already to the activities of advocacy groups and their representatives and to the tendency of senators to solicit the views of trusted advisors familiar with the Court and oftentimes with the nominee. The influence of these cues, along with those of family and confidants, cannot help but affect a senator's perception of the nomination. Senators don't need to be mathematical wizards to calculate how the support or opposition of different advocacy groups will add up in terms of a gain or loss of popularity in response to their voting decisions.

For most senators, the vast majority of these cues are mutually reinforcing. Liberal senators are more likely to interact with and trust liberal cue sources. Conservative senators are more likely to seek out and to be sought out by other conservatives. Those in the middle are more likely to be targets from both sides and to have varied cue sources. For them, any controversial nomination is likely to become an adventure, though not a welcome one. Their ultimate individual decisions are likely to represent some combination of cue sources that tip the balance one way or another.

For southern Democrats in the Bork nomination, strong constituency pressures were reinforced by the opposition advocacy groups who heightened the intensity of that pressure in conjunction with assertive leadership within the Senate, particularly from Louisiana Senator Bennett Johnston (Gitenstein 1992, 276–291). Reporter Ethan Bronner writes that at a meeting with four of the new southern Democratic senators, the three-term veteran reportedly turned to Richard Shelby and said,

> "Shelby you're not going to vote for Bork. You know why? Because you're not going to turn your back on 91 percent of the black voters in Alabama who got you here." Then Johnston pointed at others at the table and said, "I know how you're going to vote, and you, and you, and you." (Bronner 1989, 286)

And to a person they voted as he predicted.

This convergence of cues plays back into the significance of ideology and partisanship. Those two factors structure the types of cue sources that will surround a senator. They will structure a senator's perception and interpretation of events and information involving the nomination. They will structure the ultimate decision regarding the confirmation vote.

The Individual Decision

The confirmation decision for senators involves a series of steps taken in interaction with the other political actors involved in the process. Ideally, senators would prefer to have a Supreme Court justice appointed that reflects their own views about the Court, constitutional law, and justice. However, senators also recognize the constitutional prerogative of the president to make the appointment, and most senators have a default status that they will vote to confirm the nomination in the absence of information that would place the nominee outside their zone of support.

This default status of confirmation support stems in part from time-management considerations. Such a "rule" eases the problem of evaluating in detail each of the hundreds of nominations that pass through the Senate each session. There is no reason to spend much time assessing a nominee who doesn't generate controversy. Such a decisional rule further serves to justify one's vote to the constituency and to minimize others' expectations concerning the likelihood of influencing the senator's vote and consequently lowering the salience of appointments to constituent activists. Especially for those senators nearer the middle of the ideological-partisan continuum, the default status helps to lower expectations about getting that particular senator to oppose a nomination unless evidence to support opponents' claims is quite persuasive.

The tension between the default decisional rule and a senator's ideological-partisan preference for a like-minded justice also occurs within the context of a senator's desire to be reelected. To the extent that a confirmation vote will affect the senator's constituency with sufficient impact to imperil reelection, then the default position and/or the ideological-partisan preference may give way for political expediency to drive the confirmation decision.

No nominations occur outside ideological-partisan considerations. Those nominations that do not seem to raise ideological or partisan issues do so not from an avoidance of those concerns but from a balancing of them. Nominations occur within the ideological-partisan space we depicted earlier in Box 6.1. Each senator in the space has a zone of acceptability. A nominee perceived to be in that zone will be supported (see Figure 6.5). Unanimously confirmed nominees, then, are those who are perceived by all sides as neither too ideological nor too partisan in the direction of the opposition, as indicated by the shaded area of the figure.

Locating the nominee in the space does not represent the nominee's party loyalty or ideology. Rather, it designates how a senator with those levels of party support and ideological commitment perceives the attractiveness of the nominee. In reality, the location of the nominee is not a single point. A nominee is perceived differently by different people. The nominee's position in a partisan-ideology space will vary as represented by the nominee rectangle in Figure 6.5, dependent upon the success of efforts by opposing forces to define the nominee's spatial location. That definition is what the nomination discourse is largely about. The minimum ideal point

for either side is one that will attract at least a majority of the senators. For an essentially conservative nominee, as depicted here, the
goal of conservatives is to frame the nominee as sufficiently moderate and well qualified as to be within the acceptable space of a majority of the Senate. Liberal opponents to a conservative nominee
would try to characterize the nominee as falling in the far lower left

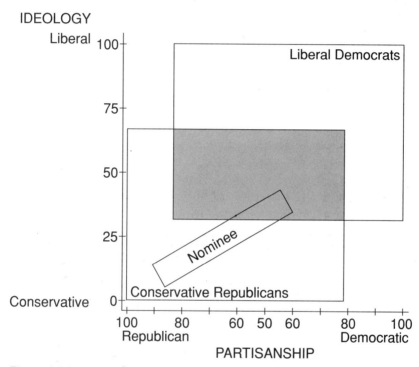

Figure 6.5 Locating the Nominee in the Ideological Partisan
Space of Senators

ADA score is the percentage of time a senator voted in accordance with positions taken by the Americans for Democratic Action (ADA 1987) (see Appendix D). Partisanship is calculated as the percentage of recorded votes in which
senators voted with their party from among those votes where a majority of
voting Democrats opposed a majority of voting Republicans. The 50 in the
middle indicates voting half the time with the Democrats and half the time
with the Republicans. Moving toward the right indicates how often one voted
with the Democrats; moving toward the left indicates how often one voted
with the Republicans.
Liberal Democrats identifies a senator at the extremes of the liberal ideological
and Democratic partisan continuums. Conservative Republicans identifies a
senator at the extremes of the conservative ideological and Republican partisan
continuums. Each resides in a rectangle that represents the zone of acceptability for a Supreme Court nominee. The shaded overlap of the two represents
mutually acceptable space. The Nominee rectangle represents the range of perceptions and characterizations of the nominee.

of the range of perceptions, presumably outside of the acceptable space of a majority of the Senate.

A key senator in the 1987 confirmation battle over Bork was Dennis DeConcini, a moderate Democrat from Arizona. His vote against Bork, both in the Judiciary Committee and subsequently on the floor of the Senate, sums up much of the individual decision-making calculus we have been talking about.

Why did Dennis DeConcini vote against the confirmation of Robert Bork? The senator explained his vote as a careful consideration of the testimony that left him in doubt concerning Bork's commitment to equal protection. A prominent anti-Bork activist in Arizona who is a friend of DeConcini credited his vote to the concerted and persuasive efforts of the local constituency. One Washington lobbyist suggested his vote was the result of strong opposition to Bork by Susie DeConcini, the senator's wife. Certain pro-Bork activists, including one of DeConcini's fellow Judiciary Committee members, explained his vote in terms of a cruder pressure, namely, that of labor leaders in Arizona who vowed to produce primary opposition to DeConcini in his upcoming 1988 reelection effort. On the other hand, the basic Senate voting model simply notes that DeConcini is a Democrat and an ideological moderate, a combination likely to oppose Bork in this ideological and partisan battle (Poole and Rosenthal 1991, 264–267).

For Senator DeConcini, the decision to oppose the confirmation of Robert Bork was not an easy one. First, he was faced with his personal default decisional rule regarding presidential nominations, which is to defer to the president unless there is an especially strong case for not doing so. In other nominations, the default has served him well. With Scalia, there was no buildup of controversy at all. O'Connor and Rehnquist were fellow Arizonans, a factor sufficient in itself to justify his confirmation support, even though DeConcini's position in the ideological-partisan space for 1986 would have predicted opposition to Rehnquist. There was insufficient controversy surrounding the nomination of David Souter to raise the expectations of any Arizona activist that DeConcini might oppose the nomination. Those low expectations also meant that DeConcini suffered no real loss of support, since his position on such relatively noncontroversial nominations is well defined.

The Bork nomination was different. There would be no default "yes" position in this confirmation vote. An evaluation on the merits of the nominee would be required. DeConcini looked to a number of cue givers, probably all of those mentioned above, for assistance in locating Bork in that middle ideological and partisan space that DeConcini occupies. His middle ground on ideological and partisan measures was indicative of his fragile constituency in Arizona. In a conservative state fairly evenly split between Democrats and Republicans, a Democrat cannot win statewide without some Republican support while attracting both liberal and conservative Democrats. DeConcini's moderate position came from deciding individual issues on grounds that do not reflect a consistent ideological or partisan direction.

To appeal to those senators like DeConcini, conservative Republicans needed to portray Bork as more centrist and liberal than many really believed him to be—toward the upper right into the zone of acceptability as illustrated by Figure 6.5—at least far enough to get the conservative and moderate Democrats as well as hold the liberal Republicans. Liberal Democrats, of course, tried to drive the perception of Bork toward the lower left, out of the zone of acceptability for DeConcini and other moderate to conservative Democrats and liberal Republicans. Given a rather large tolerance on the part of most senators for liberal or conservative justices, liberal Democrats had to frame Bork as more doctrinairely conservative than many actually believed him to be, outside the mainstream of American judicial thought.

To argue to DeConcini that Bork was merely conservative would not move him. Senators who cross ideological lines in their own voting behavior are pretty tolerant of both liberals and conservatives. It is likely, however, that these senators who occupy the middle ideological and partisan ground also see themselves as occupying such middle ground and consider it a reflection of the mainstream of American political life. To argue that a nominee is so conservative or so liberal that he is outside the mainstream is one way to gain the consideration of those senators in the middle. Such an argument places a heavy burden on those making the outside-the-mainstream argument. The nominee has only to show that he or she appears reasonably open minded and considerate of arguments from both sides of a question to demonstrate that he or she is sufficiently mainstream to rebut the claim of extremism.

Having claimed that senators in the middle are less susceptible to ideological and partisan claims, let it nevertheless clearly be understood that their evaluation of these claims will still be colored by their propensities to affiliate more with one side than another. Senator DeConcini's ADA score of 60 and Democratic party support score of 73 suggested that he could more easily accept liberal Democratic claims that someone was too conservative rather than conservative Republican claims that someone was too liberal.

DeConcini's ideological-partisan position was consistent with his explanation of his vote. For DeConcini, Bork was too conservative on the Fourteenth Amendment, an issue dear to the senator's heart and more generally dearer to the hearts of liberals than conservatives. Whether or not DeConcini's placement of Bork as out-side the senator's zone of acceptability resulted from the framing ef-forts of opposition activists, his wife, his own biases, or some other factor cannot really be determined. The various factors are so inter-twined and mutually reinforcing that not even the senator is likely to know how they all served to structure his decision.

It may well be that his vote reflected some convergence of these potential sources of influence. There was significant local con-stituency opposition from groups typically supportive of the sena-tor in Arizona, and the senator was well aware of that fact—espe-cially with his reelection time nearing in the following year. There is no doubt that Susie DeConcini opposed the confirmation of Bork and that the senator and she had discussed the nomination. We find less credible the evidence to support the claim by certain Bork sup-porters that DeConcini responded to an electoral threat from labor leaders in Arizona. Quite frankly, the status of the labor movement in Arizona, even in the more narrow politics of the Democratic party, casts that as a pretty weak threat. It makes more sense to place the labor movement with the other advocates as one of sev-eral voices calling for Bork's defeat. Finally, it comes down to the senator. He, as did many others, took his vote seriously, especially given his position on the Judiciary Committee. It placed him in the position of reading over the considerable claims of both sides and of interacting personally with the nominee. Our experience with the senator convinces us that he could have been persuaded to support Bork but that the burden DeConcini normally lays on the opposi-tion now rested on the nominee himself, a burden that Bork was unable to bear.

Epilogue

Once the vote is concluded, it is typically on to the next issue for the senators—business as usual. A nomination is just another battle in a continuing civil war that pits ideological and partisan views against each other. But it *is* a "civil" war. Feelings get hurt and egos get bruised, but wounds usually heal quickly, at least among those senators who understand the legislative game. Antagonists Kennedy and Hatch, Simpson and Metzenbaum, and Biden and Thurmond move on to other issues, some of which they will join together as fellow protagonists. On other issues, they will renew their opposition.

On the other hand, each of these battles also exacts a toll. It was evident at the hearings for Anthony Kennedy that the Bork battle had left some unhealed scars. And if there were scars from the Bork battle, the Thomas hearings were an absolute war. Nasty exchanges between Hatch and Biden, Kennedy and Specter, and others may have permanently damaged some working relationships. Changes in the makeup of the committee have already begun and many more will come before the turn of the century.

While senators generally would like to put the rancor of a controversial nomination behind them, there are constituents and political opponents who would not. The controversy generated by the Thomas-Hill confrontation deeply affected certain political landscapes. "All of the meetings of the women's movement over the past twenty years . . . didn't have the impact of that Judiciary Committee photo," according to Ann Lewis, a Democratic political consultant (CQ 1992, 3269). The image of an all-male Judiciary Committee sitting in judgment of Anita Hill's sexual harassment charge encouraged a number of the record 11 women who competed in elections for the Senate in 1992. One of them, Carol Moseley-Braun, now sits on that Judiciary Committee.

In what manner confirmation hearings will change remains to be seen. We can be reasonably certain, however, that while the politics of the Supreme Court appointment process may change, the fact that the process is political will not.

CHAPTER SEVEN

Nomination Politics: A Reprise and a Foreword

> The scenes from the Senate bore little resemblance to the tidy leg-islative process that we all studied in school and we describe to our children, now, maybe to our grandchildren. . . . And the process seemed unreal, more like a satire than like the govern-ment in which all of you, in which I, take so much pride, more like a burlesque show than a civics class.
>
> *President George Bush*

> The root of the current collapse of the confirmation process is the administration's campaign to make the Supreme Court the agent of an ultraconservative social agenda which lacks support in the Congress or in the country.
>
> *Senator Joseph Biden*

The previous six chapters reprise the old adage that the more things change the more they stay the same. Certainly, the way in which the constitutional system of selecting justices actually operates has changed significantly over the years. Television has become an im-portant participant; the Judiciary Committee has emerged as a pre-eminent determinant of nominee qualifications; and participation by general-interest groups like the AFL-CIO has been supplemented by advocacy groups that are specifically interested in the nomina-tion process. However, what has not changed is the underlying real-ity that the nomination process is and always has been political. Presidents have always selected nominees on the basis of their po-litical and legal philosophy. Similarly, the Senate has always fac-tored political concerns into its calculus of whether to oppose or support a nominee. Finally, there have always been political groups and advocates who were interested in the nomination process and sought to influence it.

In this chapter we first summarize the politics of the current nomination process. Then, against the backdrop of constancy and change in that process, we briefly catalog and evaluate various pro-

posals that have been offered to "reform" the way we select
Supreme Court justices.

Supreme Court Nominations as a Spectator Sport

Throughout this book we have tried to portray the complex web of
political interactions that define a Supreme Court nomination. In
so doing, we have relied upon numerous historical examples. However, if we have achieved our goal, we have also provided at least a
rudimentary framework for understanding future nominations as
they occur.

As you read this chapter, assume that you hear on the radio that
a current member of the Supreme Court has decided to retire. What
should you watch for as the nomination process unfolds over the
next few months? The most important question to ask is whether
this nomination will become controversial, that is, will there be
substantial opposition to the nomination or will the nominee be
easily confirmed by the Senate. The discussion in the previous six
chapters suggests three interrelated processes that must be kept in
mind and observed in order to understand whether a nomination
will become controversial. The processes are (1) the nomination
setting, (2) the basic realities of the nomination process, and (3) the
ongoing discourse about the nominee.

The Nomination Setting

As discussed in Chapter 2, the content of the nomination discourse
will be initially influenced by the situation at the time of a vacancy.
Therefore, an initial factor to consider when a vacancy is announced
is how favorable the current political situation is to the president. If
the president's party controls the Senate, if the Senate seems largely
supportive of the president's policies, if public opinion seems favorable to the president, and if there are no characteristics about the vacancy that will raise the normal level of concern about the nomination, then the potential for controversy is considerably dampened.

On the other hand, to the extent that any of these factors are
not favorable to the president, then a breeding ground for opposition to the nominee is established. As the political setting becomes
less and less favorable to the president, the potential for a controversial nomination is substantially increased. So the first step in
watching the nomination process is to ask how strong is the president's current position and, therefore, how fertile is the ground for
the emergence of opposition to a nominee.

The Basic Realities of the Nomination Process

It is an accepted reality of modern politics that a Supreme Court nomination can become truly controversial only if the nominee is perceived as unqualified in some way. We have given numerous examples of how presidents in unfavorable settings have avoided controversy by selecting a nominee widely respected as having suitable stature for the Supreme Court. However, we have also argued that nominee qualifications are a political and social construct. The definition and perception of qualifications are politically motivated. It is this discontinuity between the political basis of nominee opposition and the rationales that are presented to justify that opposition on the basis of the nominee's "qualifications" that is the Rosetta stone of the modern nomination process.

As the nomination process unfolds, it is paramount to remember that the president, senators, advocacy groups, and media will engage in a discourse about the nominee in which each of them seeks not merely to "find" the truth about the nominee's qualifications but rather to "create" that truth. Therefore, the key to watch for in the nomination process is the emergence and effectiveness of negative characterizations of the nominee's qualifications. In the absence of the development of a negative discourse, the nomination will likely move easily to confirmation.

The Nomination Discourse

While the potential for nomination conflict is originally shaped by the political setting at the time of the vacancy, the final resolution of the nomination depends upon an ongoing discourse about the qualifications of the nominee. This discourse has four distinct but interrelated stages that need to be observed in order to understand the ultimate outcome of the nomination.

Presidential Selection and Justification

Chapter 3 showed that by selecting a particular nominee a president can expand or reduce the opportunity for negative discourse that is inherent in the nomination setting. Similarly, the way in which the president describes a nominee serves to set the initial tone of the nomination discourse. For example, does the president seek to emphasize the nominee's background, as President Bush did in announcing the Clarence Thomas nomination, or the nominee's "objective merit" as President Reagan did in announcing the Robert Bork nomination? Therefore, when the nominee is announced, we ought to pay special attention to the experience of the nominee and the way in which the president chooses to frame the nomination.

The Interim Period

Our examples in Chapter 4 demonstrated that the immediate responses to a nominee by advocacy groups, the media, senators, and others indicate whether controversy is forthcoming. They also provide clues as to the key qualification issues that will animate the remainder of the discourse. Overwhelming positive reaction to the nominee at this stage may discourage opposition and signal a noncontroversial nomination. The careful observer ought to be able to have some inkling of what is to come based on these early reactions.

The portion of the interim period between the initial reaction to the nominee and the beginning of Senate consideration is dominated by advocacy groups and media who attempt to "define" the nominee. For unknown nominees this period is characterized by digging activities. For better-known nominees it is devoted to decisions of whether to support, oppose, or remain neutral toward the nominee and the appropriate implementations of those decisions through framing and spinning techniques. By the end of this period, there is usually a good indication of whether controversy will emerge and, if it will, what the focus of that controversy will be.

The Judiciary Committee

In modern times, as Chapter 5 demonstrated, the Judiciary Committee exercises the formal responsibility for evaluating and defining the nominee's qualifications. The character of the definitional process, however, is strongly affected by the media and advocacy-group activity during the interim period. If no substantial opposition has emerged during the interim period, the nomination is unlikely to become controversial in the Judiciary Committee. However, if controversy has arisen, the committee then becomes the focal point of the discourse. While the confirmation hearings will provide the most public forum for the discourse, important clues as to the likely outcome will emerge in the days and weeks immediately before the hearings when the senators begin to stake out their positions and indicate what roles they will play at the hearings.

If controversy has emerged, the Judiciary Committee vote will likely fall along partisan and ideological lines. The observer ought to pay particular attention to these lines because they will be helpful in predicting the number and types of senators who will oppose the nominee in the full Senate.

The Full Senate

The perception of the nominee's qualifications held by a majority of the Senate ultimately determines the nominee's fate. As discussed in Chapter 6, however, the Judiciary Committee has served an important cueing role for the full Senate in recent years. A strongly positive Judiciary Committee will rarely be followed by major conflict in the Senate. Conversely, a controversial outcome in the Judiciary Committee ensures a similar fate in the Senate. When a nomination is controversial, it is useful to examine which senators on the Judiciary Committee supported and which opposed the nomination. What is the political party affiliation of those who opposed or supported? What is the ideology of those senators? These factors provide important clues to the voting of similarly situated members of the full Senate.

In a truly close nomination it is particularly important to look for various key swing votes in the Senate. These are often moderates who are not strongly partisan. Their very moderation makes predicting their votes more problematic, but the outcome of the nomination will depend on the way these senators choose to vote.

What's Ahead?

With the assumption of the presidency by Bill Clinton in 1993, a period of divided government, in which one party held the presidency and the other controlled the Senate, came to an end. The control by the Democratic party of both constitutional actors in the appointment process provided the potential to reduce the level of nomination controversy considerably. It is true that united government does not guarantee success, as evident for example with Lyndon Johnson's failure with Abe Fortas in 1968. However, President Clinton revealed a Supreme Court appointment style of making greater concessions than required by his nomination settings in an effort to avoid any opposition, let alone controversy, in his first two nominations. This style may bode well for the president, because the 1994 Senate elections have reminded us that the potential of divided government is never more than an election away. As in all things political, the only constant is change. As 1995 approaches, we are returning to a divided government with a Republican Senate and Democratic president. We hope that the framework suggested throughout this book, and just summarized, will help the interested observer to make sense of nomination politics in the face of this constancy of change.

Is It Broken? Should the Appointment Process Be Changed?

In recent years, many voices—including presidents, senators, the general public, media representatives, and scholars—have called for changes in the way we appoint Supreme Court justices. The heated battles over the Bork and Thomas nominations are put forward to support the proposition that the nomination system is broken and needs to be fixed. Others feel that the system is working as it should and don't believe any reform is in order. We began this book by saying that the system of selecting Supreme Court justices is important because who sits on the Court is important. Having now extensively discussed the nomination process in action, we believe it appropriate to end the book by asking whether changes in that process are in fact needed.

The Case for Change

Underlying the claim that the nomination process has broken down seems to be the belief that it has become too political. Many of the examples we have used throughout this book support this claim: the extensive involvement of political advocacy groups in recent nominations; the media "circus" that characterized the Bork and Thomas nominations; the partisan wrangling between Democratic and Republican members of the Judiciary Committee; the injection of race into the confirmation process for Clarence Thomas; and— most notably—the spectacle of Judiciary Committee members on live television discussing porno movie stars and crude sexual innuendoes with Clarence Thomas and Anita Hill.

Certainly these examples and many others show that the nomination process is political. However, to say the process has become "too" political requires some demonstration that negative consequences flow from the current level and form of nomination politics. Advocates of change perceive at least two such consequences as (1) the nomination process has become so politically charged that it can no longer achieve its primary goal of selecting the most qualified justices, and (2) the public increasingly perceives the nomination process as illegitimate—simply "dirty politics as usual."

The Selection Process Fails in Its Primary Purpose

There are various forms of the argument that the process is now so political that it does not select the best-qualified nominees. The first contention is that the current politically charged environment results in the Senate rejecting the most qualified nominees. So the argument goes, the best-qualified nominees will have an extensive track record or paper trail that will permit those who politically oppose the nominee to find at least some material that can be used to construct a negative portrait of the nominee's competency, integrity, and/or temperament. Conversely, less well qualified nominees will have a smaller paper trail, will be less subject to negative characterization, and therefore will be less likely to be rejected. Many supporters of Robert Bork argue that he was rejected because he was so well qualified rather than because he was not qualified.

The second contention follows from the first and argues that presidents will seek to avoid such negative characterizations of more prominent individuals by selecting less well qualified nominees with minimal paper trails. Many have argued that such a strategy explains the appointment of the so-called "stealth" nominee, David Souter.

Finally, some have contended that the increasingly rigorous and rancorous scrutiny of nominees will discourage the best-qualified potential nominees from accepting a nomination. For example, one survey of sitting judges found that almost half of the respondents would not want to be nominated to the Supreme Court "given the rancorous four-month Thomas nomination and confirmation process" (National Law Journal, 1991).

The Public Perceives the Process as Lacking Legitimacy

The argument that the nomination process is too political because the public perceives it as such goes directly to two fundamental tenets of democratic government. First, government should reflect the goals and views of the public. Second, when the public perceives that a governmental process is unresponsive to its needs, that public increasingly views government as lacking legitimacy and unworthy of support.

This public discontent theory was bolstered by the public response to the Clarence Thomas hearings. Survey data consistently showed that the public was dissatisfied with the partisan wrangling. For example, a majority of the American public opposed the way in which the Thomas hearings were handled. When asked whether they thought the hearings were a good thing or a bad thing, 59 percent said bad (Hugick 1991a, 26). Even more significant for the proposition that public dissatisfaction will reduce the perceived legitimacy of government are polls that showed that as a result of the Thomas nomination process 48 percent of those surveyed had less confidence in Congress than before the hearings and 28 percent had less confidence in the president (Hugick 1991a, 26).

Who's to Blame? What Should Be Changed?

While reformers agree that some changes are needed, there has been much more finger-pointing than constructive suggestions for change as is evident from the statements made by President Bush and Judiciary Committee Chair Joseph Biden with which we began this chapter.

Those who blame the chief executive seem to suggest three related presidential "sins."

> 1. Presidents have focused too much on their own political agendas when appointing nominees and not enough on selecting the best-qualified nominees.
> 2. Presidents have assumed sole responsibility for selecting nominees and have ignored the constitutional mandate to seek the advice of the Senate.
> 3. Presidents have politicized the process by using inflammatory rhetoric to justify and defend their nominees.

Those who blame the Senate make parallel attacks.

> 1. The recent confirmation voting of the Senate has reflected political motives and ignored whether in fact the nominee is qualified.
> 2. Senators have engaged in inflammatory public rhetoric and character assassination to accomplish their goals.
> 3. Senators and their staffs have destroyed the legitimacy of the process by leaking confidential information and manipulating the media.

Finally, there are some who cast blame on advocacy groups and the media. From this perspective, the process has become too political due to the dirt-digging of politically motivated advocacy groups and the sensation-seeking of "investigative" journalists.

Admonitions for Change

The problem with taking action on these perceived flaws is that the offending behaviors (with the possible exception of information leaks) are perfectly constitutional and legal. Therefore, the many calls for change are really only admonitions that presidents, senators, or the media shouldn't behave the way they have. For example, some have said that the president should pick the very best person and ignore politics. Others have said that the Senate should presume that the president's nominee is acceptable and only vote no if there is an overwhelming and qualification-based reason to do so.

These types of admonitions can only produce change if they are acted upon politically. Ultimately, they require the electorate to hold presidents and/or senators accountable for failing to follow these mandates. Polling during and immediately after the Thomas hearings and the 1992 Senate races show at least some public willingness to hold elected official accountable for their confirmation behavior. For example, a Gallup poll during the hearings found that more than 40 percent of those surveyed said that their senator's vote on the Thomas nomination would influence their decision of whether to support or oppose that senator for reelection (Hugick 1991b, 33).

The 1992 Senate races also showed at least some willingness on the part of certain constituencies to hold their senator accountable for confirmation behavior. For example, Pennsylvania Senator and Judiciary Committee member Arlen Specter faced extremely stiff competition from a Democratic candidate, Lynn Yeakel, who was motivated to enter the race by Specter's support of Clarence Thomas and his vigorous questioning of Anita Hill. Similarly, Carol Moseley-Braun defeated Illinois incumbent Alan Dixon at least in part by appealing to anger over Dixon's support of Thomas (Palley 1993).

A Reform Agenda
While the calls for reform in the wake of the Bork and Thomas nominations have often been politically motivated, fragmented, and mere admonitions, it is nonetheless useful to draw them together into an overall reform agenda that can provide the basis for a systematic public debate about whether changes are needed in the nomination process. Three types of reforms have been suggested: approaches that envision major reforms in the process; attacks suggesting only incremental changes in confirmation procedures; and views focusing on personnel changes that would diversify the actors involved formally in the process.

Major Process Reforms. Many observers have called for fundamental changes in the relationship between the president and the Senate. These proposals seek to foster consensus between the two by encouraging or forcing presidents to coordinate more explicitly with the Senate when making nominations. Two of the specific reform proposals that have been suggested in this regard include:

> Reform Proposal (1) Formalize the "advice" role of the Senate by establishing a procedure for the Senate (or some panel of experts) to recommend potential nominees to the president.

> Reform Proposal (2) Place the burden of proof for confirmation on the nominee and make it acceptable to oppose nominees on purely political grounds.

The logic of the first proposal is straightforward: We can decrease nomination controversy by forcing presidents to select nominees who are clearly meritorious or at least clearly acceptable to the Senate. From the perspective of the second proposed reform, the solution to nomination controversy is not the attempt to make the Senate process nonpolitical but to make it explicitly political. Opposition could then be as simple as "I don't like the nominee's politics," negating the need to assault personal ethics, competency, or temperament. This approach seems quite compatible with George Washington's assertion that opposition to a nominee requires no justification, just as the president's appointments require no justification (Harris 1953, 39). By being explicitly political, the process arguably would become more civil.

Incremental Procedural Reforms. The Thomas nomination led to suggestions for a variety of incremental changes in the way the Senate Judiciary Committee evaluates nominees. These reforms are primarily aimed at increasing both civility and attention to nominee quality rather than changing the role of politics.

> *Reform Proposal (3)* Replace committee questioning with designated questioners (as used in the second round of the Thomas hearings) or have the equivalent of a special counsel to question the nominee.
>
> *Reform Proposal (4)* Reduce participation of advocacy groups by limiting their hearing participation to written statements only.
>
> *Reform Proposal (5)* Limit media and public access to sensitive material by (1) minimizing staff access to such material; (2) formalizing and strictly enforcing Senate rules against leaks; and (3) holding some questioning in a closed session.

While not addressing the fundamental political problem of the relationship between the president and the Senate, each of these incremental proposals goes to the heart of most people's objections to the Thomas hearings by seeking to reduce the circus atmosphere of modern nominations. For example, the rationale for using special counsel or designated questioners at nomination hearings results from the public perception that the questioning by senators at the Bork and Thomas hearings was at best political grandstanding and at worst mudslinging.

Other incremental changes seek to reduce politics by decreasing the influence of outside interests such as advocacy groups, the media, and the public. Presumably these political actors contribute to the politicization of the process. Limiting their participation would permit a greater focus on qualifications and protect nominees from hearsay and other inflammatory accusations that should not be aired in public. Proponents argue that these reforms face directly the current problems with the system and would both increase the quality of justices and improve the public's evaluation of and support for the process.

Because these proposed reforms were a direct response to dissatisfaction with the Thomas hearings, at least some of them received formal attention soon after those hearings. For example, in February 1992 President Bush and the Judiciary Committee reached new agreements on the extent to which staff should have access to nominee FBI files and took additional steps to prevent the leaking of such material (Gray, Biden, and Thurmond 1992). The committee chair, Senator Biden, also announced a policy of holding a closed session at which the committee would meet to hear any allegations of impropriety, even if none were anticipated. As promised, he did in fact hold a closed session of the committee during the time of Ruth Ginsburg's hearings, laying the foundation for yet another change in the confirmation process.

Personnel Reforms. A fundamentally different type of reform than those previously mentioned also resulted from the Thomas hearings. The spectacle of 14 middle-aged and elderly white men judging charges of sexual harassment between two African Americans did not go unnoticed by much of the American public and resulted in the following proposal.

> *Reform Proposal (6)* Increase the diversity of the Judiciary Committee for Supreme Court nominations by either adding women and minorities to the committee and/or by employing special counsel who would bring greater diversity to the process.

As a result of the 1992 election, it became possible and in fact politically inevitable that this reform would be implemented. One of the first acts of the Senate in January 1993 was to expand the size of the Judiciary Committee to permit the addition of newly elected Democratic Senators Carol Moseley-Braun and Diane Feinstein. In order to maintain the ratio of Democrats to Republicans on the committee without asking any current member of the committee to resign, these additions were accomplished by adding two more Republicans to the committee—William Cohen and Larry Pressler. Thus, as of January 1993 the committee was composed of 18 members and for the first time had both female and African-American representation.

It is unlikely that a Supreme Court confirmation hearing will ever again be conducted by an all-white and male group of questioners. Even were the committee to lack diversity again at some time in the future, there is no reason not to seek representation from the Senate as a whole to participate in these most important hearings. There is precedent at least as recent as William Brennan's nomination in 1956 for allowing noncommittee members to question a nominee. In that instance, the questioner was Joseph McCarthy, who sought assurance that Brennan was an anticommunist. Surely such outside participation could be accommodated in the name of racial and gender diversity.

Theories of Nomination Reform. There are two basic approaches to reforming the process as reflected in the proposals mentioned above. One is to reduce the amount of politics in the process; the other is not only to permit politics to continue as a key part of the process but even to expand its role.

The politics reduction approach proceeds on three fronts. The first is to reduce conflict between the Senate and the president by suggesting (or mandating) that one branch defer to the other. This can be manifested in a presidential-centered model where the Senate is expected to defer to the president's choice (Reynolds 1991), a presumption that many senators accept. No one seriously proposes actual Senate control over appointments in which the president would acquiesce to the Senate, but there have been proposals for the president to appoint from a list of nominees acceptable to a group of senators.

The second way in which the politics presumably can be removed from the appointment process is by the use of a nonpartisan selection committee that would screen potential nominees and develop a list of suitable nominees from which the president would select and the Senate would confirm. This effort attempts to reduce the political gamesmanship of both the president and the Senate. The acquiescence of the president in such a plan would pressure the Senate to do likewise.

The third route to reducing politics is to decrease public awareness of the process. The public could be shut out by having closed hearings. With no media to pander to, senators—according to this logic—could now simply focus on the qualifications of the nominee. The influence of advocacy groups could be reduced by limiting their access to testify. Least restrictive of this particular politics reduction approach is limiting interrogation by the senators in favor of special counsel or a designated questioner for each party. Each of these reforms is designed to strip the process of its "dirty politics" appearance.

The alternative theory of reform calling for increased politics is represented by reform proposals that recognize politics as a legitimate basis of evaluating a nominee. This theoretical approach underlies the proposal to establish a confirmation committee that provides representation more in line with the diversity in our population—or at least the considerably limited diversity within the Senate itself. Other proposals that would permit rationales for the rejection of nominees based on explicitly ideological and/or political grounds are also based on an underlying premise that politics is an inevitable and desirable part of the process (Melone 1991). From this perspective, politics is only problematic if some views are suppressed or artificially submerged and replaced by character assassination under the guise of the nominee's lack of qualifications.

If It Ain't Broke, Don't Fix It: A Personal Conclusion

At first, and maybe even at second, glance the contentions that there is too much politics in the confirmation process and that reforms are needed to reduce the amount political influence seem persuasive. However, we believe that the description and analysis of the confirmation process presented in this book provide the basis for a compelling argument against these calls for reduced politics and, in fact, endorse the view that if any change is appropriate it is toward a more explicitly political process and not one that is less political. Our argument rests on the contention that politics, even at times extreme politics, is both an inevitable and a useful part of the selection process (Sinclair 1992).

Attempts to make the selection of Supreme Court justices an "objective merit" decision rather than a political decision are doomed to failure. In Chapter 1 we reviewed why who sits on the Supreme Court is so important. That importance results from the significance of the Supreme Court in our constitutional system of government as well as from the fact that the political and legal attitudes justices bring to the Court will inevitably affect the types of decisions that they will make there. Given these realities, whether one supports or opposes the views of a nominee will inevitably affect one's perception of the nominee's qualifications. "Qualifications" always have been and always will be defined politically.

In addition, the notion that a president or the Senate will voluntarily give up their constitutional prerogatives is highly unrealistic. No president will voluntarily relinquish his autonomy in choosing a nominee. During the 1992 election campaign, candidate Bill Clinton was asked whether the president should select nominees from a list of highly qualified Americans chosen by a commission of lawyers and other citizens. He responded just as we should expect any president to respond: "It's an interesting idea and worth consideration. Ultimately, however, judicial appointments are the fundamental responsibility of the president" (Richert 1992, 100).

It is interesting, however, that the fundamental contribution of President Clinton to the nomination process is his greater involvement of the public and the Senate in the selection process. With the public announcement of individuals under consideration, the president has invited scrutiny and reactions from the public as well as political advocates and senators. Indeed, it was the equally public negative response to Interior Secretary Bruce Babbitt by Senators Hatch and Simpson, important Republican members of the Senate Judiciary Committee, that presumably persuaded the president to back away from Babbitt in favor of nominating Stephen Breyer in 1994. Those two western senators objected to some of Babbitt's actions as Interior Secretary regarding the use of public lands in the West. Ironically, it was the response of environmental advocates who supported Babbitt that apparently persuaded the president not to appoint Babbitt for the first vacancy awarded the administration in 1993, deciding that Babbitt was more important for the moment in his Cabinet position.

Similarly, senators who are not from the president's party or are ideologically in conflict with the president cannot be expected to say "I don't like this nominee's views, but it's up to the president." In fact, the Senate seems more and more poised to move away from the unstated norm that opposition to a nominee must be articulated in terms of the nominee's lack of qualifications, defined as integrity, as integrity, professional competence, and judicial temperament. The promise of opposition by Senators Hatch and Simpson to a 1994 Babbitt nomination was linked to actions of Babbitt as Interior Secretary, not to an assessment of his qualifications for the Court. Whether such overt political opposition to an actual nominee becomes more acceptable among senators and the public remains to be seen.

Even if the president or Senate were to relinquish their authority in the nomination process, many calls for change are undesirable because of their patently undemocratic consequences, namely, the consolidation of power within a single institution and/or reduced public awareness of and participation in the process. Whether the call is for a president-centered or a Senate-centered selection system the result is the same: Political conflict will be eliminated at the cost of varying points of view and the need for compromise.

There is great ingenuity in our separation-of-powers system. In periods of considerable consensus in the country, the executive and legislative branches tend to reflect that consensus by being controlled by the same political party and ideological view. The political process then moves more quickly, as democratic theory suggests it should, in the absence of fundamental disagreements over issues. Presidential nominees are more readily accepted by the Senate, and nominations are least likely to generate controversy.

Conversely, a period of political conflict, often reflected by— perhaps even defined as—divided government in which the presidency is controlled by one party and the House and/or the Senate by a different party is precisely a time when the democratic process is designed to slow down. In the midst of fundamental disagreements over the direction the nation should go, this democratic system struggles to find a compromise that can permit the nation to move forward in a way that is at least tolerable to most if not exactly desirable. Public debate becomes relatively more critical in order to find the most acceptable solution for the situation at hand.

Consequently, those proposals that seek to consolidate power in the presidency or the Senate or otherwise diminish the political discourse are democratically flawed. They attempt to rein in the political process precisely during those times in which we are most in need of an open and comprehensive political discourse. Consolidation of power in a single institution inevitably means that one significant point of view in society will be ignored in the selection process. The abandonment of power by both the president and the Senate is an abandonment of representative democracy. It is only through interinstitutional conflict and the threat of conflict that compromise emerges. From a democratic perspective, a compromise nominee may be exactly what is appropriate during periods of divided government.

Similarly, the calls for closed sessions or other means to decrease public awareness or advocacy-group participation would inevitably decrease the public's role in the selection process if acted upon. Yet in a democratic society the public ought to have a role to play in the selection of justices for this highest of courts (Frankfurter and Landis 1928, 185–186). Given the presumptive lifetime tenure of the appointment, if there is no public role at the selection stage, there is no role for the public at all.

Attempts to close the doors of the process block the public's fundamental right to know. Once again, efforts to limit the public's participation are directed at precisely those situations in which the public's participation is most needed. It takes conflict and controversy to arouse public awareness, as it did with the Bork and Thomas nominations, and it is here that the representative institutions should seek the public's views. In this regard advocacy groups and the media play crucial roles by putting the cases for opposition and support before the people and thereby foster democratic participation. To hide the process from the public or artificially eliminate conflict by consolidating selection power in a single institution will decrease political conflict but will also decrease the public's opportunity to be informed of and participate in deciding whether this is the person they want to sit on the Court for the next generation.

As to the specific claim that the current level of political conflict has resulted in Court members that are less than the best-qualified justices, we see little empirical evidence to support the contention that the recently appointed justices are less well qualified on some objective measure of merit than justices of the past. Moreover, we reiterate that qualifications are, by definition, subjective. This may mean that during a period of political controversy, the best-qualified nominee is the consensus nominee. From this perspective, Warren Burger was probably a better-qualified chief justice for the time period than was Abe Fortas. Following the same logic, Anthony Kennedy was a better-qualified justice for the late 1980s than was Robert Bork. Who is "qualified" is and should be a political question. During a period of divided government the definition of qualifications should reflect those differences.

The charge that the current process has reduced public support cannot be so easily rejected. Most poll results showed a dissatisfied public after the Thomas nomination. Countering the significance of these negative perceptions, however, are two realities about the public's response to the Thomas hearings. First, while many people were apparently disgusted with the process, they watched the hearings in record numbers. Eighty-eight percent of the public reported watching some part of the Thomas hearings (Hugick 1991a, 23). In an ironic sort of way, the controversy and the "dirty politics" resulted in greater public awareness and attention than to probably any other nomination in history. In our view such attention cannot be considered a total negative in a democratic society (Alter 1991).

The negative response to the Thomas hearings can also be put in perspective by asking what was the source of the dissatisfaction. We believe the discontent may have resulted as much from false expectations as from what actually happened. Those expectations reflected the "common wisdom" and accepted rationales about why nominees are rejected or accepted, namely, that nominees who are highly qualified are accepted while those who are unqualified are rejected. As a result, the public expected an antiseptic "trial-like" process rather than the rough-and-tumble reality of the political process.

We believe the discontinuity between the expectations and the reality of the nomination process ought to be resolved in favor of accepting that process for what it is—political. Then we need to educate the public about that reality—and its significance—rather than futilely seeking to achieve some apolitical expectation. The statement by President Bush that opened this chapter was right. The Thomas nomination didn't represent any civics lesson that most people received in school, but it is the one they should have received, and the president should help to see that they get it. If the president wants to appoint a person of color to what would otherwise have been an all-white Court, then he should say that's the right thing to do and do it. And if he wants a conservative on the Court, he should say that. For presidents to initiate the discourse with language designed to mask, not reveal, is harmful to the process.

Who is on the Court is an important political question. Explicit political conflict about a nominee should be considered legitimate and appropriate. Senators should not ignore questions of ethics, competency, or temperament, but they should be encouraged to jettison attempts to wrap their support or opposition in these terms if in fact their objections are grounded in political and ideological objections. As we suggested earlier, an explicitly political process would, we believe, actually civilize the nomination process. It would have been much more civil for a senator to have told Robert Bork , "I disagree with your conservative views and the conservative implications that derive from your jurisprudence, and I will not support putting you on the Court" rather than seeking to impugn his character in order to establish a rationale for opposing the nomination.

In addition, the public should be educated to realize the significance of the political process and to recognize that at least during periods of divided government conflict may result and, if so, that conflict is a necessary and important step toward ensuring that all political points of view are reflected. Here as elsewhere the media and advocacy groups have roles to play in civic education by helping us to understand the political bases for opposition and the legitimacy of those bases. The answer is not to hide that conflict or prevent it from emerging by consolidating power but to let it play itself out. Educate the public to understand the political stakes of the process and the competing political forces that will inevitably be involved—to be observant, not disgusted, and active, not alienated.

Finally, academics and educators have an obligation as well to educate our present and future citizens about the nature of democratic politics. We hope that in at least a small way this book contributes to such a public understanding of the confirmation process because ultimately it is the American people that shape America.

Supreme Court Cases Cited

The following is a listing of the Supreme Court cases that are cited throughout this book:

Arizona v. *Fulminante*	111 S.Ct. 1246	(1991)
Baker v. *Carr*	369 U.S. 186	(1962)
Baker v. *Glen Theatre*	111 S.Ct.2456	(1991)
Bray v. *Alexandria*		
Women's Health Clinic	113 S.Ct.753	(1993)
Brown v. *the Board of Education*	347 U.S. 483	(1954)
Communist Party v. *SAC Board*	367 U.S. 1	(1961)
Engel v. *Vitale*	370 U.S. 421	(1962)
Hamelin v. *Michigan*	111 S.Ct. 1120	(1991)
Harris v. *McRae*	448 U.S. 297	(1980)
Mallory v. *U.S.*	354 U.S. 449	(1957)
Marbury v. *Madison*	5 U.S. 137	(1803)
Maxwell v. *Bishop*	398 F2d 138	(1968)
Miranda v. *Arizona*	384 U.S. 436	(1966)
Mu'Min v. *Virginia*	111 S.Ct. 1899	(1991)
Payne v. *Tennessee*	111 S.Ct. 2597	(1991)
Planned Parenthood v. *Casey*	112 S.Ct. 2791	(1992)
R. A. V. v. *St. Paul*	112 S.Ct. 2538	(1992)
Regents v. *Bakke*	438 U.S. 265	(1978)
Reynolds v. *Sims*	377 U.S. 533	(1964)
Richmond v. *Croson*	488 U.S. 469	(1989)
Riverside v. *McLaughlin*	111 S.Ct. 1661	(1991)
Roe v. *Wade*	410 U.S. 113	(1973)
Scales v. *U.S.*	367 U.S. 203	(1961)
Texas v. *Johnson*	491 U.S. 397	(1989)
U.S. v. *Eichman*	496 U.S. 310	(1990)
U.S. v. *Wade*	388 U.S. 218	(1967)
Washington Legal Foundation v.		
U.S. Department of Justice	491 U.S. 440	(1989)
Webster v. *Reproductive Health*	492 U.S. 490	(1989)

References

ABC and Washington Post. 1991a. ABC News/Washington Post Clarence Thomas Hearing Poll, September 1991. Radnor, PA: Chilton Research Services. Data provided through the Interuniversity Consortium for Political and Social Research. Ann Arbor: University of Michigan.

———. 1991b. ABC News/Washington Post Clarence Thomas Vote Delay Polls, October 1991. Radnor, PA: Chilton Research Services. Data provided through the Interuniversity Consortium for Political and Social Research. Ann Arbor: University of Michigan.

Abraham, Henry J. 1983. "A Bench Happily Filled: Some Historical Reflections on the Supreme Court Appointment Process." Judicature 66, no. 7:282–95.

———. 1985. Justices and Presidents. 2nd ed. New York: Oxford University Press.

Abraham, Henry J., and Bruce Allen Murphy. 1976. "The Influence of Sitting and Retired Justices on Presidential Supreme Court Nominations." Hastings Constitutional Law Quarterly. 3:37–63.

Abrahamson, Jeffrey B., Christopher Arterton, and Gary R. Orren. 1988. The Electronic Commonwealth. New York: Basic Books.

Alsop, Joseph, and Turner Catledge. 1938. The 168 Days. New York: Doubleday, Doran & Co.

Alter, Jonathan. 1991. "Why There Isn't a Better Way." Newsweek. October 21:45.

Altheide, David L. 1976. Creating Reality. Beverly Hills, CA: Sage Publications.

American Bar Association. 1972. Code of Judicial Conduct. Chicago: American Bar Association.

———. 1991. Standing Committee on Federal Judiciary: What It Is and How It Works. Chicago: American Bar Association.

Americans for Self Reliance. 1991. "By the Time Clarence Thomas was 10 Years Old, He'd Gotten an Education That Would Last a Lifetime." Washington Post. September 12:A7.

Arnold, R. Douglas. 1990. The Logic of Congressional Action. New Haven, CT: Yale University Press.

Baker, Richard Allan. 1988. The Senate of the United States. Malabar, FL: Robert E. Krieger Publishing.

Berry, Jeffrey M. 1977. Lobbying for the People: The Political Behavior of Political Interest Groups. Princeton, NJ: Princeton University Press.

Biden, Joseph R. 1987. "Advice and Consent: The Right and Duty of the Senate to Protect the Integrity of the Supreme Court." Los Angeles Daily Journal Report 100 (August 21):3–12

———. 1992. "Reforming the Confirmation Process: A New Era Must Dawn." June 25. Washington, D.C.: Office of Senator Biden.

Blaustein, Albert P., and Roy M. Mersky. 1978. The First One Hundred Justices: Statistical Studies on the Supreme Court of the United States. Hamden, CT: Archon Books.

Bork, Robert. 1971. "Neutral Principles and Some First Amendment Problems." Indiana Law Journal 47:1–56.

———. 1990. The Tempting of America: The Political Seduction of the Law. New York: The Free Press.

Brace, Paul, and Barbara Hinckley. 1992. Follow the Leader: Opinion Polls and the Modern Presidents. New York: Basic Books.

Brock, David. 1993. The Real Anita Hill. New York: The Free Press.

Bronner, Ethan. 1989. Battle for Justice: How the Bork Nomination Shook America. New York: W. W. Norton.

Bryant, Irving. 1972. Impeachment: Trials and Errors. New York: Alfred A. Knopf.

Bullock, Charles S., and David W. Brady. 1983. "Party, Constituency, and Roll-Call Voting in the U.S. Senate." Legislative Studies Quarterly 8:29–43.

Bush, George. 1990. Weekly Compilation of Presidential Documents. July 30. Vol. 26, no. 30. Washington: Office of the Federal Register.

———. 1991a. Weekly Compilation of Presidential Documents. July 8. Vol. 27, no. 27. Washington, D.C.: Office of the Federal Register.

———. 1991b. Weekly Compilation of Presidential Documents. October 28. Vol. 27, no. 43. Washington: Office of the Federal Register.

Cameron, Charles, Albert Cover, and Jeffrey Segal. 1989. "The Puzzle of Roll Call Voting on Supreme Court Nominees: A Neoinstitutional Analysis." Paper presented at Midwest Political Science Association meeting. Chicago, IL: March.

———. 1990. "Senate Voting on Supreme Court Nominees: A Neoinstitutional Model." American Political Science Review. 84:525–534.

Cannon, Lou and Howard Kurtz. 1987. "Senate Leaders Given List of 10 Possible Nominees." Washington Post. July 1:A1, A9.

Canon, Bradley C. 1982. "A Framework for the Analysis of Judicial Activism." In Supreme Court Activism and Restraint, edited by S. C. Halpern and C. M. Lamb, 385–419. Lexington, MA: D. C. Heath.

———. 1991. "Justice John Paul Stevens: The Lone Ranger in a Black Robe." In The Burger Court: Political and Judicial Profiles, edited by C. M. Lamb and S. C. Halpern, 63–99. Urbana, IL: University of Illinois Press.

Cardozo, Benjamin Nathan. 1922. The Nature of the Judicial Process. New Haven, CT: Yale University Press.

Carson, Richard T., and Joe A. Oppenheimer. 1984. "A Method of Estimating the Personal Ideology of Political Representatives," American Political Science Review 78:163–178.

CBS and New York Times. 1987a. Bork/Arms Control Poll. Conducted September 9–10. Data provided through the Roper Center for Public Opinion Research. Storrs, CT.: University of Connecticut.

———. 1987b. Bork/Persian Gulf Survey. Conducted September 21–22. Data provided through the Roper Center for Public Opinion Research. Storrs, CT: University of Connecticut.

Charns, Alexander. 1989. "How the FBI Spied on the High Court." Washington Post. December 3:C1, C4.

Chrisman, Robert and Robert L. Allen. eds. 1992. Court of Appeal: The Black Community Speaks Out on the Racial and Sexual Politics of Clarence Thomas vs. Anita Hill. New York: Ballantine Books.

Clausen, Aage. 1973. How Congressmen Decide: A Policy Focus. New York: St. Martin's Press.

Clinton, William J. 1993. Weekly Compilation of Presidential Documents. June 14. Vol. 29, no. 24. Washington: Office of the Federal Register.

———. 1994. "President Clinton: Supreme Court Nominee Announcement." Legi-Slate. Transcript ID 1071857. May 13. Washington D.C.: Federal Information Systems Corporation.

Congress. 1854. Annals of the Congress of the United States, Fourteenth Congress—Second Session. Washington, D.C.: Gales and Seaton.

———. 1969. Congressional Record. Ninety Five Congress, First Session. Washington, D.C.: GPO.

———. 1991. Congressional Record. One Hundred Second Congress, First Session. Washington, D.C.: GPO.

Congressional Quarterly. 1956. "Southern Congressmen Present Segregation Manifesto." Congressional Quarterly Almanac. Washington, D.C.: Congressional Quarterly. 12:416–417.

———. 1959. "1959 Presidential Nominations." Congressional Quarterly Almanac. Washington, D.C.: Congressional Quarterly. 15:664

———. 1968. "Attempt to Stop Fortas Debate Fails by 14-Vote Margin." Congressional Quarterly Almanac. 24:531–540.

———. 1980. "GOP Wins Senate Control for First Time in 28 Years." Congressional Quarterly Almanac. Washington, D.C.: Congressional Quarterly. 36:7B–9B.

———. 1986. Congressional Quarterly Almanac. Washington, D.C.: Congressional Quarterly.

———. 1988. Congressional Quarterly Almanac. Washington, D.C.: Congressional Quarterly.

———. 1992. Congressional Quarterly Weekly. 50:3269. (October 17th).

Danelski, David J. 1964. A Supreme Court Justice Is Appointed. New York: Random House.

———. 1990. "Ideology as a Ground for the Rejection of the Bork Nomination." Northwestern University Law Review. 84:900–920.

Davidson, Roger H. 1990. "The Legislative Reorganization Act of 1946." Legislative Studies Quarterly. 15:357–373.

Duke, Lynne. 1991a. "Mixed Feelings Are Voiced by Rights Leaders." Washington Post. July 2: A6.

———. 1991b. "NAACP Defers Decision on Thomas." Washington Post. July 9: A4.

Dunne, Gerald T. 1970. Justice Joseph Story and the Rise of the Supreme Court. New York: Simon and Schuster.

Edelman, Murray. 1977. Political Language. New York: Academic Press.

———. 1988. Constructing the Political Spectacle. Chicago: University of Chicago Press.

Elling, Richard C. 1982. "Ideological Change in the U.S. Senate: Time and Electoral Responsiveness." Legislative Studies Quarterly 7:75–92.

Federal Bureau of Investigation. 1969a. Memo from JHG to the Attorney General regarding Clemont [sic] Haynsworth. July 1, 1969.

———. 1969b. Memo from W. V. Cleveland to Mr. DeLoach. October 15, 1969.

Fitzpatrick, John C., Ed. 1940. The Writings of George Washington. Vol. 34. Washington, D.C.: GPO.

Frank, John P. 1991. Clement Haynsworth, the Senate, and the Supreme Court. Charlottesville, VA: University Press of Virginia.

Frankfurter, Felix, and James M. Landis. 1928. The Business of the Supreme Court. New York: Macmillan.

Friedman, Leon and Fred L. Israel. 1969. The Justices of the United States Supreme Court 1789–1969. 5 vols. New York: Chelsea House Publishers.

Gallup, George, Jr. 1987. The Gallup Poll. Wilmington, DE: Scholarly Resources.

Gamson, William A. 1992. Talking Politics. New York: Cambridge University Press.

Gates, John B. 1992. The Supreme Court and Partisan Realignment: A Macro- and Microlevel Perspective. Boulder, CO: Westview Press.

Gitenstein, Mark. 1992. Matters of Principle: An Insider's Account of America's Rejection of Robert Bork's Nomination to the Supreme Court. New York: Simon & Schuster.

Godwin, R. Kenneth. 1992. "Money, Technology, and Political Interests: The Direct Marketing of Politics." In The Politics of Interest: Interest Groups Transformed. edited by M. P. Petracca. Boulder, CO: Westview Press. 308–325.

Goldman, Sheldon. 1982. "Judicial Selection and the Qualities that Make a 'Good' Judge." Annals of the American Academy of Social and Political Science 112:113–14.

———. 1987. Constitutional Law: Cases and Essays. 2nd ed. New York: Harper & Row.

———. 1989. "Reagan's Judicial Legacy: Completing the Puzzle and Summing Up." Judicature 72:318–29.

Grassley, Charles E, Orrin G. Hatch, Gordon Humphrey, and Alan K. Simpson. 1990. "Letter to Attorney General Richard Thornburgh." Reprinted as "End the ABA's Judicial Selection Role." Legal Times. (March 26):21.

Gray, C. Boyden, Joseph Biden, and Strom Thurmond. 1992. Memorandum of Understanding: Senate Judiciary Committee and White House Counsel. February 7. Unpublished memo.

Grey, Thomas C. 1974. "Do We Have an Unwritten Constitution?" Stanford Law Review 27 (1974–75):703–718.

Grossman, Joel B. 1965. Lawyers and Judges. New York: John Wiley and Sons.

Grossman, Joel B., and Stephen L. Wasby. 1972. "The Senate and Supreme Court Nominations—Some Reflections." Duke Law Journal. 1972:557–591.

228

Halpern, Stephen C., and Charles M. Lamb, eds. 1982. Supreme Court Activism and Restraint. Lexington, MA.: D.C. Heath.

Hamilton, Alexander. 1987. The Federalist Papers. Nos. 76 and 78. In The Constitution Papers, CD-ROM. Electronic Text Corp.

Harris, Joseph P. 1953. The Advice and Consent of the Senate. Berkeley: University of California Press.

Harris, Richard. 1971. Decision. New York: Dutton.

Harvard Law Review. 1985. "The Supreme Court 1984 Term." Harvard Law Review 99 (November):9–330.

———. 1986. "The Supreme Court 1985 Term." Harvard Law Review 100 (November):4–311.

———. 1987. "The Supreme Court 1986 Term." Harvard Law Review 101 (November):10–370.

Hatch, Orrin G. 1987. "A Response to Senator Biden: The Dangers of Politicizing Supreme Court Selections." Los Angeles Daily Journal Report 100 (August 21):13–25.

Haynes, George H. 1960. The Senate of the United States. 2 vols. New York: Russell and Russell.

Heller, Francis H., ed. 1980. The Truman White House. Lawrence: Regents Press of Kansas.

Hughes, Charles Evans. 1916. Addresses of Charles Evans Hughes, 1906–1916. New York: G.P. Putnam's Sons.

———. 1928. The Supreme Court of the United States. New York: Columbia University Press.

Hugick, Larry. 1991a. "One Night Before Vote, Support for Thomas Remains Strong." The Gallup Poll Monthly. (October):23–27.

———. 1991b. "Political Fallout from the Thomas Hearings." The Gallup Poll Monthly. (October):28–33.

Hugick, Larry, and Graham Hueber. 1991. "Two-thirds Oppose Supreme Court's Latest Abortion Ruling." The Gallup Poll Monthly. 309 (June):36–39.

Jacob, Kathryn Allamong and Bruce A. Ragsdale, editors-in-chief. 1989. Biographical Directory of the United States Congress 1774–1989. US:GPO.

Janda, Kenneth, Jeffrey M. Berry, and Goldman, Sheldon. 1992. The Challenge of Democracy. Boston: Houghton Mifflin.

Kalt, Joseph P., and Mark A. Zupan, 1990. "The Apparent Ideological Behavior of Legislators: Testing for Principal-Agent Slack in Political Institutions." Journal of Law and Economics 33:103–131.

Kaufman, Andrew L. 1979. "Cardozo's Appointment to the Supreme Court." Cardozo Law Review 1:23–53.

Keene, Karlyn H., and Everett Carll Ladd eds. 1991. "Public Opinion and Demographic Report: The Bush Barometer." The American Enterprise (September/October):92.

Kiley, Tom. 1987. A National Survey of Attitudes Toward the Supreme Court and the Bork Nomination. Boston, MA: Marttila and Kiley.

Kingdon, John W. 1989. Congressmen's Voting Decisions. 3rd ed. Ann Arbor: University of Michigan Press.

Knoke, David. 1990. Organizing for Collective Action. New York: Aldine de Gruyter.

Kravitz, Walter. 1990. "The Legislative Reorganization Act of 1970." Legislative Studies Quarterly. 15:375–399.

Kuklinski, James H. 1978. "Representativeness and Elections: A Policy Analysis." American Political Science Review. 72:165–177.

Kurz, Howard. 1991. "Reporter Quits Over Rewrite of Story." Washington Post. (October 16): C1, C9.

LaFraniere, Sharon. 1991. "Despite Achievement Thomas Felt Isolated." Washington Post. (September 9):A1, A6.

Lamb, Charles. 1982. "Judicial Restraint on the Supreme Court." In Supreme Court Activism and Restraint, edited by S. C. Halpern and C. M. Lamb. 7–36. Lexington, MA: D. C. Heath.

Lancaster, John, and Sharon LaFraniere. 1991. "Thomas: Growing Up Black in a White World." Washington Post. (September 8):A1, A20.

Laski, Harold J. 1927. Communism. London: Williams and Norgate.

Lasswell, Harold. 1958. Politics: Who Gets What, When, and How. New York: Meridian Books.

Legal Times. 1990. "End the ABA's Judicial Selection Role." Legal Times. (March 26):21.

Leuchtenburg, William E. 1985. "FDR's Court Packing Plan: A Second Life, A Second Death." Duke Law Journal 1985:673–689.

Lipset, Seymour Martin, and Ben J. Wattenberg, editors. 1989. "Opinion Roundup: Closing the Book on the Reagan Presidency." Public Opinion. (January/February):40.

Lodge, Henry Cabot. 1925. Selections from the Correspondence of Theodore Roosevelt and Henry Cabot Lodge, 1884–1918. 2 vols. New York: Charles Scribner's Sons.

McCarthy, Coleman. 1991. ". . . And the Insults." Washington Post. July 6:A19.

McFeeley, Neil D. 1987. Appointment of Judges: The Johnson Presidency. Austin: University of Texas Press.

McGuigan, Patrick B., and Randall R. Rader, eds. 1981. A Blueprint for Judicial Reform. Washington, D.C.: Free Congress Research and Education Foundation.

McGuigan, Patrick B., and Dawn M. Weyrich. 1990. Ninth Justice: The Fight for Bork. Washington, D.C.: Free Congress Research and Education Foundation.

MacKenzie, G. Calvin. 1981. The Politics of Presidential Appointments. New York: The Free Press.

Malbin, Michael J. 1980. Unelected Representatives. New York: Basic Books.

Marcus, Maeva, and James R. Perry, eds. 1985. Appointments and Proceedings. Vol. 1, Part 1 of The Documentary History of the Supreme Court of the United States, 1789–1800, 2 vols. New York: Columbia University Press.

Marcus, Ruth. 1987. "Hatch Assails ABA Dissenters on Bork Vote." Washington Post. (September 11):A20.

———. 1991a. "NAACP Opposes Thomas." Washington Post. (August 1):A1.

Marcus, Ruth. 1991b. "Backers of Thomas Unveil Add Attacking 3 Democrats." Washington Post (September 4):A1, A13.

Marcus, Ruth, and Gwen Ifill. 1987. "Lobbying Groups Gathering Steam for Bork Confirmation Battle." Washington Post. (July 7):A4.

Marcus, Ruth, and Al Kamen. 1987. "ABA Endorses Bork As Panel Splits Vote." Washington Post. (September 10):A1, A20.

Marke, Julius. J., ed. 1964. The Holmes Reader. New York: Oceana.

Markus, Gregory B. 1974. "Electoral Coalitions and Senate Roll Call Behavior: An Ecological Analysis." American Journal of Political Science. 18:595–607.

Mason, Alpheus Thomas. 1946. Brandeis: A Free Man's Life. New York: Viking Press.

———. 1956. Harlan Fiske Stone: Pillar of the Law. New York: Viking Press.

———. 1965. William Howard Taft: Chief Justice. London: Oldbourne.

Massaro, John. 1990. Supremely Political: The Role of Ideology and Presidential Management in Unsuccessful Supreme Court Nominations. Albany: State University of New York Press.

Melone, Albert P. 1991. "The Senate's Confirmation Role in Supreme Court Nominations and the Politics of Ideology Versus Impartiality." Judicature. 75:68–79.

Metzenbaum, Howard. 1981. Personal interview by author. September 10, Washington, D.C.

Miller, Merle. 1973. Plain Speaking. New York: Berkeley Publishing.

Moore, David W. 1993. "Clinton's Job Ratings Fall, But Character Ratings Remain High." Gallup Poll Monthly. (June):6–7.

Morgenroth, Joyce. 1987. Dance Improvisations. Pittsburgh, PA: University of Pittsburgh Press.

Morrison, Toni, ed. 1992. Race-ing Justice, En-gendering Power: Essays on Anita Hill, Clarence Thomas, and the Construction of Social Reality. New York: Pantheon Books.

Murphy, Bruce Allen. 1988. Fortas: The Rise and Ruin of a Supreme Court Justice. New York: W. Morrow.

National Law Journal. (1991). "Hearings Turn Off Judges." National Law Journal 14 (October 28):1.

NBC and Wall Street Journal. 1987. National Poll, September, 1987. Data provided through the Roper Center for Public Opinion Research. Storrs, CT: University of Connecticut.

Neuman, W. Russell, Marion R. Just, and Ann N. Crigler. 1992. Common Knowledge: News and the Construction of Political Meaning. Chicago: University of Chicago Press.

Newmeyer, R. Kent. 1985. Supreme Court Justice Joseph Story. Chapel Hill: University of North Carolina Press.

Nimmo, Dan, and James E. Combs. 1990. Mediated Political Realities. New York: Longman.

Nixon, Richard. 1969. Weekly Compilation of Presidential Documents, August 25. Vol. 5, no. 34. Washington, D.C.: Office of the Federal Register.

———. 1970. Weekly Compilation of Presidential Documents, February 2. Vol. 6, no. 5. Washington, D.C.: Office of the Federal Register.

O'Brien, David. 1989. "Filling Justice William O. Douglas's Seat: President Gerald R. Ford's Appointment of Justice John Paul Stevens." Yearbook 1989 Supreme Court Historical Society. 20–39. Washington, D.C.: Supreme Court Historical Society.

———. 1990. Storm Center: The Supreme Court in American Politics. 2nd ed. New York: W. W. Norton.

O'Connor, Karen and Lee Epstein. 1989. Public Interest Law Groups. New York: Greenwood Press.

O'Connor, Karen, and Bryant Scott McFall. 1992. "Conservative Interest Group Litigation in the Reagan Era and Beyond." In The Politics of Interest: Interest Groups Transformed, edited by M. P. Petracca. 263–281. Boulder, CO: Westview Press.

Overby, L. Martin, Beth Henschen, Julie Strauss, and Michael Walsh. 1992. "Courting Constituents? An Analysis of the Senate Confirmation Vote on Clarence Thomas." American Political Science Review 86:997–1003.

Palley, Marian Lief. 1993. "Elections 1992 and the Thomas Appointment." PS: Political Science and Politics. 26:28–31.

Pertschuk, Michael, and Wendy Schaetzel. 1989. The People Rising: The Campaign Against the Bork Nomination. New York: Thunder's Mouth Press.

Petracca, Mark P. 1992. "The Rediscovery of Interest Group Politics." In The Politics of Interest: Interest Groups Transformed, edited by M. P. Petracca. 3–31. Boulder, CO: Westview Press.

Phelps, Timothy M., and Helen Winternitz. 1992. Capitol Games: Clarence Thomas, Anita Hill, and the Story of a Supreme Court Nomination. New York: Hyperion.

Polk, James K. 1952. Polk: The Diary of a President. London: Longmans, Green and Co.

Polsby, Nelson W. 1990a "Political Change and the Character of the Contemporary Congress." In The New American Political System, edited by A. King. 2nd version. 29–46. Washington, D.C.: The AEI Press.

———. 1990b. "Public Opinion is Led." Northwestern University Law Review. 84:1031–1032.

Poole, Keith T., and Howard Rosenthal. 1991. "Patterns of Congressional Voting." American Journal of Political Science 35, no. 1:228–278.

Popeo, Daniel J., and Paul D. Kammenar. 1989. "The Questionable Role of the American Bar Association in the Judicial Selection Process." In The Judges War, edited by P. B. McGuigan and J. P. O'Connell. 177–190. Washington, D.C.: Free Congress Research and Education Foundation.

Powe, L. A., Jr. 1976. "The Senate and the Court: Questioning a Nominee." Texas Law Review 4:891–901.

Randolph, Eleanor. 1993. "Husband Triggered Letters Supporting Ginsburg for Court." Washington Post (June 16):A25.

Ranney, Austin. 1990. "Broadcasting, Narrowcasting, and Politics." In The New American Political System, edited by A. King. 2nd version. 175–201. Washington, D.C.: The AEI Press.

Reagan, Ronald. 1981. Weekly Compilation of Presidential Documents, July 13. Vol. 17, no. 28. Washington, D.C.: Office of the Federal Register.

Rees, Grover, III. 1981. "The American Bar Association: Its Cause and Cure." In A Blueprint for Judicial Reform, edited by Patrick B. McGuigan and Randall R. Rader. Washington, D.C.: Free Congress Research and Education Foundation.

————. 1983. "Questions for Supreme Court Nominees at Confirmation Hearings: Excluding the Constitution." Georgia Law Review. 17:913–967.

————. 1988. "The Next Bork." National Review. 40(December 9):32, 34.

Remini, Robert V. 1984. Andrew Jackson and the Course of American Democracy, 1833–1845. Vol. 3. New York: Harper & Row.

Reske, Henry J. 1987. "Did Bork Say Too Much." American Bar Association Journal 73:74–76.

Reynolds, William Bradford. 1991. "The Confirmation Process: Too Much Advice and Too Little Consent." Judicature 75:80–82.

Richardson, Elmo. 1979. The Presidency of Dwight D. Eisenhower. Lawrence: Regents Press of Kansas.

Richert, David, ed. 1992. "Bill Clinton States Positions on the Federal Judiciary." Judicature 76:97, 100.

Ross, William G. 1987a. "The Questioning of Supreme Court Nominees at Senate Confirmation Hearings: Proposals for Accommodating the Needs of the Senate and Ameliorating the Fears of the Nominees." Tulane Law Review. 62:109–174.

————. 1987b. "The Functions, Roles, and Duties of the Senate in the Supreme Court Appointment Process." William and Mary Law Review 28:633–682.

Russakoff, Dale. 1990. "Hunting for Souter's 'Smoking Gun'." Washington Post. (July 26):A25.

Rutkus, Denis Steven. 1993. The Supreme Court Appointment Process: Should It Be Reformed? Washington, D.C.: Congressional Research Service.

Salisbury, Robert H. 1990. "The Paradox of Interest Groups in Washington—More Groups, Less Clout." In The New American Political System, edited by A. King. 2nd version. 203–229. Washington, D.C.: The AEI Press.

Salisbury, Robert H., John P. Heinz, Robert L. Nelson, and Robert O. Laumann. 1992. "Triangles, Networks, and Hollow Cores: The Complex Geometry of Washington Interest Groups." In The Politics of Interest: Interest Groups Transformed, edited by M. P. Petracca. Boulder: 130–49. Boulder, CO: Westview Press.

Schlozman, Kay Lehman, and John T. Tierney. 1986. Organized Interests and American Democracy. New York: Harper & Row.

Schneider, Jerrold E. 1979. Ideological Coalitions in Congress. Westport, CT: Greenwood Press.

Schwartz, Bernard. 1983. Super Chief, Earl Warren and His Supreme Court. New York: New York University Press.

Schwartz, Herman. 1988. Packing the Courts. New York: Charles Scribner's Sons.

Segal, Jeffrey A., Charles M. Cameron, and Albert D. Cover. 1992. "A Spatial Model of Roll Call Voting: Senators, Constituents, Presidents, and

Interest Groups in Supreme Court Confirmations." American Journal of Political Science 36:96–121.

Senate. 1939. Nomination of Felix Frankfurter to be Associate Justice of the Supreme Court of the United States. Senate Judiciary Committee. Seventy-Sixth Congress, First session. Washington, D.C.: GPO.

Senate. 1957. Nomination of William Joseph Brennan, Junior, of New Jersey, to be Associate Justice of the Supreme Court of the United States. Senate Judiciary Committee. Eighty-Fifth Congress, First session. Washington, D.C.: GPO.

Senate. 1959. Nomination of Potter Stewart to be Associate Justice of the Supreme Court of the United States. Eighty-Sixth Congress, First session. Washington, D.C.: Ward and Paul.

Senate. 1967. Nomination of Thurgood Marshall of New York to be Associate Justice of the United States. Senate Judiciary Committee. Ninetieth Congress, First session. Washington, D.C.: GPO.

Senate. 1969a. Nomination of Abe Fortas, of Tennessee, to be Chief Justice of the United States. Senate Judiciary Committee. Ninetieth Congress, Second session. Washington, D.C.: GPO.

Senate. 1969b. Nomination of Clement Haynsworth, Jr., of South Carolina, to be Associate Justice of the Supreme Court of the United States. Senate Judiciary Committee. Ninety-First Congress, First session. Washington, D.C.: GPO.

Senate. 1970. Nomination of George Harrold Carswell Report. Executive report no. 91–14. Ninety-First Congress, Second session. Washington, D.C.: GPO.

Senate. 1981. Nomination of Sandra Day O'Connor to be Associate Justice of the Supreme Court of the United States. Senate Judiciary Committee. Ninety-Seventh Congress, First session. Washington, D.C.: GPO.

Senate. 1987. Nomination of Judge Antonin Scalia to be Associate Justice of the Supreme Court of the United States. Senate Judiciary Committee. Ninety-Ninth Congress, Second session. Washington, D.C.: GPO.

Senate. 1988. Nomination of Anthony M. Kennedy to be Associate Justice of the Supreme Court of the United States. Senate Judiciary Committee. One Hundredth Congress, First session. Washington, D.C.: GPO.

Senate. 1989. Nomination of Robert H. Bork to be Associate Justice of the Supreme Court of the United States. Senate Judiciary Committee. One Hundredth Congress, First session. Washington, D.C.: GPO.

Senate. 1990. ABA Role in the Judicial Nomination Process. Senate Judiciary Committee. One Hundred First Congress, Second session. Washington, D.C.: GPO.

Senate. 1991a. Nomination of David H. Souter to be Associate Justice of the Supreme Court of the United States. Senate Judiciary Committee. One Hundred First Congress, Second session. Washington, D.C.: GPO.

Senate. 1991b. Nomination of Clarence Thomas to the Supreme Court. Sept. 10, 1991. Electronic transcript 750478.

Senate. 1991c. Nomination of Clarence Thomas to be an Associate Justice of the United States Supreme Court: Report Together with Additional and Supplemental Views. Executive Report 102–115. Senate Judiciary Committee. One Hundred Second Congress, First session. Washington, D.C.: GPO.

Shapiro, Catherine R., David W. Brady, Richard A. Brody, and John A. Ferejohn. 1990. "Linking Constituency Opinion and Senate Voting Scores: A Hybrid Explanation." Legislative Studies Quarterly 15:599–621.

Shogan, Robert. 1972. A Question of Judgment. Indianapolis, IN: Bobbs Merrill.

Simon, James F. 1973. In His Own Image: The Supreme Court in Richard Nixon's America. New York: David McKay.

———. 1980. Independent Journey: The Life of William O. Douglas. New York: Harper & Row.

Simon, Paul. 1992. Advice and Consent. Washington, D.C.: National Press Books.

———. 1993. "The Exercise of Advice and Consent." Judicature 76:189–191.

Simon, Todd F., Frederick Fico, and Stephen Lacy. 1989. "Covering Conflict and Controversy: Measuring Balance, Fairness, Defamation." Journalism Quarterly 66:427–434.

Sinclair, Barbara. 1992. "Senate Process, Congressional Politics, and the Thomas Nomination," PS: Political Science and Politics. 25:477–480.

Smith, Eric R. A. N., Richard Herrerra, and Cheryl L. Herrerra. 1990. "The Measurement Characteristics of Congressional Roll-Call Indexes." Legislative Studies Quarterly 15, no. 2:283–295.

Smith, Hendrick. 1988. The Power Game. New York: Random House.

Smith, Steven S., and Christopher J. Deering. 1984. Committees in Congress. Washington, D.C.: CQ Press.

Sorauf, Frank J. 1984. "Political Action Committees in American Politics: An Overview." In What Price PACS? Report of the Twentieth Century Fund Task Force on Political Action Committees. New York: Twentieth Century Fund.

Sparks, Phil. 1989. Personal interview with the author. Washington, D.C.

Stern, Robert. 1988. "The Court Packing Plan and the Commerce Clause." Yearbook 1988 Supreme Court Historical Society. 91–97. Washington D.C.: The Supreme Court Historical Society.

Stookey, John, and George Watson. 1988. "The Bork Hearings: Rocks and Roles." Judicature 71:194–96.

Swisher, Carl B. 1974. The Taney Period, 1836–64. In The History of the Supreme Court, edited by Paul A. Freund. Vol. 5. New York: Macmillan.

Theoharis, Athan G., and John Stuart Cox. 1988. The Boss: J. Edgar Hoover and the Great American Inquisition. Philadelphia, PA: Temple University Press.

Torry, Saundra. 1991. "ABA Panel Judges Thomas 'Qualified' for High Court." Washington Post. (August 28):A1.

Totenburg, Nina. 1988. "The Confirmation Process and the Public: To Know or Not to Know." Harvard Law Review 101:1213–1229.

Tribe, Lawrence H. 1985. God Save This Honorable Court: How the Choice of Supreme Court Justices Shapes Our History. New York: Random House.

Tribe, Laurence H. and Michael C. Dorf. 1991. On Reading the Constitution. Cambridge: Harvard University Press.

Tyler, Harold R. 1987. Letter of September 21 to Joseph R. Biden, Chairman, Committee on the Judiciary.

UPI. 1987. "NAACP Plans 'All-Out' Fight Against Bork." Washington Post. (July 6):A3.

Warren, Charles. 1935. The Supreme Court in United States History. Rev. ed. 2 vols. Boston, MA: Little, Brown.

Wasby, Stephen L. 1991. "Justice Harry A. Blackmun: Transformation from Minnesota Twin to Independent Voice." In The Burger Court: Political and Judicial Profiles, edited by C. M. Lamb and S. C. Halpern. 63–99. Urbana, IL: University of Illinois Press.

Washington Post. 1974. "The Name was Renchburg?" Washington Post (July 19):A12.

Washington Post. 1987. "Biden Plans to Oppose Bork; Hearings Set for September." Washington Post. (July 9):A1.

Watson, George, and John Stookey. 1988. "Supreme Court Confirmation Hearings: A View from the Senate." Judicature 71:186–193.

Wilson, Woodrow. (1913) 1885. Congressional Government. 15th ed. Boston, MA: Houghton Mifflin Co.

Witt, Elder. 1990. Congressional Quarterly's Guide to the United States Supreme Court. 2nd ed. Washington, D.C.: Congressional Quarterly.

Wolpe, Bruce C. 1990. Lobbying Congress: How the System Works. Washington, D.C.: Congressional Quarterly.

Wood, Floris W., ed. 1990. An American Profile: Opinions and Behavior, 1972–1989 Detroit, MI: Gale Research, Inc.

Woodward, Bob. 1991. "Quayle Says Thomas Can Shun Queries." Washington Post (July 6):A1, A9.

Wright, Charles Alan. 1990. "Authenticity of 'A Dirtier Day's Work' Quote in Question." The Supreme Court Historical Society Quarterly 13 (Winter):6–7.

APPENDIX A

Justices of the United States Supreme Court

Justice[1]	Justice's Party[2]	President	President's Party[2]	Year Appointed	Year Departed	Years Served	Age Appointed	Departure	Seat Number[4]	Years Judge[5]	Rating[5]
1. Jay, John	F	Washington	F	1789	1795	6	43	Rs	1	2	C
2. Rutledge, John	F	Washington	F	1789	1791	1	50	Rs	2	6	C
3. Cushing, William	F	Washington	F	1789	1810	20	57	D	3	29	C
4. Wilson, James	F	Washington	F	1789	1798	8	47	D	4	0	C
5. Blair, John	F	Washington	F	1789	1796	6	57	Rs	5	11	C
6. Iredell, James	F	Washington	F	1790	1798	9	38	D	6	1	C
7. Johnson, Thomas	F	Washington	F	1791	1793	1	59	Rs	2	2	D
8. Paterson, William	F	Washington	F	1793	1806	13	47	D	2	0	C
9. Chase, Samuel	F	Washington	F	1796	1811	15	54	D	5	8	C
10. Ellsworth, Oliver	F	Washington	F	1796	1800	4	50	Rs	1	5	C
11. Washington, Bushrod	F	Adams	F	1798	1829	31	36	D	4	0	C
12. Moore, Alfred	F	Adams	F	1799	1804	4	44	Rs	6	1	D
13. Marshall, John	F	Adams	F	1801	1835	34	45	D	1	0	A
14. Johnson, William	D	Jefferson	D	1804	1834	30	32	D	6	6	B
15. Livingston, Brockholst	D	Jefferson	D	1806	1823	16	49	D	2	0	C

Continued

#	Name		President									
16.	Todd, Thomas	D	Jefferson	D	1807	1826	18	42	D	7	6	C
17.	Duvall, Gabriel	D	Madison	D	1811	1835	23	58	Rs	5	0	C
18.	Story, Joseph	D	Madison	D	1811	1845	33	32	D	3	6	A
19.	Thompson, Smith	D	Monroe	D	1823	1843	20	55	D	2	16	C
20.	Trimble, Robert	D	Adams, JQ	D	1826	1828	2	49	D	7	11	D
21.	McLean, John	D	Jackson	D	1829	1861	32	44	D	7	6	C
22.	Baldwin, Henry	D	Jackson	D	1830	1844	14	50	D	4	0	C
23.	Wayne, James	D	Jackson	D	1835	1867	32	45	D	6	5	C
24.	Taney, Roger	D	Jackson	D	1836	1864	28	59	D	1	0	A
25.	Barbour, Philip	D	Jackson	D	1836	1841	5	52	D	5	8	D
26.	Catron, John	D	Jackson	D	1837	1865	28	51	D	8	10	C
27.	McKinley, John	D	Van Buren	D	1837	1852	15	57	D	9	0	C
28.	Daniel, Peter	D	Van Buren	D	1841	1860	19	56	D	5	4	C
29.	Nelson, Samuel	D	Tyler	W	1845	1872	27	52	Rt	2	22	C
30.	Woodbury, Levi	D	Polk	D	1845	1851	5	56	D	3	6	C
31.	Grier, Robert	D	Polk	D	1846	1870	23	53	Rt	4	13	C
32.	Curtis, Benjamin	W	Fillmore	W	1851	1857	6	42	Rs	3	0	B
33.	Campbell, John	D	Pierce	D	1853	1861	8	41	Rs	9	0	C
34.	Clifford, Nathan	D	Buchanan	D	1858	1881	23	54	D	3	0	C
35.	Swayne, Noah	R	Lincoln	R	1862	1881	19	57	Rt	7	0	C
36.	Miller, Samuel	R	Lincoln	R	1862	1890	28	46	D	5	0	B
37.	Davis, David	R	Lincoln	D	1862	1877	14	47	Rs	9	14	C
38.	Field, Stephen	R	Lincoln	D	1863	1897	34	46	Rt	10	6	B
39.	Chase, Salmon	R	Lincoln	R	1864	1873	8	56	D	1	0	B
40.	Strong, William	R	Grant	R	1870	1880	10	61	Rt	4	11	C
41.	Bradley, Joseph	R	Grant	R	1870	1892	21	57	D	6	0	B
42.	Hunt, Ward	R	Grant	R	1872	1882	9	62	Rt	2	8	C

43.	Waite, Morrison	R	Grant	1874	14	1888	57	D	1	0	B
44.	Harlan, John	R	Hayes	1877	34	1911	44	D	9	1	A
45.	Woods, William	R	Hayes	1880	6	1887	56	D	4	12	D
46.	Matthews, Stanley	R	Garfield	1881	7	1889	56	D	7	4	C
47.	Gray, Horace	R	Arthur	1881	20	1902	53	D	3	18	C
48.	Blatchford, Samuel	R	Arthur	1882	11	1893	62	D	2	15	C
49.	Lamar, Lucius	D	Cleveland	1888	5	1893	62	D	4	0	C
50.	Fuller, Melville	D	Cleveland	1888	21	1910	55	D	1	0	C
51.	Brewer, David	R	Harrison	1889	20	1910	52	D	7	28	C
52.	Brown, Henry	R	Harrison	1890	15	1906	54	Rt	5	16	C
53.	Shiras, George	R	Harrison	1892	10	1903	60	Rt	6	0	C
54.	Jackson, Howell	R	Harrison	1893	2	1895	60	D	4	7	D
55.	White, Edward	D	Cleveland	1894	16	1910	48	P	2	2	B
56.	Peckham, Rufus	D	Cleveland	1895	13	1909	57	D	4	9	C
57.	McKenna, Joseph	R	McKinley	1898	27	1925	54	Rt	10	5	C
58.	Holmes, Oliver	R	Roosevelt, T	1902	29	1932	61	Rt	3	20	A
59.	Day, William	R	Roosevelt, T	1903	19	1922	53	Rt	6	7	C
60.	Moody, William	R	Roosevelt, T	1906	4	1910	52	Rt	5	0	C
61.	Lurton, Horace	D	Taft	1909	4	1914	65	D	4	26	C
62.	Hughes, Charles	R	Taft	1910	5	1916	48	Rs	7	0	A
55.	White, Edward	D	Taft	1910	10	1921	65	D	1	18	B
63.	Van Devanter, Willis	R	Taft	1910	26	1937	51	Rt	2	8	E
64.	Lamar, Joseph	D	Taft	1910	5	1916	53	D	5	2	C
65.	Pitney, Mahlon	R	Taft	1912	10	1922	54	Rt	9	11	E
66.	McReynolds, James	D	Wilson	1914	26	1941	52	Rt	4	0	C
67.	Brandeis, Louis	D	Wilson	1916	22	1939	59	Rt	5	0	A

Continued

68.	Clarke, John	D	1916	1922	5	59	Rs	7	2	C
69.	Taft, William	R	1921	1930	8	63	Rt	1	13	B
70.	Sutherland, George	R	1922	1938	15	60	Rt	7	0	B
71.	Butler, Pierce	D	1922	1939	16	56	D	6	0	E
72.	Sanford, Edward	R	1923	1930	7	57	P	9	14	C
73.	Stone, Harlan	R	1925	1941	16	52	Rt	10	0	A
62.	Hughes, Charles	R	1930	1941	11	67	Rs	1	5	A
74.	Roberts, Owen	R	1930	1945	15	55	D	9	0	C
75.	Cardozo, Benjamin	D	1932	1938	6	61	Rt	3	18	A
76.	Black, Hugo	D	1937	1971	34	51	Rt	2	2	A
77.	Reed, Stanley	D	1938	1957	19	53	Rt	7	0	C
78.	Frankfurter, Felix	D	1939	1962	23	56	Rt	3	0	A
79.	Douglas, William	D	1939	1975	36	40	Rt	5	0	B
80.	Murphy, Frank	D	1940	1949	9	49	D	6	7	C
81.	Byrnes, James	D	1941	1942	1	62	Rs	4	0	E
73.	Stone, Harlan	R	1941	1946	5	68	D	1	15	A
82.	Jackson, Robert	D	1941	1954	13	49	D	10	0	B
83.	Rutledge, Wiley	D	1943	1949	6	48	D	4	4	B
84.	Burton, Harold	R	1945	1958	13	57	Rt	9	0	E
85.	Vinson, Fred	D	1946	1953	7	56	D	1	5	E
86.	Clark, Tom	D	1949	1967	18	49	Rt	6	0	C
87.	Minton, Sherman	D	1949	1956	7	58	Rt	4	8	E
88.	Warren, Earl	R	1953	1969	16	62	Rt	1	0	A
89.	Harlan, II John	R	1955	1971	16	55	Rt	10	1	B
90.	Brennan, William	D	1956	1990	34	50	Rt	4	7	B
91.	Whittaker, Charles	R	1957	1962	5	56	Rt	7	3	E
92.	Stewart, Potter	R	1958	1981	23	43	Rt	9	4	C

#												
93.	White, Byron	D	Kennedy	D	1962	1993	31	44	Rt	7	0	C
94.	Goldberg, Arthur	D	Kennedy	D	1962	1965	3	54	Rs	3	0	C
95.	Fortas, Abe	D	Johnson, L	D	1965	1969	4	55	Rs	3	0	B
96.	Marshall, Thurgood	D	Johnson, L	D	1967	1991	24	59	Rt	6	4	C
97.	Burger, Warren	R	Nixon	R	1969	1986	17	61	Rt	1	13	
98.	Blackmun, Harold	R	Nixon	R	1970	1994	24	61	Rt	3	11	
99.	Powell, Lewis	D	Nixon	R	1971	1987	16	64	Rt	2	0	
100.	Rehnquist, William	R	Nixon	R	1971	1986	16	47	P	10	0	
101.	Stevens, John	R	Ford	R	1975		21	55		5	5	
102.	O'Connor, Sandra	R	Reagan	R	1981		14	51		9	6	
100.	Rehnquist, William	R	Reagan	R	1986		9	61		1	15	
103.	Scalia, Antonin	R	Reagan	R	1986		9	50		10	4	
104.	Kennedy, Anthony	R	Reagan	R	1988		7	51		2	11	
105.	Souter, David	R	Bush	R	1990		5	51		4	12	
106.	Thomas, Clarence	R	Bush	R	1991		4	43		6	1	
107.	Ginsburg, Ruth	D	Clinton	D	1993		2	60		7	14	
108.	Breyer, Stephen	D	Clinton	D	1994		1	55		3	14	
	Average (Median)						15	54			6	

Notes

[1] As of 1994 there have been 112 appointments to the Court, not counting the interim appointment of John Rutledge in 1793, who ultimately was rejected by the Senate. However, Stephen Breyer was only the one hundred and eighth person to be appointed. Four justices have filled positions twice, three of whom were elevated from an associate justice to chief justice. The fourth was Charles Evans Hughes, who was reappointed to the Court after having resigned.

[2] Party abbreviations: D for Democratic, F for Federalist, R for Republican, and W for Whig.

[3] Abbreviations for the methods of a justice's departure from the Court are: D for death, Rs for resigned, Rt for retired, and P for promoted (from associate to chief justice).

[4] Seats on the Court are assigned numbers to facilitate following the line of succession from one justice to the next. The original six seats were assigned in order of the list submitted by President Washington. Note that while the Court currently has nine justices, the original eighth seat was eliminated when the Court shrank from 10 to nine members in 1865.

[5] This column indicates the number of years of judicial experience a justice had at the time of appointment to the Supreme Court.

[6] Ratings of the justices on a scale from A to E are based on a 1970 survey of Court scholars as reported in Blaustein and Mersky (1978, 32–51). The A rating is defined as "great", B is "near-great", C is "average", D is "below average", and E is rather ungraciously listed as "failure." Anyone serving after 1970 is unranked.

APPENDIX B
Failed Nominations

	Nominee	Year Nominated	President	How Nomination Failed
1.	Harrison, Robert	1789	Washington	Declined (even though confirmed)
2.	Paterson, William	1793	Washington	Withdrawn (resubmitted and confirmed later in the year)
3.	Rutledge, John	1795	Washington	Rejected by 10 to 14 Senate vote (after serving as interim chief justice)
4.	Cushing, William	1796	Washington	Declined (even though confirmed)
5.	Jay, John	1800	Adams	Declined (even though confirmed)
6.	Lincoln, Levi	1811	Madison	Declined (even though confirmed)
7.	Wolcott, Alexander	1811	Madison	Rejected by 9 to 24 Senate vote
8.	Adams, John Q.	1811	Madison	Declined (even though confirmed)
9.	Crittenden, John J.	1828	Adams, JQ	Postponed
10.	Taney, Roger	1835	Jackson	Postponed (subsequently confirmed as chief justice)
11.	Smith, William	1837	Jackson	Declined (even though confirmed)
12.	Spencer, John	1844	Tyler	Rejected by 21 to 26 Senate vote
13.	Walworth, Reuben	1844	Tyler	Withdrawn after Senate postponement
14.	King, Edward	1844	Tyler	Postponed

Continued

	Name	Year	President	Outcome
15.	King, Edward	1844	Tyler	Withdrawn after Senate postponement (having been renominated)
16.	Read, John	1845	Tyler	No action taken by Senate
17.	Woodward, George	1845	Polk	Rejected by 20 to 29 Senate vote
18.	Bradford, Edward	1852	Fillmore	No action taken by Senate
19.	Badger, George	1853	Fillmore	Postponed
20.	Micou, William	1853	Fillmore	No action taken by Senate
21.	Black, Jeremiah	1861	Buchanan	Rejected by 25 to 26 Senate vote
22.	Stanbery, Henry	1866	Johnson	No action (no vacancy existed because Senate reduced size of Court)
23.	Hoar, Ebenezer	1869	Grant	Rejected by 24 to 33 Senate vote
24.	Stanton, Edwin	1869	Grant	Died (after confirmation but before taking oath)
25.	Williams, George	1873	Grant	Withdrawn before Senate consideration
26.	Cushing, Caleb	1874	Grant	Withdrawn before Senate consideration
27.	Matthews, Stanley	1881	Hayes	No action (resubmitted by President Garfield and confirmed)
28.	Conkling, Roscoe	1882	Arthur	Declined (even though confirmed)
29.	Hornblower, William	1893	Cleveland	Rejected by 24 to 30 Senate vote
30.	Peckham, Wheeler	1894	Cleveland	Rejected by 32 to 41 Senate vote
31.	Parker, John	1930	Hoover	Rejected by 39 to 41 Senate vote
32.	Fortas, Abe	1968	Johnson, LB	Withdrawn (for chief justice, after Senate cloture vote failed, 45 to 43)
33.	Thornberry, Homer	1968	Johnson, LB	Withdrawn (no vacancy existed after Fortas withdrawal)
34.	Haynsworth, Clement	1969	Nixon	Rejected by 45 to 55 Senate vote
35.	Carswell, Harrold	1969	Nixon	Rejected by 45 to 51 Senate vote
36.	Bork, Robert	1987	Reagan	Rejected by 42 to 58 Senate vote
37.	Ginsburg, Douglas	1987	Reagan	Withdrawn before Senate action

APPENDIX C

Senate Judiciary Committee

The Senate Judiciary Committee is a standing committee, which means that it operates from one session of Congress to the next, typically with little change in membership. In 1993, however, the Committee was expanded by four members in order to place two women on the Committee without bumping any members already serving on the Committee. Adding two female Democrats (Feinstein and Moseley-Braun) necessitated adding two additional Republicans, both male (Cohen and Pressler). With the Republican takeover in 1995, the Republican leadership decided to maintain the Committee at 18 members, only now with 10 Republicans and 8 Democrats. The two Republicans who were added in 1993 were permitted to drop off the Committee in recognition of their greater interest and more senior status on other committees. This resulted in the appointment of four freshmen Republican senators. On the Democratic side, Moseley-Braun was permitted to drop and one new Democrat was appointed. The Committee had already lost two Democrats for 1995 through retirement (Metzenbaum and DeConcini).

Committees operate on a somewhat modified seniority system. The majority party controls the committee and subcommittee chair positions. Within the controlling party, the Committee Chair is typically the one with the longest service on the Committee. Within the minority party group, the one with the longest service on the Committee is typically designated the ranking minority member. However, because a senator may chair or be designated as ranking member of only one major standing committee, neither the current chair (Hatch) nor the ranking member (Biden) of the Judiciary Committee are the most senior within their respective parties. Senators Thurmond and Kennedy both relinquished their claim to Judiciary Committee leadership in order to fulfill similar roles on other committees.

When members join the Committee and the same time, there are numerous methods for ranking seniority. In 1995, Thompson, Kyl, DeWine, and Abraham all joined the Committee as new Republicans. The initial priority for ranking is length of service in the Senate. Because Thompson was sworn in on December 9, 1994, rather than the conventional first working day in January, he gained seniority over the other three. This was prompted by the early resignation of Harlan Matthews, appointed to the Senate as an interim replacement for Al Gore, who vacated the seat to become vice president in 1993. Among the other three senators, Kyl and DeWine both had served four terms in the House of Representatives, so they had seniority over Abraham, who was new to Congress in 1995. For Committee seniority between Kyl and DeWine, it came down to a coin flip. Kyl won and now has a Committee position senior to DeWine.

244

Presented below are the 1995–1996 Judiciary Committee senators, along with their times of entry to the Senate and the Committee. In addition, their votes on Supreme Court nominees over time are listed. In all instances involving these particular Committee members, their votes in Committee regarding the nominee and their votes on the Senate floor concerning confirmation have been identical.

Senate Judiciary Committee Members for 1995–1996 by Party and in Order of Seniority

Republicans

Orrin Hatch, a Republican from Utah, has served in the Senate and on the Committee since 1977. He assumed the ranking minority position in 1993 when Strom Thurmond stepped aside to assume such a position on a different committee. Hatch became chair of the Committee in 1995 as a result of the Republican majority in the Senate established in the 1994 elections. During the Reagan-Bush presidencies, Hatch took a very proactive position in leading support for the nominees during the Committee hearings.

Supported confirmation of   O'Connor (1981); Rehnquist (1986); Scalia (1986); Bork (1987); Kennedy (1987); Souter (1990); Thomas (1991); Ginsburg (1993); Breyer (1994)

Opposed confirmation of

Strom Thurmond is a Republican senator from South Carolina serving since 1954. Thurmond was actually a Democratic senator from 1954–1964, when he switched to the Republican party. He has served on the Judiciary Committee since 1967 and chaired the Committee between 1981–1986, which covered the nominations of O'Connor, Rehnquist as Chief Justice, and Scalia. While senior among the Republican Committee members, he relinquished his ranking member status in 1993 in favor of serving in that capacity on the Armed Services Committee.

Supported confirmation of   Burger (1969); Haynsworth (1969); Carswell (1970); Blackmun (1970); Rehnquist (1971); Powell (1971); Stevens (1975); O'Connor (1981); Rehnquist (1986); Scalia (1986); Bork (1987); Kennedy (1987); Souter (1990); Thomas (1991); Ginsburg (1993); Breyer (1994)

Opposed confirmation of   Harlan (1955); Stewart (1959); Goldberg (1962); Fortas (1965); Marshall (1967); Fortas (1968)

Alan Simpson, a Republican from Wyoming, entered the Senate and the Committee in 1979. Characterized by his droll humor that surfaces in the hearings, Simpson has joined with the conservative Republican bloc in support of the controversial nominations of Rehnquist, Bork, and Thomas.

Supported confirmation of   O'Connor (1981); Rehnquist (1986); Scalia (1986); Bork (1987); Kennedy (1987); Souter (1990); Thomas (1991); Ginsburg (1993); Breyer (1994)

Opposed confirmation of

Charles Grassley, a Republican from Iowa, began his career in the Senate and on the committee in 1981. While ultimately supporting her nomination, Grassley joined with two other committee members to raise doubts about the O'Connor nomination, based largely on uncertainties about her position on abortion, hoping for a nominee who would vote to overturn *Roe* v. *Wade.* Ultimately, he voted to confirm her nomination.

Supported confirmation of   O'Connor (1981); Rehnquist (1986); Scalia (1986); Bork (1987); Kennedy (1987); Souter (1990); Thomas (1991); Ginsburg (1993); Breyer (1994)

Opposed confirmation of

Arlen Specter, a Republican from Pennsylvania, entered the Senate and the Committee in 1981. By Republican standards, relatively liberal, Specter's questioning of Robert Bork and his ultimate decision to oppose may have been critical to the defeat of the nomination. On the other hand, his aggressive critical questioning of Anita Hill in the Thomas nomination nearly cost him re-election in 1992.

Supported confirmation of   O'Connor (1981); Rehnquist (1986); Scalia (1986); Kennedy (1987); Souter (1990); Thomas (1991); Ginsburg (1993); Breyer (1994)

Opposed confirmation of   Bork (1987)

Hank Brown, a Republican from Colorado, entered the Senate and the Committee in 1991, after having served four terms in the House of Representatives. He has voted to confirm the only three nominees on which he has had an opportunity to vote.

Supported confirmation of   Thomas (1991); Ginsburg (1993); Breyer (1994)

Opposed confirmation of

Fred Thompson, a Republican, was elected and took office in 1994 for the Tennessee seat formerly held by Vice President Al Gore. Thompson was chief minority counsel for the Senate Watergate Committee in the early 1970s and subsequently played strong attorney roles in some major movies.

Jon Kyl, a Republican, effectively replaces Dennis DeConcini in 1995 both as senator from Arizona and on the Judiciary Committee. Kyl served in the House of Representatives since 1987, where he established a record as a solid conservative in the Gingrich mold.

Mike DeWine, a Republican, succeeds Howard Metzenbaum in 1995 as a senator from Ohio and a Judiciary Committee member. The switch from Metzenbaum, one of the most liberal members of the Senate, to DeWine, who established strong conservative credentials in a four-term House of

Representatives record, epitomizes the change in the Senate and the Committee as a result of the 1994 elections.

Spencer Abraham, a Republican from Michigan, is an attorney who has been actively involved in Republican politics all of his adult life, serving as the state's party chair from 1983 to 1990. Abraham briefly taught law at the Thomas Cooley School of Law in Lansing. This 1995 Senate position is his first elective office.

Democrats

Joseph Biden has served as a Democratic senator from Delaware since 1973 and a member of the Judiciary Committee since 1977. He chaired the Committee from 1987 through 1994 and presided over the Committee during the nominations of Bork, Kennedy, Souter, Thomas, Ginsburg. Biden worked hard to maintain cordial working relationships with the Republican minority despite fundamental differences between the members of the two parties on the suitability of certain nominees to the Court.

Supported confirmation of	Stevens (1975); O'Connor (1981); Scalia (1986); Kennedy (1987); Souter (1990); Ginsburg (1993); Breyer (1994)
Opposed confirmation of	Rehnquist (1986); Bork (1987); Thomas (1991)

Edward (Ted) Kennedy, Democratic senator from Massachusetts since 1962, has also served on the Judiciary Committee during that time. He chaired the Committee from 1979–1980 but declined to chair it again in 1987 when the Democrats regained control of the Senate, preferring to chair the Committee on Labor and Human Resources instead. He led the opposition to Robert Bork, was the only Committee member to oppose Souter, opposed William Rehnquist as Chief Justice, and voted against Clarence Thomas, as well as certain Nixon nominees from an earlier era.

Supported confirmation of	White (1962); Goldberg (1962); Fortas (1965); Marshall (1967); Fortas (1968); Burger (1969); Blackmun (1970); Powell (1971); Stevens (1975); O'Connor (1981); Scalia (1986); Kennedy (1987); Ginsburg (1993); Breyer (1994)
Opposed confirmation of	Haynsworth (1969); Carswell (1970); Rehnquist (1971); Rehnquist (1986); Bork (1987); Souter (1990); Thomas (1991)

Patrick Leahy, a Democrat from Vermont, began service in the Senate in 1975 and on the Committee in 1979. With fairly consistent liberal ratings in his Senate votes, he opposed the Rehnquist, Bork, and Thomas nominations.

Supported confirmation of	O'Connor (1981); Scalia (1986); Kennedy (1987); Souter (1990); Ginsburg (1993); Breyer (1994)
Opposed confirmation of	Rehnquist (1986); Bork (1987); Thomas (1991)

Howell Heflin is a Democrat from Alabama who began his Senate career and service on the Committee in 1979. He is the only member of the current Committee who has been a judge, serving as Chief Justice of the Alabama Supreme Court from 1971–1977. Considered one of the more conservative Democrats, Heflin nonetheless has views of what a Justice should be that led him to oppose both the Bork and Thomas nominations, while departing from his more liberal colleagues to support the Rehnquist elevation to Chief Justice.

Supported confirmation of   O'Connor (1981); Rehnquist (1986); Scalia (1986); Kennedy (1987); Souter (1990); Ginsburg (1993); Breyer (1994)

Opposed confirmation of   Bork (1987), Thomas (1991)

Paul Simon, a Democrat from Illinois, came to the Senate and the Committee in 1985. Since then, he has joined the liberal bloc of the Committee in opposition to the Rehnquist, Bork, and Thomas nominations. Simon's extensive journalistic background is unique to the Committee and has resulted in his writing a book that deals with the appointment process.

Supported confirmation of   Scalia (1986); Kennedy (1987); Souter (1990); Ginsburg (1993); Breyer (1994)

Opposed confirmation of   Rehnquist (1986); Bork (1987); Thomas (1991)

Herbert Kohl, a Democrat from Wisconsin, began his service in the Senate and on the Committee in 1989. He joined the liberal bloc of the Committee in opposing the Thomas nomination.

Supported confirmation of   Souter (1990); Ginsburg (1993); Breyer (1994)

Opposed confirmation of   Thomas (1991)

Diane Feinstein, a Democrat from California, was sworn in to her Senate seat in November of 1992, and began service on the Committee in 1993. One of four new women elected to the Senate in 1992, her appointment to the Committee in 1993, along with Carol Moseley-Braun, reflected the Committee's response to criticism regarding the situation in which an all-male committee was hearing allegations of sexual harassment from a female against a male nominee to the Court.

Supported confirmation of   Ginsburg (1993); Breyer (1994)

Opposed confirmation of

Russell Feingold, a Democrat, represents Wisconsin as does fellow Committee member, Herb Kohl. Feingold came to the Senate in 1993, scoring an upset victory first in the Democratic primary and then unseating incumbent Senator Bob Kasten. In his first two years in the Senate, Feingold has established a strong liberal voting record. He is a new 1995 appointee to the Committee, in effect replacing Carol Moseley-Braun who chose to leave the Committee.

Supported confirmation of   Ginsburg (1993); Breyer (1994)

Opposed confirmation of

Departing Committee Members from 1993–1994

William Cohen, a Republican from Maine, took his Senate seat in 1979 but did not begin service on the Committee until 1993 when the Committee was expanded. Exhibiting a relatively moderate voting record, Cohen nonetheless has supported all nominees to the Court since coming to the Senate. Cohen left the Committee to make way for new Republican members and to focus on work in other committees.

Supported confirmation of   O'Connor (1981); Rehnquist (1986); Scalia (1986); Bork (1987); Kennedy(1987); Souter (1990); Thomas (1991); Ginsburg (1993); Breyer (1994)

Opposed confirmation of

Larry Pressler, a Republican from South Dakota, came to the Senate in 1979 and was appointed to the Committee in 1993 as part of the Committee expansion. Pressler's voting record in the senate is regarded as a conservative one, and he has supported all nominees to the Court since coming to the Senate. Pressler left the Committee to make way for new Republican members and to focus on working on other committees.

Supported confirmation of   O'Connor (1981); Rehnquist (1986); Scalia (1986); Bork (1987); Kennedy(1987); Souter (1990); Thomas (1991); Ginsburg (1993); Breyer (1994)

Opposed confirmation of

Howard Metzenbaum, a Democrat from Ohio, has served in the Senate and on the Committee since 1977. (He was actually sworn in to the Senate on December 28, 1976.) Recognized as one of the Senate's more consistently liberal members, he joined the Committee's liberal bloc in opposing the nominations of Rehnquist, Bork, and Thomas. Metzenbaum retired with the expiration of his term at the end of 1994.

Supported confirmation of   O'Connor (1981); Scalia (1986); Kennedy (1987); Souter (1990); Ginsburg (1993); Breyer (1994)

Opposed confirmation of   Rehnquist (1986); Bork (1987); Thomas (1991)

Dennis DeConcini, a Democrat from Arizona, has served in the Senate and on the Committee since 1977. His middle position on the ideology scale has placed him between more liberal Democrats and more conservative Republicans, appropriately reflected in his opposition to Bork but support of Clarence Thomas. DeConcini retired with the expiration of his term at the end of 1994.

Supported confirmation of   O'Connor (1981); Rehnquist (1986); Scalia (1986); Kennedy (1987); Souter (1990); Thomas (1991); Ginsburg (1993); Breyer (1994)

Opposed confirmation of   Bork (1987)

Carol Moseley-Braun, a Democrat from Illinois, began her service in the Senate and on the Committee in 1993. Her election campaign against the Democratic incumbent had made his support of Clarence Thomas and the need for female representation in such matters an issue. Her appointment to the Committee, along with that of Feinstein, reflected the Committee's recognition of the need for women on the Committee. However, it was not a committee she preferred and she left when given that opportunity in 1995.

Supported confirmation of   Ginsburg (1993); Breyer (1994)
Opposed confirmation of

APPENDIX D

Measuring Political Ideology

Political ideology in American politics revolves around individual preferences regarding fundamental values like equality, freedom, and order
(Janda, Berry, and Goldman 1992, 27–28). Kenneth Janda and his colleagues
define liberals as individuals who prefer equality over freedom and freedom
over order. Conservatives reverse the priorities of that list. While these
scholars use their framework to expand out to other logical ideological
groupings, the discourse of American politics remains largely imbued with
conservatives and liberals as the dominant ideological groupings, and those
terms remain common in considerations involving the Supreme Court appointment process.

There are any number of measures of conservatism and liberalism
(Smith, Herrerra, and Herrerra 1990). Many of them are connected to the
voting behavior of the senators. Of these, the one most commonly used in
the literature is probably the liberalism quotient of the Americans for Democratic Action (ADA). This liberal group selects issues before the Senate
that it considers significant, typically about twenty, and constructs a measure based on whether the senator voted in accordance with the presumably liberal stand taken by the ADA on the issue. The result is a percentage
score that ranges from 0 to 100 and indicates how frequently the senator
voted in the liberal direction. Of course, a score of 100 indicates having
voted "liberal" on all of the issues; a score of 50 means that the senator
voted as a liberal on only half.

One major problem that arises in assigning these scores is how to deal
with the problem of nonvoting. While absenteeism is not generally a problem, it arises somewhat systematically as the presidential primary season
approaches and certain senators are away from Washington trying to fulfill
their presidential aspirations. In some instances, a senator's absenteeism
can produce a misleading score. The ADA has traditionally calculated their
liberalism percentage using the total number of issues identified for its
scale and not the number of issues actually voted on by each individual
senator. For example, if 20 issues were identified for the scale and a senator
voted as a liberal on 12, a conservative on 3, and did not vote at all on the
other 5, then that senator's score would be 60 rather than 80—arrived at by
dividing the 12 liberal votes by the 20 available votes and not by the 15
votes actually cast.

While the ADA procedure places an emphasis on a senator's total
support for their liberal causes, the result is unsatisfactory for those who
wish to get a clearer assessment of a senator's ideology. For example, in 1987
Senator Paul Simon, a Democratic Judiciary Committee member from Illinois, was present and voting on only 7 of the 20 ADA-selected issues. He
voted in the liberal ADA direction on all 7, but his resulting score of 35 identified him as a moderate conservative and the most conservative of the Democrats. It would be clearly misleading to characterize Simon in that way.

To deal with this anomaly of the ADA scoring procedures, we checked all ADA scores used to see if absenteeism could produce a score of 20 or more points different from a score based on the number of votes actually cast by the senator. Simon's score of 35, for example, deviates by 65 points from the 100 he scored if you divide his 7 liberal votes by the 7 votes he actually took. In those instances, we evaluated the senator's suspect score by comparing it with scores from the years immediately preceding and following the one being evaluated. If those scores deviated by more than 20 points, we analyzed them more closely to see if some correction to the suspect score might be warranted. Simon's scores for 1986 and 1988 were both 85, which was 50 points higher than the suspect score. At that point we assigned a score that seemed consistent with the four scores under consideration. In Simon's case, we used the 85 from 1986, the 35 assigned by the ADA in 1987, the 100 obtained for 1987 by basing the percentage on actual votes cast, and the 85 score for 1988. We ultimately assigned an 85 for 1987, more accurately reflecting Simon's liberal record and standing within the Senate.

Other than Simon in 1987, the only other instances in which we observed serious flaws in using the posted ADA scores were in 1968. Again, because deviations of greater than 20 points were involved, we altered the scores of four senators in the following ways when we analyzed ideology for 1968:

Frank Church	Democrat	from 43 to 67
Ted Kennedy	Democrat	from 71 to 100
Eugene McCarthy	Democrat	from 21 to 100
George McGovern	Democrat	from 43 to 67

APPENDIX E

Measuring Partisanship

Partisanship is conceptualized as support for one's political party in partisan votes in the Senate. Partisan votes are votes on issues in which a majority of Republicans vote and a majority of Democrats vote on opposite sides of the issue. Our measure of partisanship stems from the "party unity" scores reported through *Congressional Quarterly* (CQ). Our needs, however, dictate a couple of modifications in the use of their scores.

First, until 1987 the CQ scores were based on the total number of partisan votes cast in the Senate and not just the number of votes taken by each individual senator. Absenteeism cuts heavily into a senator's partisanship score in a way that is inappropriate for assessing a senator's commitment to party. From 1987 on, we used the CQ party unity scores based on the number of partisan votes for which a senator was present and voting. For the years prior to 1987, we estimated the number of partisan votes participated in by adding CQ's party unity and party opposition scores. For example, in 1986 Senator Jake Garn voted in support of the Republicans only 73 percent of the time, certainly less than would be expected for this staunch Republican. On the other hand, his party opposition score was 4, specifying voting in opposition to his Republican party only 4 percent of the time. This suggests that Senator Garn voted in only 77 percent of those partisan votes. For senators voting in fewer than 90 percent of these partisan recorded votes, we recalculated the party unity score by diving it by the sum of the unity and opposition scores. In Garn's case, this meant dividing 73 by 77 to derive a partisanship score of 95 in support of Republicans, a score much more consistent with the 93 recorded for him in 1987.

A second modification involves the handling of CQ scores that are less than 50. In order to provide a meaningful visual continuum of partisanship, we established a scale that ranges from 100 on the left (indicating the level of support for the Republicans) to 50 in the middle of the continuum (indicating split support for both parties) to 100 on the right end of the continuum (which represents the level of support for the Democrats). A Republican with a Republican party unity score of 40 would be equivalent to a Democrat with a unity score of 60. That visual representation of partisanship is based on a simple transformation of the data used for the statistical calculations. The scale used for the calculations recorded the percentage of support for the Democrats. A score of 0 indicated no support for the Democrats and 100 percent support for the Republicans.

INDEX